PIANO • VOCAL • GUITAR

POP
THE BEST OF CONTEMPORARY CHRISTIAN MUSIC

D0762526

ISBN 978-1-4234-5636-0

HAL•LEONARD®
CORPORATION
7777 W. BLUEMOUND RD. P.O. BOX 13819 MILWAUKEE, WI 53213

Visit Hal Leonard Online at
www.halleonard.com

ALL WE NEED

Words and Music by CHRISTINE DENTE,
SCOTT DENTE and CHARLIE PEACOCK

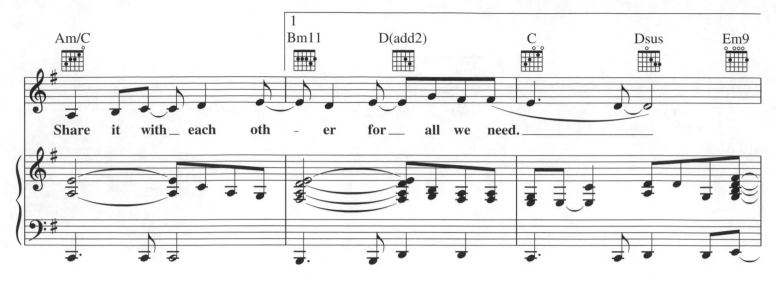

Share it with____ each oth - er for____ all we need.____

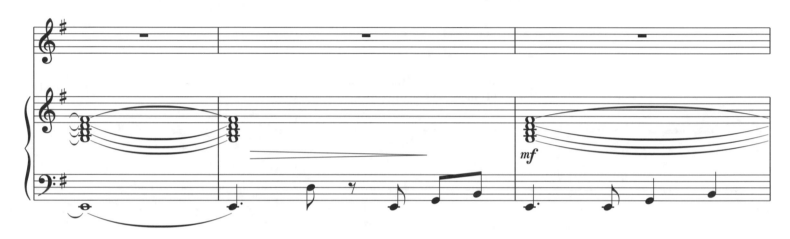

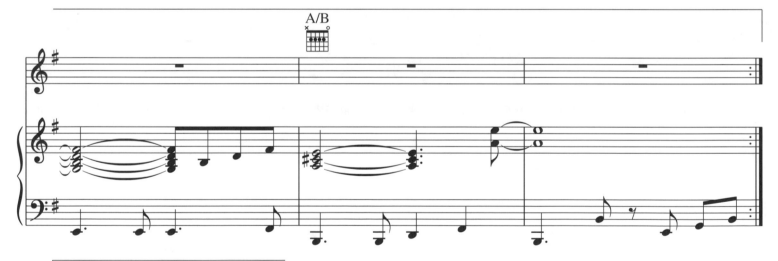

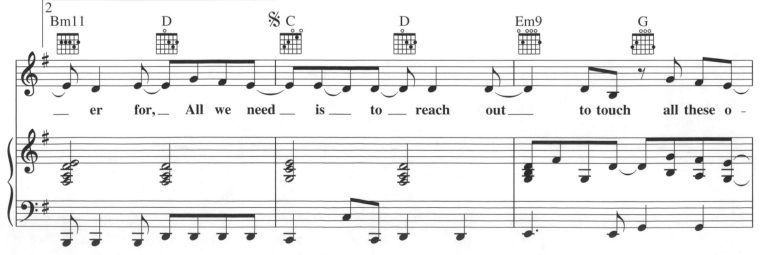

____ er for,____ All we need____ is____ to____ reach out____ to touch all these o -

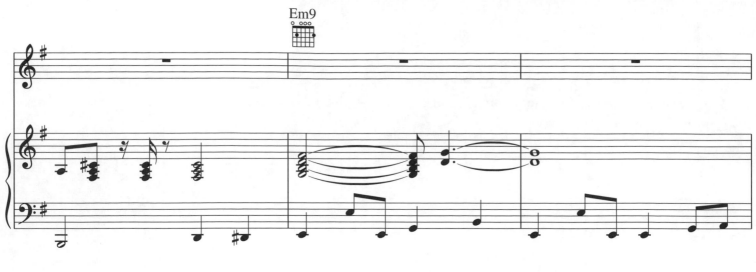

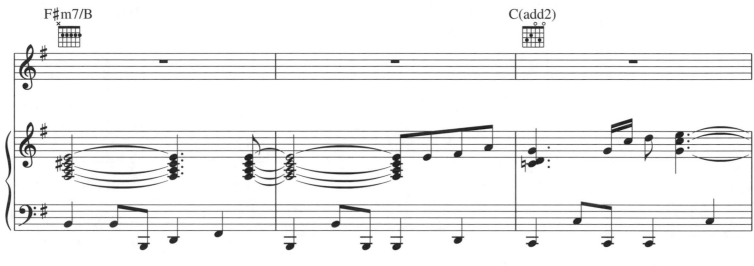

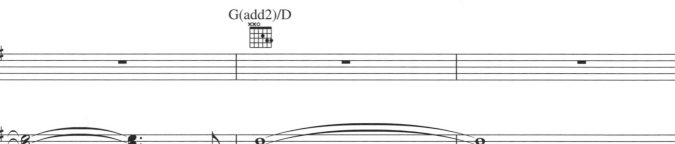

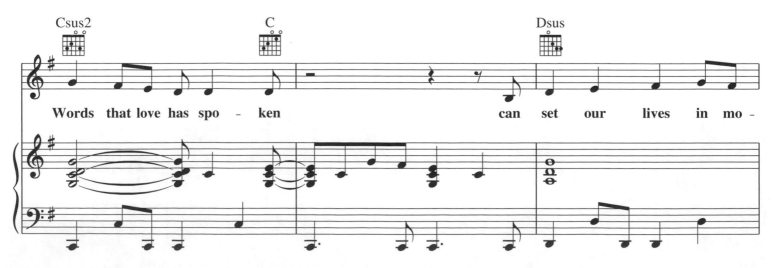

Words that love has spo - ken   can set our lives in mo -

ALWAYS HAVE, ALWAYS WILL

Words and Music by GRANT CUNNINGHAM,
NICK GONZALES and TOBY McKEEHAN

Moderately bright

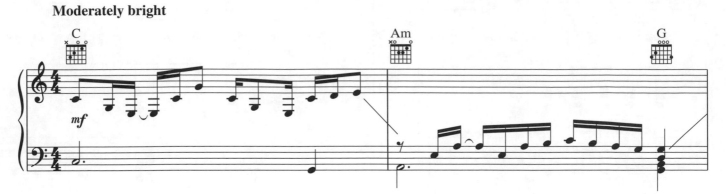

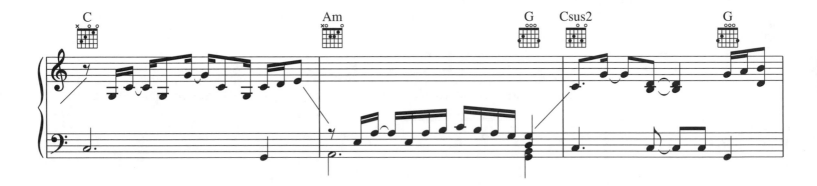

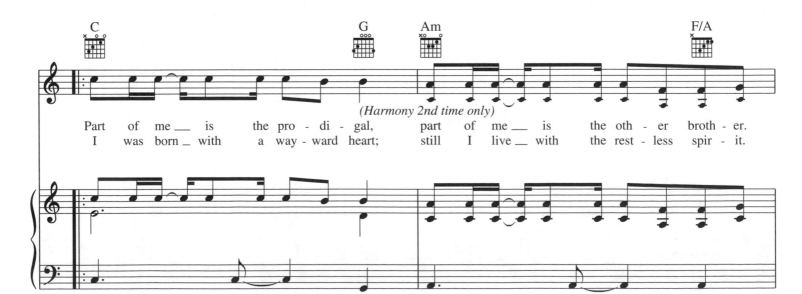

(Harmony 2nd time only)

Part of me ___ is the pro - di - gal, part of me ___ is the oth - er broth - er.
I was born ___ with a way - ward heart; still I live ___ with the rest - less spir - it.

do as ___ I please.
run back ___ to you. } I ___ al - ways ___ have. ___ I al - ways ___ will. ___ You saved ___

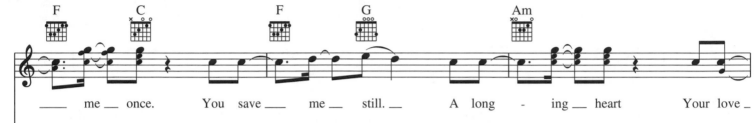

___ me once. You save ___ me ___ still. ___ A long - ing ___ heart Your love ___

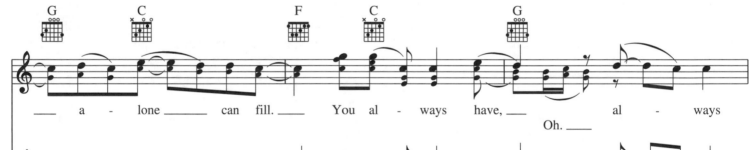

___ a - lone ___ can fill. ___ You al - ways have, ___ al - ways
Oh. ___

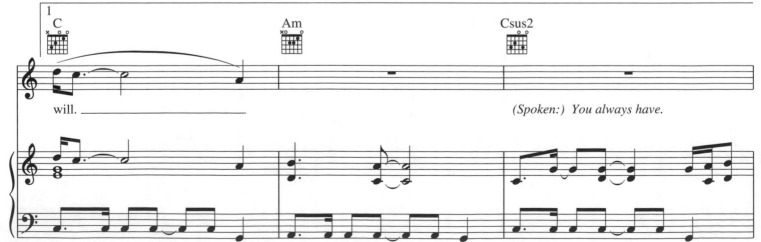

will. _____

(Spoken:) You always have.

I'm go - in' where You have gone. _____

I'm go - in' where You have gone, _____ yeah. ___

I'm let - ting You lead me, I'm let - ting You lead me home. _

I'm let - ting You lead me home. _____

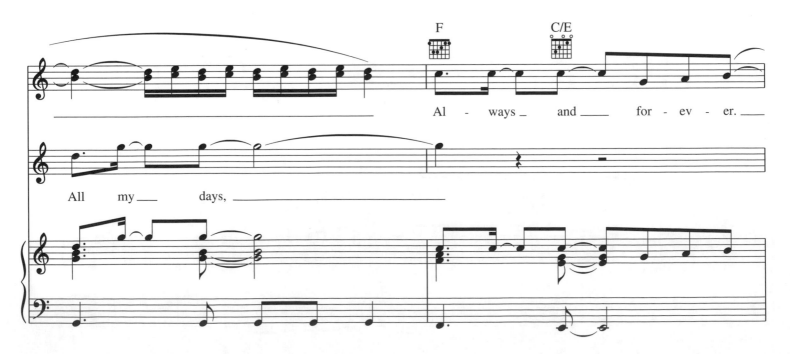

Al - ways _ and _ for - ev - er. _

All my _ days, _____

Love __ you ____ yeah __ yeah. _____ I

al - ways __ have. ___ I al - ways __ will. ___ You saved __

____ me __ once. You save ____ me still. ___ My long -

- ing __ heart your love ____ a - lone _____ can fill. __

You al - ways ___ have _____
Oh. _____
I

al - ways ___ have. ___ I al - ways ___ will. ___ You saved ___

___ me ___ once. I know you'll save me _____ still. ___
Oh. _____
My long -

- ing ___ heart _____ your love _____ a - lone _____ can fill. ___

You al - ways have, _____ al - ways

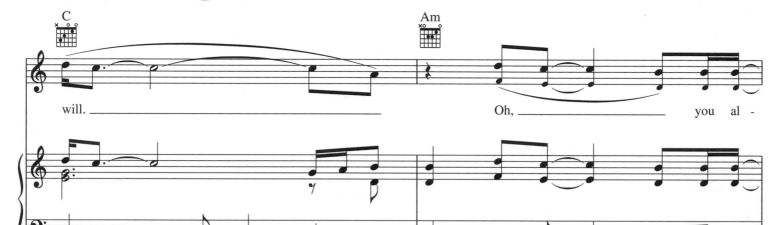

will. _____ Oh, _____ you al -

- ways will. _____ You al - ways _____ will. _____

BEAUTIFUL

Words and Music by BETHANY DILLON
and ED CASH

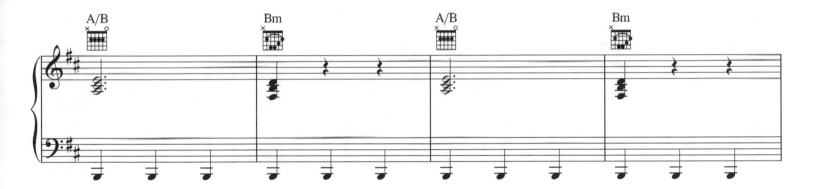

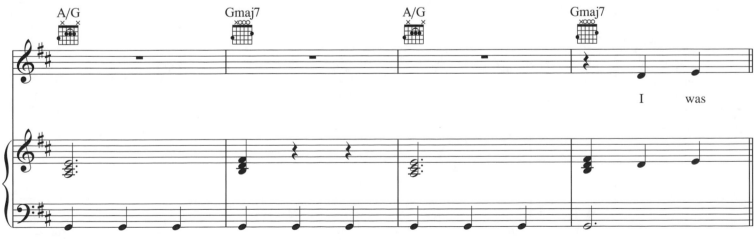

I was

*Recorded a half step lower.

so u - nique, ___ now I feel ___

skin deep.

Count on the make - up ___ to cov - er it ___

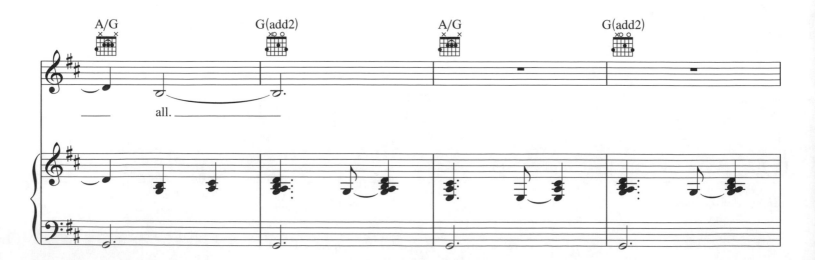

___ all. ___

Cry - ing my - self to sleep ___ 'cause I can - not

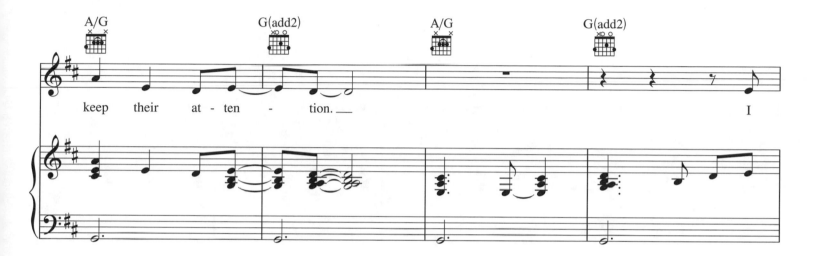

keep their at - ten - tion. ___ I

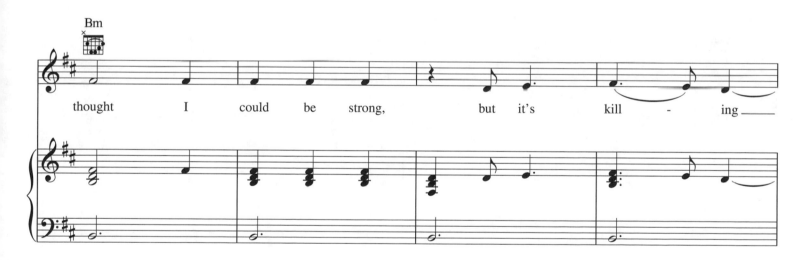

thought I could be strong, but it's kill - ing ___

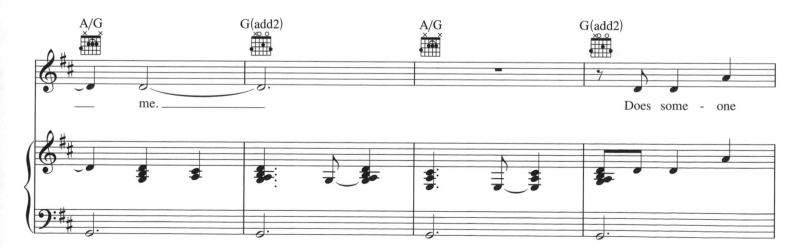

___ me. ___ Does some - one

hear _____ my cry? _____ I'm

dy - ing _____ for new _____ life. _____ I wan - na be

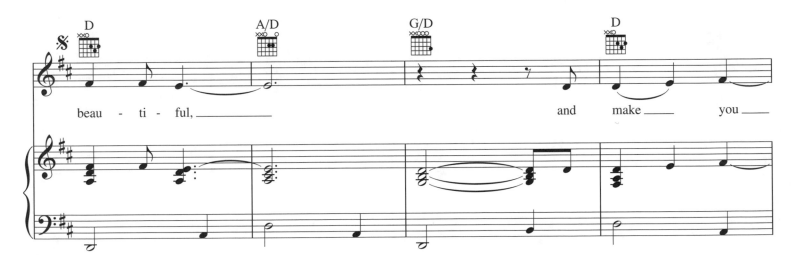

beau - ti - ful, _____ and make _____ you _____

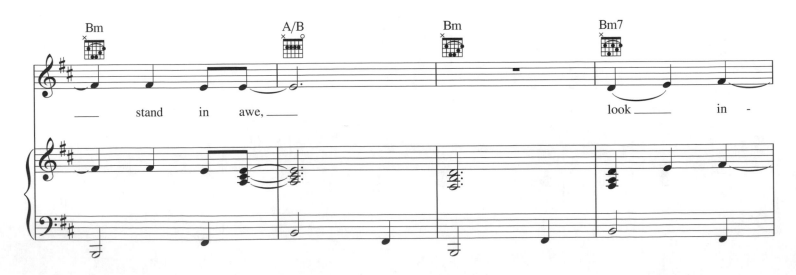

_____ stand in awe, _____ look _____ in -

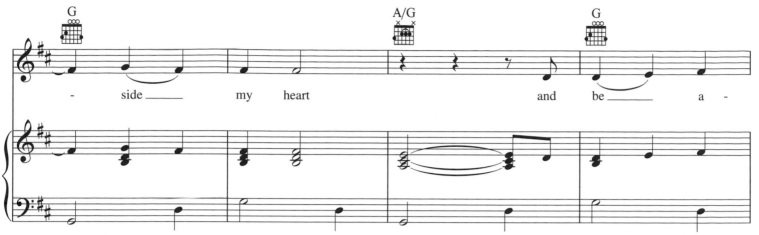

-side my heart and be a-

-mazed. I want to

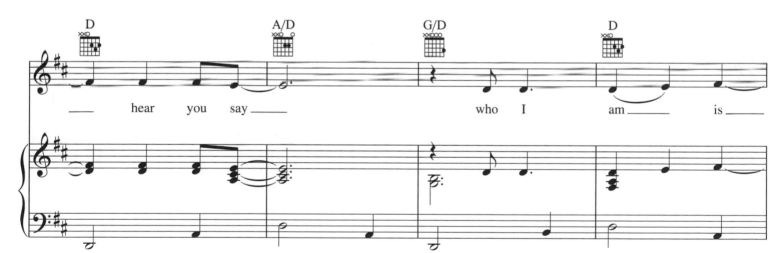

hear you say who I am is

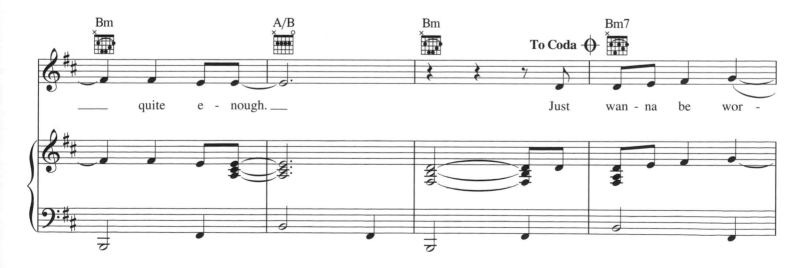

quite e-nough. Just wan-na be wor-

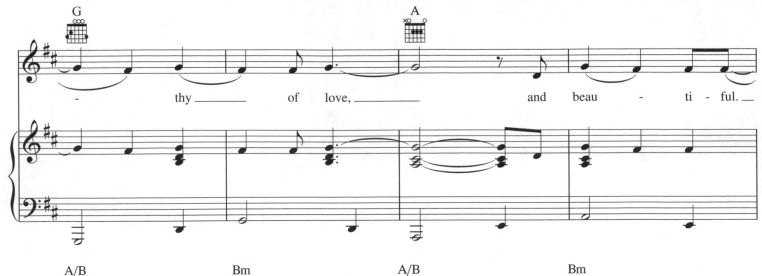

-thy _____ of love, _____ and beau - ti - ful. _____

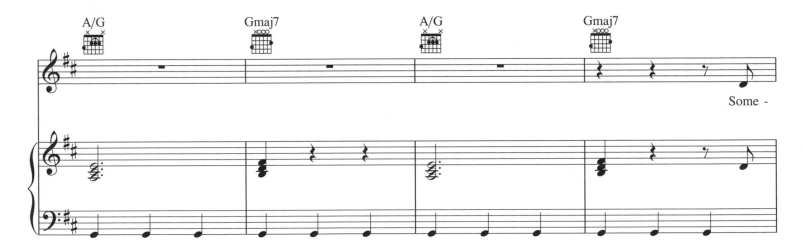

Some -

times I _____ wish I was some - one _____ oth - er than _____

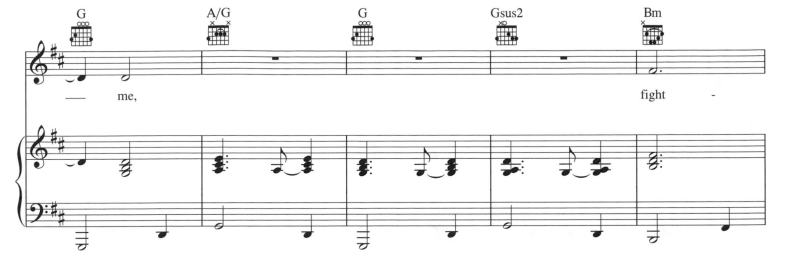

me, fight -

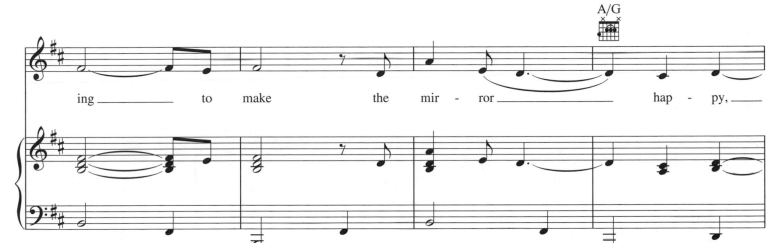

ing _____ to make the mir - ror _____ hap - py, _____

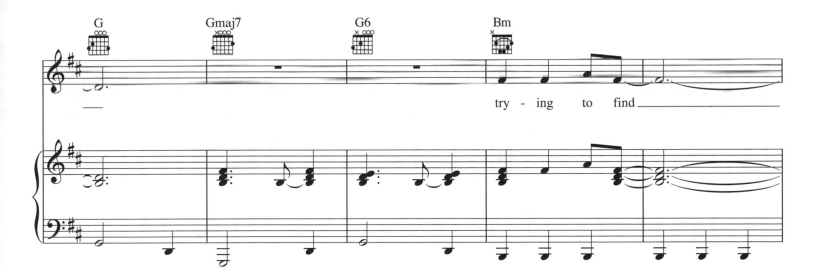

_____ try - ing to find _____

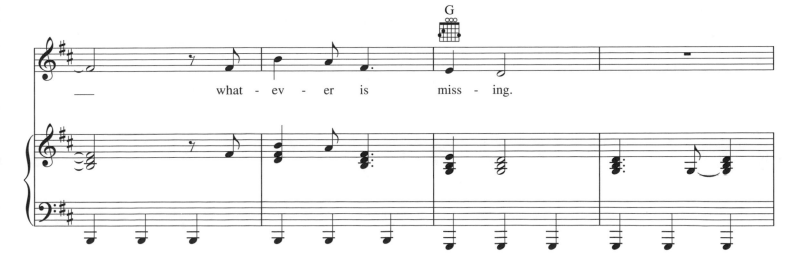

_____ what - ev - er is miss - ing.

Won't You help me ___ back to glo - ry? I

D.S. al Coda

wan - na be

CODA

wan - na be wor - thy ___ of love. ___

___ You make me ___ beau - ti - ful, ___

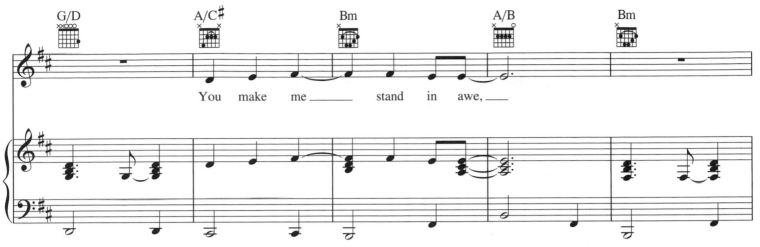

You make me _____ stand in awe, _____

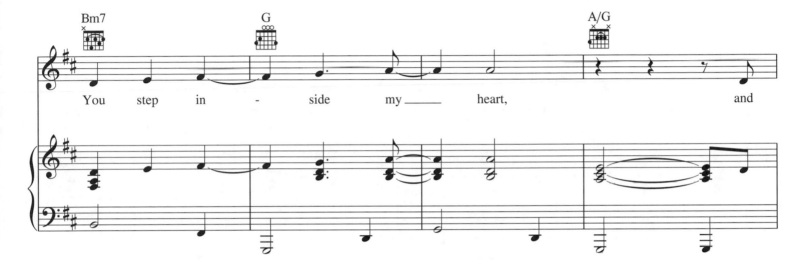

You step in - side my _____ heart, and

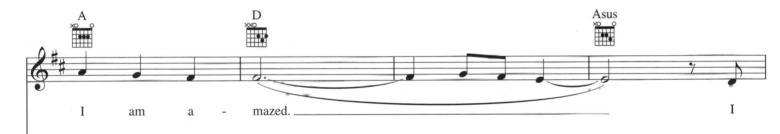

I am a - mazed. _____ I

love _____ to _____ hear You say _____ who I

am _____ is _____ quite e - nough. _____

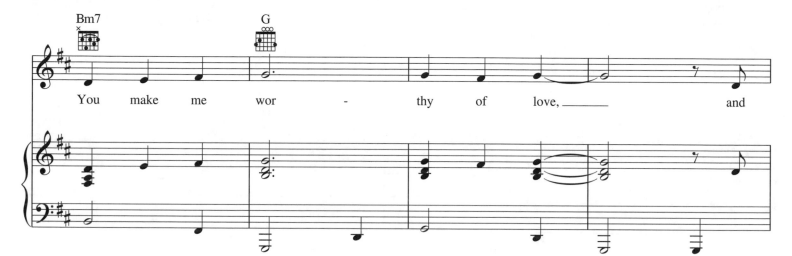

You make me wor - thy of love, _____ and

beau - ti - ful. _____ You make me

wor - thy _____ of love, _____ and beau - ti - ful. __

Beau - ti - ful.

(Vocal 1st time only)

Repeat and Fade

Optional Ending

BETWEEN YOU AND ME

Words and Music by TOBY McKEEHAN
and MARK HEIMERMANN

Medium Pop Rock

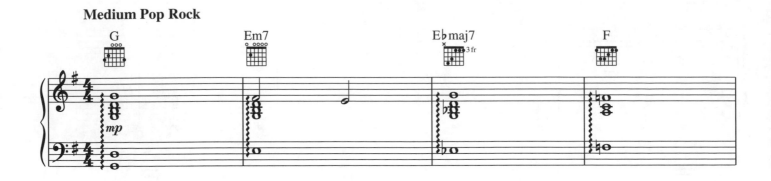

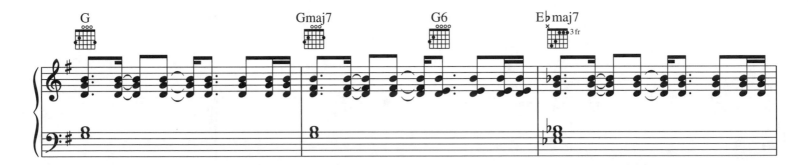

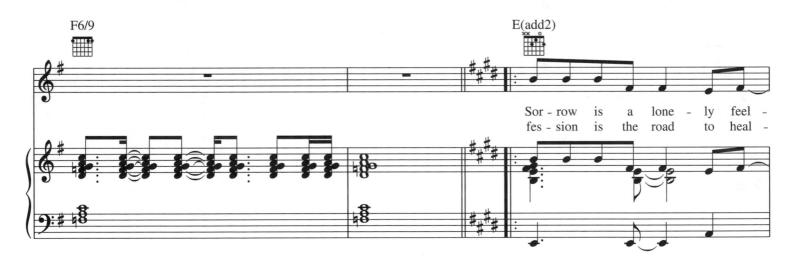

Sor-row is a lone-ly feel-
fes-sion is the road to heal-

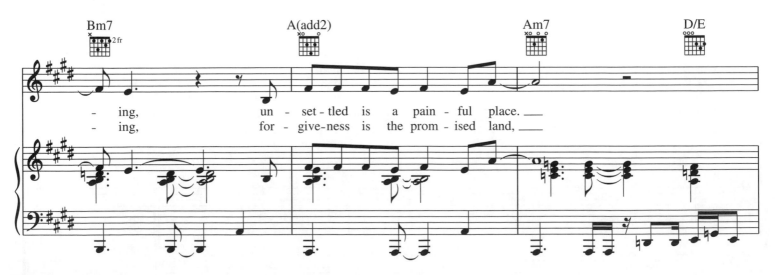

-ing, un-set-tled is a pain-ful place. ___
-ing, for-give-ness is the prom-ised land, ___

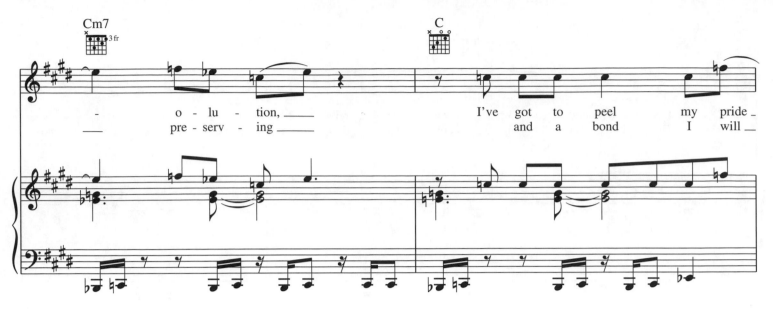

o - lu - tion, _____ I've got to peel my pride _____
_____ pre - serv - ing _____ and a bond I will _____

_____ a - way. _____ Just be - tween you and me
_____ de - fend. _____

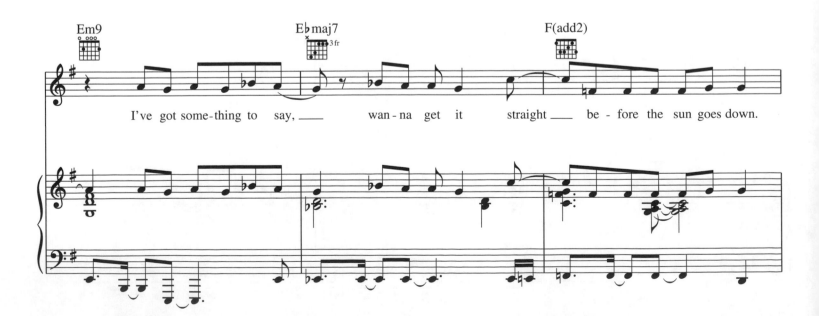

I've got some-thing to say, _____ wan - na get it straight _____ be - fore the sun goes down.

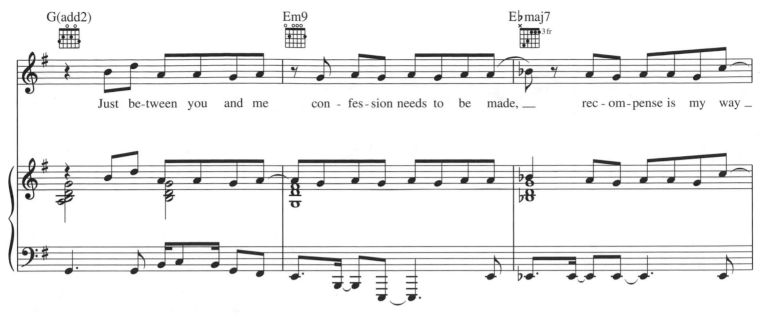

Just be-tween you and me con-fes-sion needs to be made, __ rec-om-pense is my way __

__ to free - dom now. Just be-tween you and me I've got some-thing to say. __

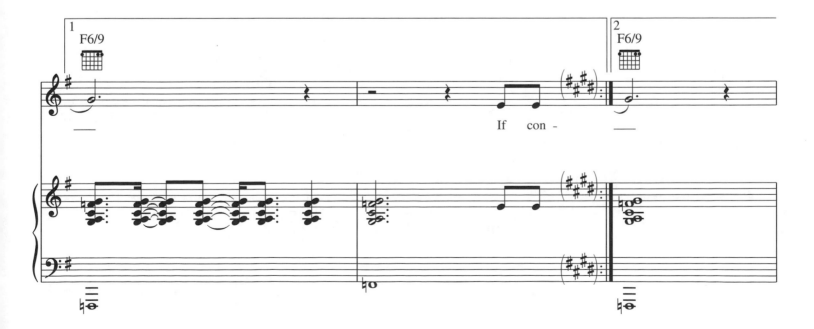

If con- __

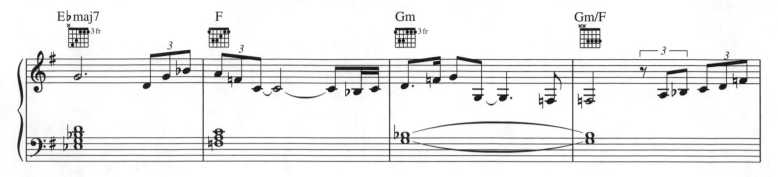

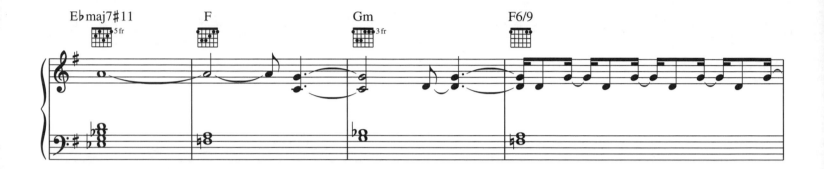

In my pur-suit of God, I thirst for ho-li-ness, as I ap-proach the Son,

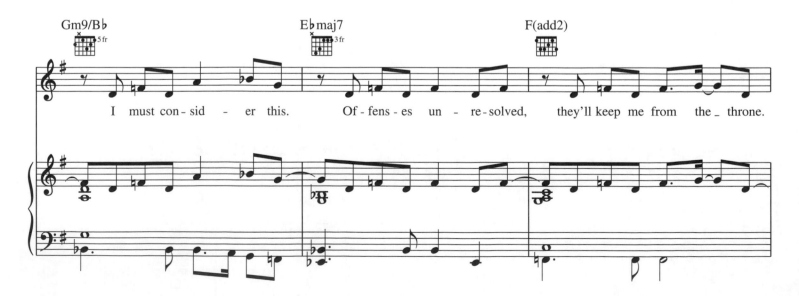

I must con-sid-er this. Of-fens-es un-re-solved, they'll keep me from the throne.

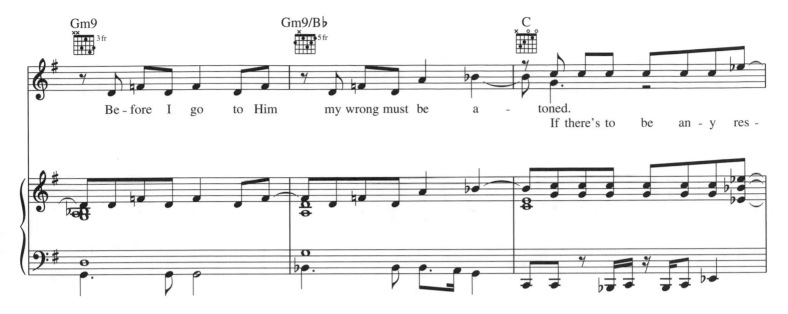

Be - fore I go to Him my wrong must be a - toned.
If there's to be an - y res-

- o - lu - tion, __ I've got to peel __ this pride __ a - way. __

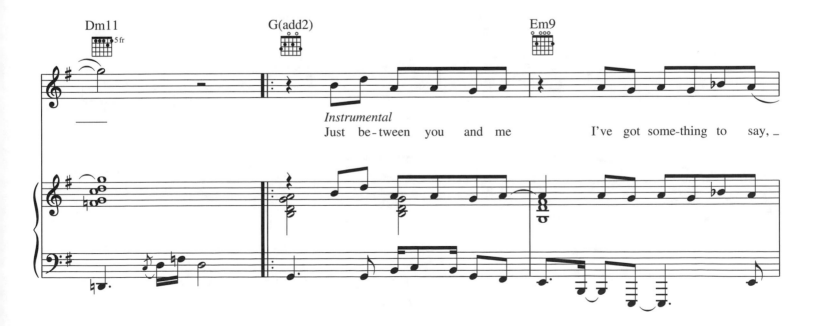

Instrumental
Just be - tween you and me I've got some-thing to say, __

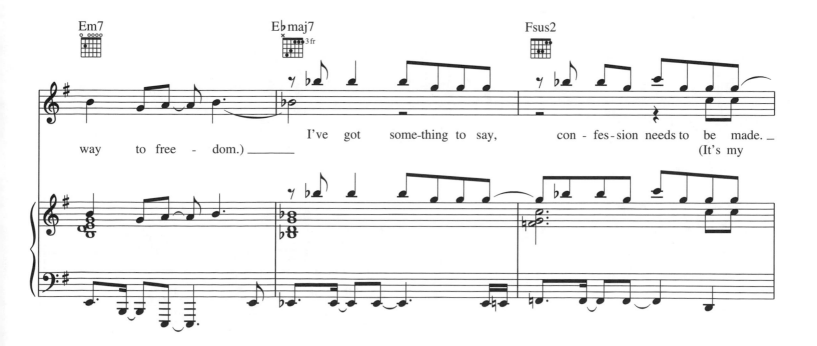

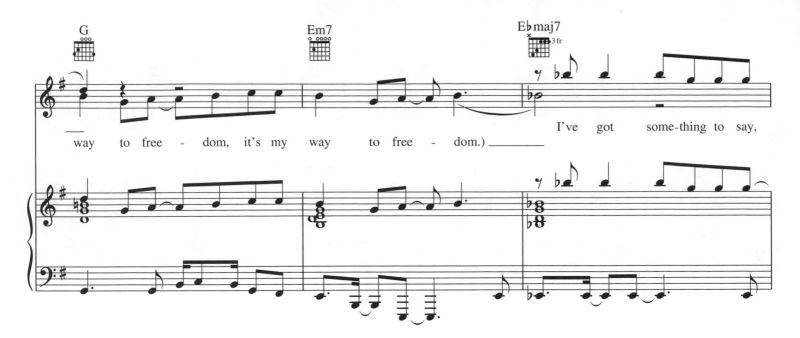

way to free - dom, it's my way to free - dom.) _____ I've got some-thing to say,

con - fes - sion needs to be made. _____ I've got
(It's my way to free - dom, it's my way to free - dom.) _____

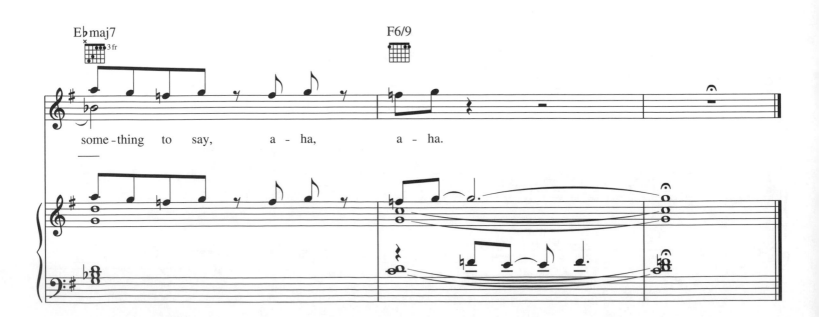

some-thing to say, a - ha, a - ha.

BRAVE

Words by NICHOLE NORDEMAN
Music by NICHOLE NORDEMAN and JAY JOYCE

Brightly

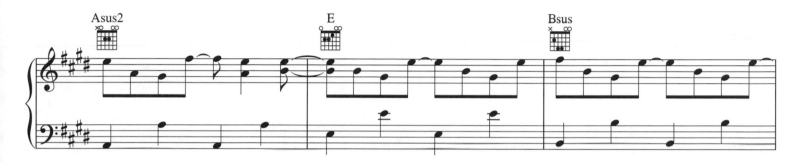

The gate is wide, _

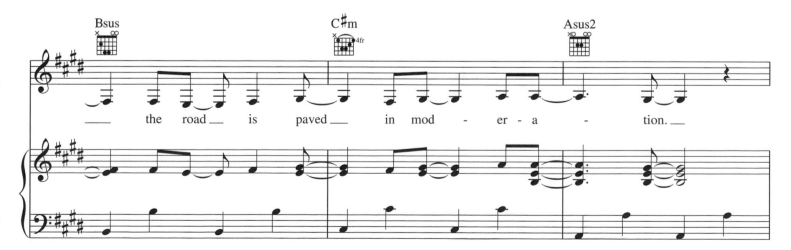

_ the road _ is paved _ in mod - er - a - tion. _

The crowd is kind and quick to pull you in.

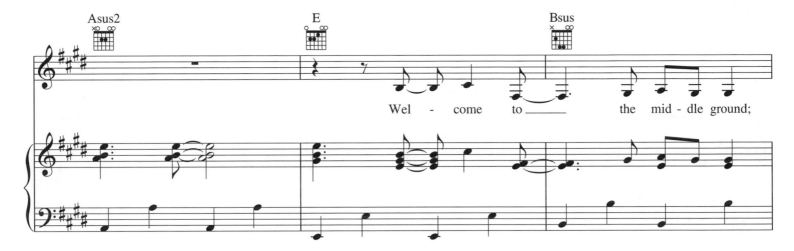

Wel - come to the mid - dle ground;

it's safe and sound, and un - til now

it's where I've been. 'Cause it's been

fear that ties _____ me down __ to ev - 'ry - thing. _____

But it's _____ been love, _____ Your _____ love, _____ that

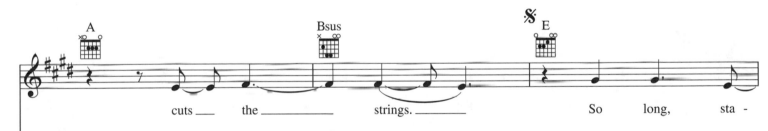

cuts ___ the _____ strings. _____ So long, sta -

- tus quo, ___ I think __ I just ___ let go. _____

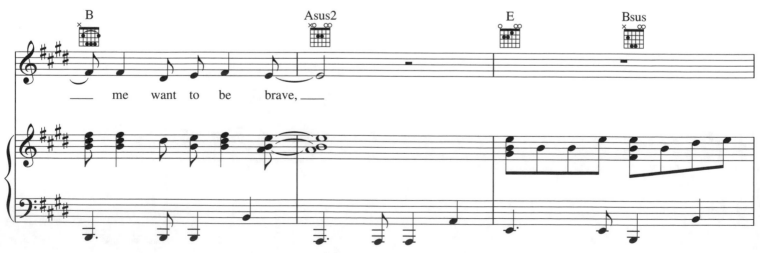

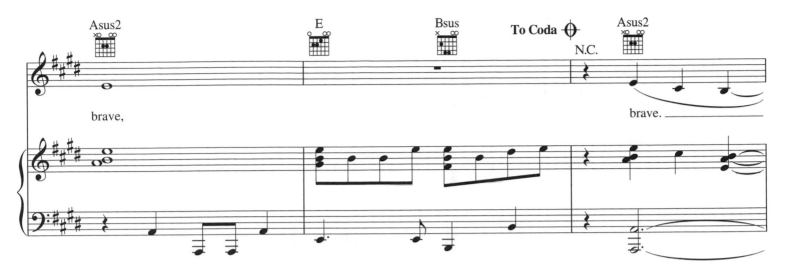

brave,   brave. _____

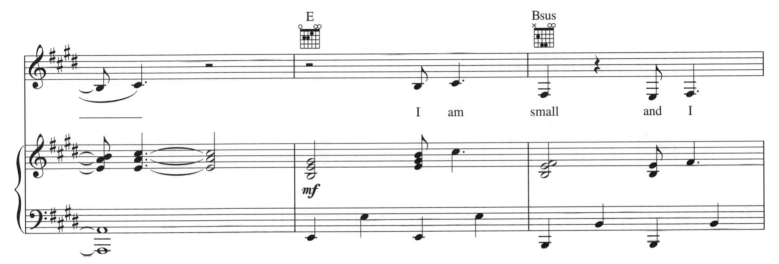

I am   small   and   I

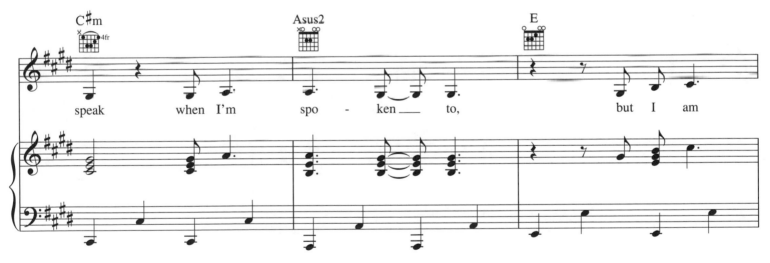

speak   when I'm   spo - ken ___ to,   but I am

will - ing   to   risk ___ it ___ all.

I say___ Your name,___ just___ Your name,___ and I'm

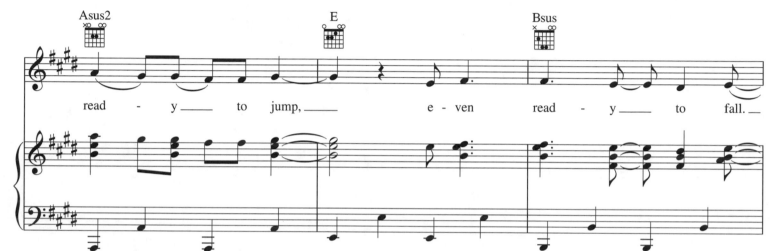

read - y ___ to jump, ___ e - ven read - y ___ to fall. ___

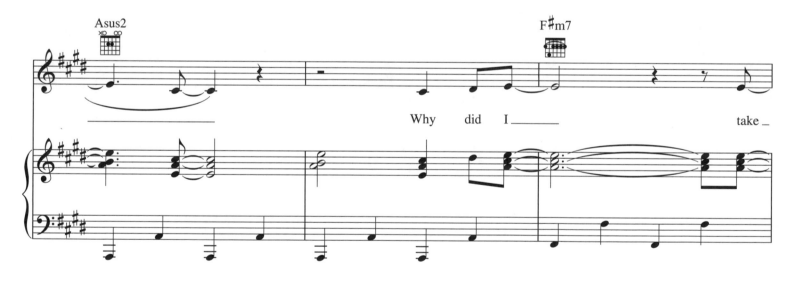

_____ Why did I _____ take _

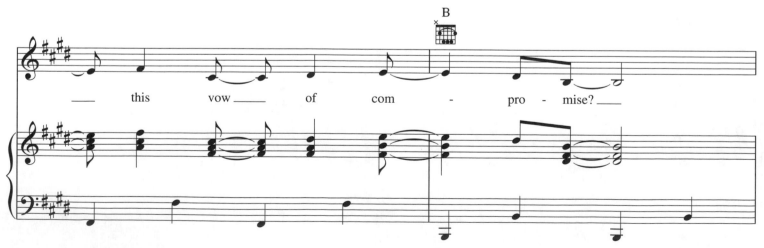

___ this vow ___ of com - pro - mise? ___

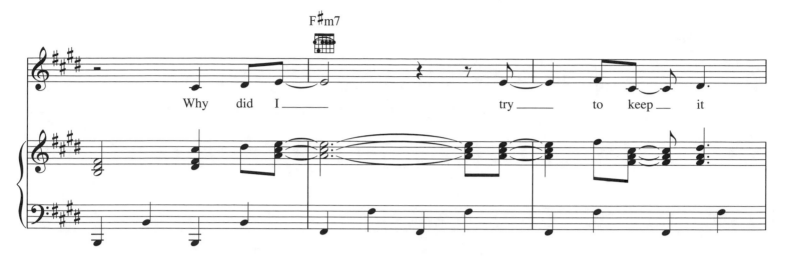

Why did I _____ try _____ to keep ___ it

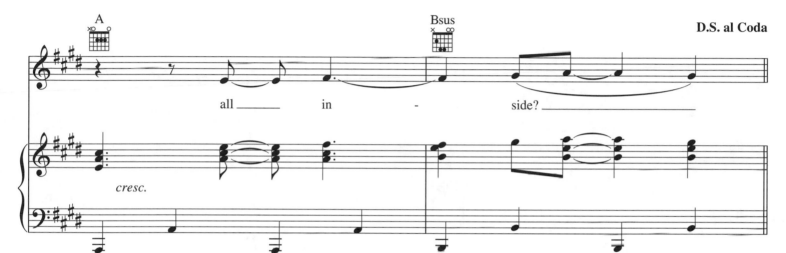

D.S. al Coda

all _____ in - side? _____

cresc.

CODA

A G#

N.C.

brave. ___ I've nev - er known ___

C#m

___ a fire _____ that did - n't be - gin with ___ a flame. ___

Ev - 'ry storm ___ will start ___ with just ___ a drop ___ of rain. ___

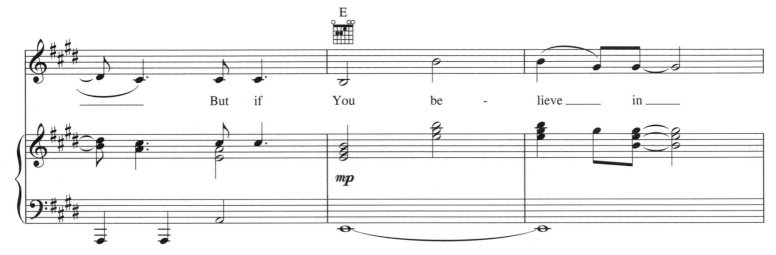

But if You be - lieve ___ in ___

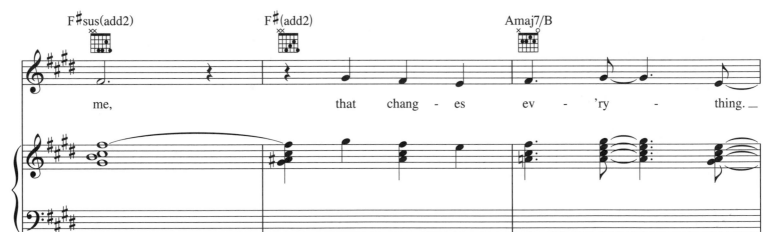

me, that chang - es ev - 'ry - thing. ___

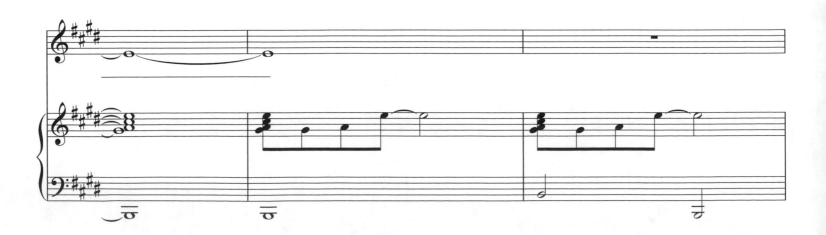

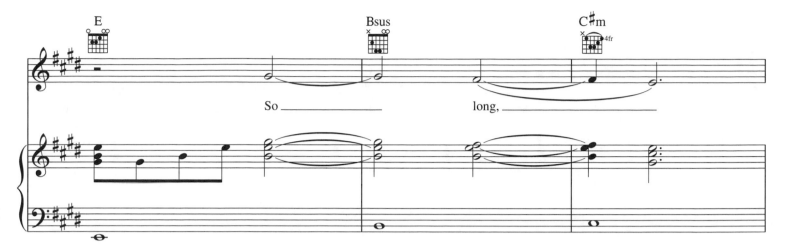

So _____ long, _____

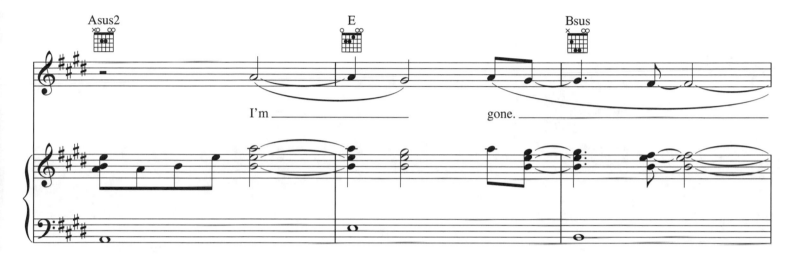

I'm _____ gone. _____

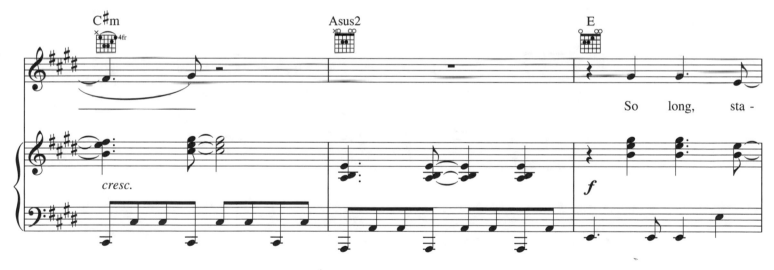

_____ So long, sta-

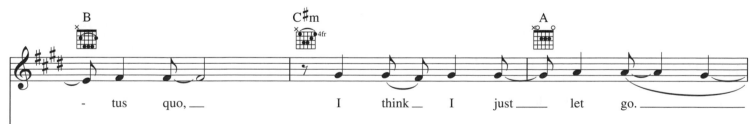

-tus quo, ___ I think ___ I just ___ let go. _____

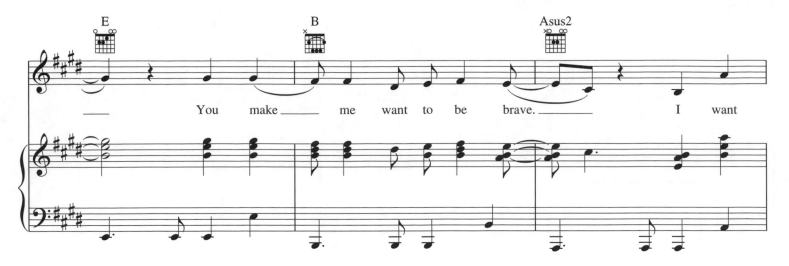

You make ___ me want to be brave. ___ I want

to be brave. ___ The way ___ it al - ways was ___

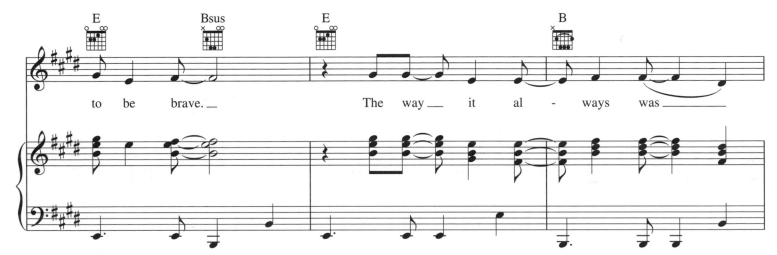

is no long - er good ___ e - nough. ___ You make ___

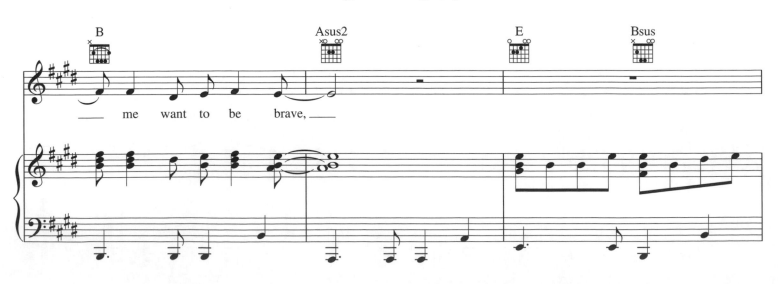

___ me want to be brave, ___

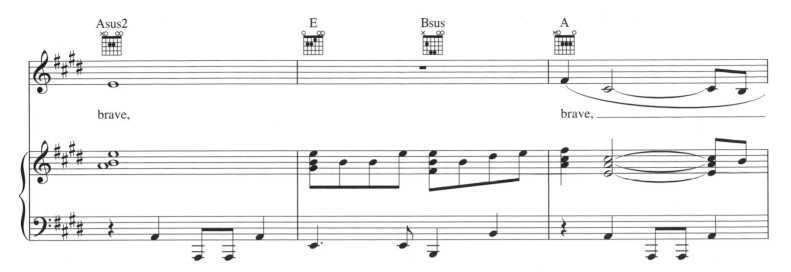

brave,   brave, _____

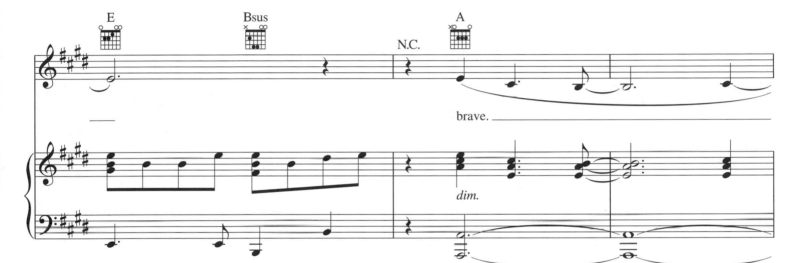

_____   brave. _____

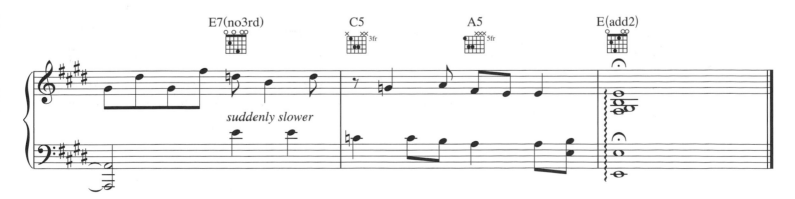

CHILDREN OF THE WORLD

Words and Music by TOMMY SIMS,
WAYNE KIRKPATRICK and AMY GRANT

Vocal written one octave higher than sung.

Red and yel - low, black and white, _____

they are pre - cious in the Fa - ther's eyes. _____

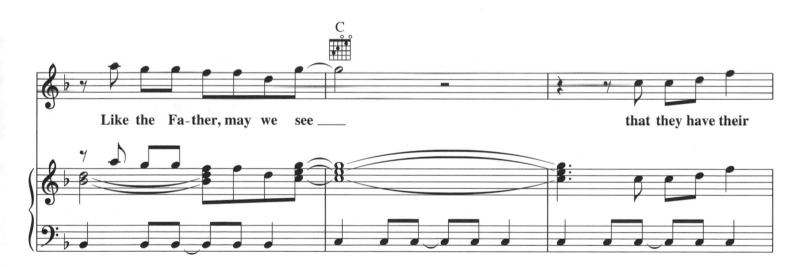

Like the Fa-ther, may we see _____ that they have their

des - ti - ny, _____ yeah, _____ and give them _ the light _____ of love _

To Coda ⊕

and we must have faith for these. ___

Red and yel - low, black and white, _____

they are pre - cious in the Fa - ther's eyes. _____

Like the Fa - ther, may we see ___ that they have their

CIRCLE OF FRIENDS

Words and Music by DOUGLAS McKELVEY
and STEVE SILER

We were made to love and be loved,
If you weep, I will weep with you.
If you

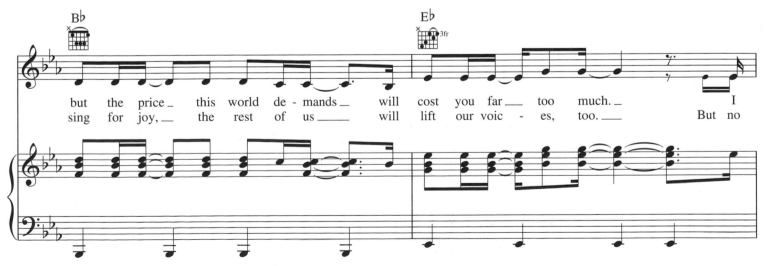

but the price this world de-mands will cost you far too much. I
sing for joy, the rest of us will lift our voic-es, too. But no

spent so man - y lone - ly years___ just try - ing to___ fit in.___ Now I've
mat - ter what you feel___ in - side,___ there's no need to___ pre - tend.___ That's the

found a place___ in this cir - cle___ of friends.___
way it is___ in this cir - cle___ of friends.___ In a cir - cle___ of friends,___

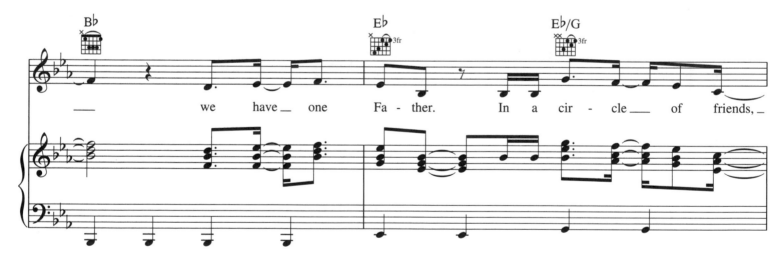

___ we have___ one Fa - ther. In a cir - cle___ of friends,___

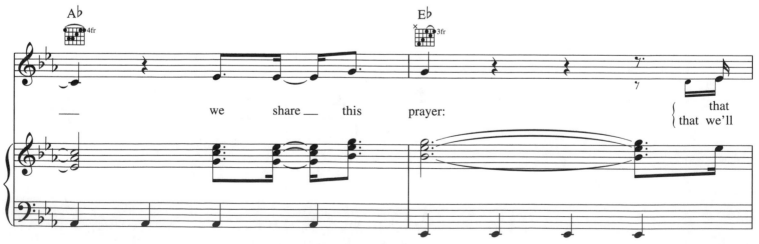

___ we share___ this prayer: { that { that we'll

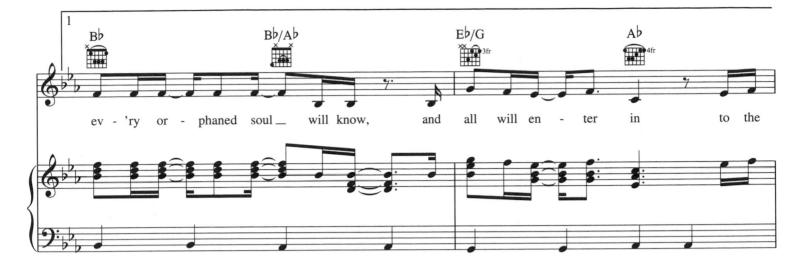

ev - 'ry or - phaned soul __ will know, and all will en - ter in to the

shel - ter of __ this cir - cle __ of friends. __

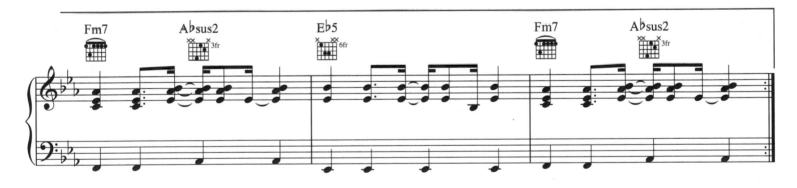

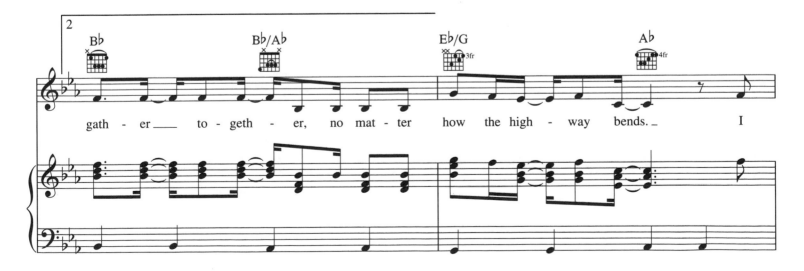

gath - er __ to - geth - er, no mat - ter how the high - way bends. __ I

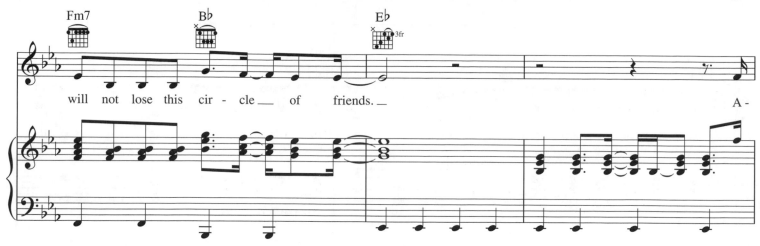

will not lose this cir - cle __ of friends. __ A-

mong the na - tions, tribes __ and tongues, __ we have sis - ters __ and broth - ers. And

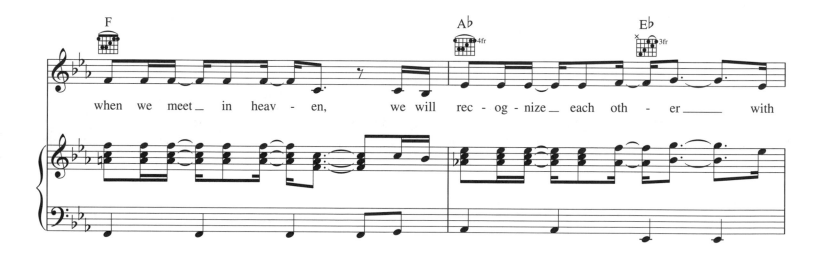

when we meet __ in heav - en, we will rec - og - nize __ each oth - er _____ with

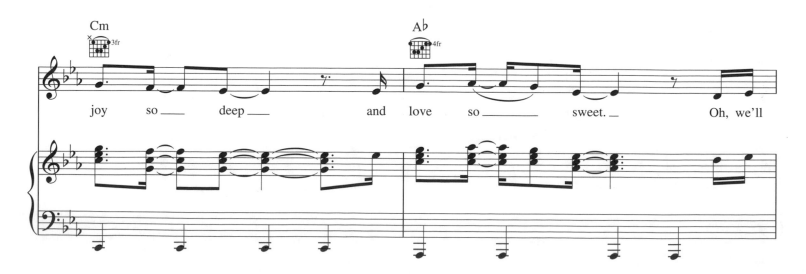

joy so __ deep __ and love so _____ sweet. __ Oh, we'll

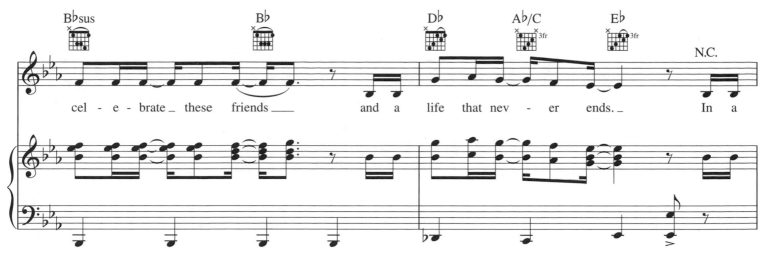

cel - e - brate _ these friends _ and a life that nev - er ends. _ In a

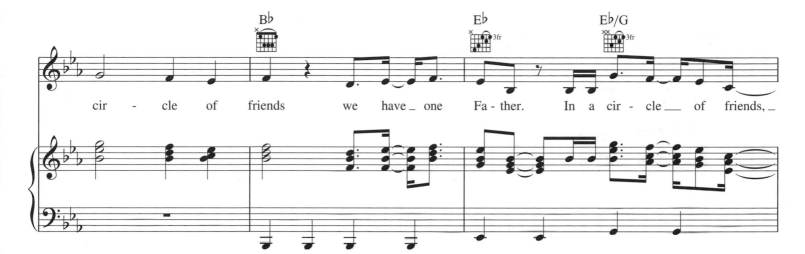

cir - cle of friends we have _ one Fa - ther. In a cir - cle _ of friends, _

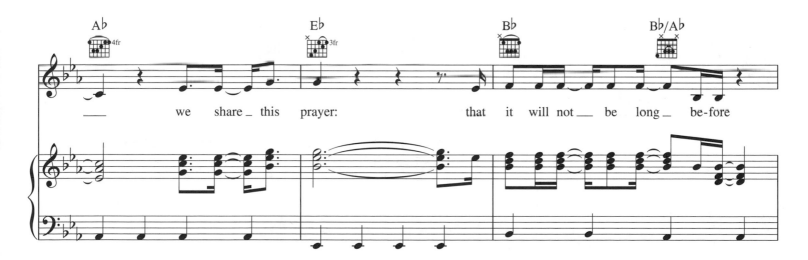

_ we share _ this prayer: that it will not _ be long _ be-fore

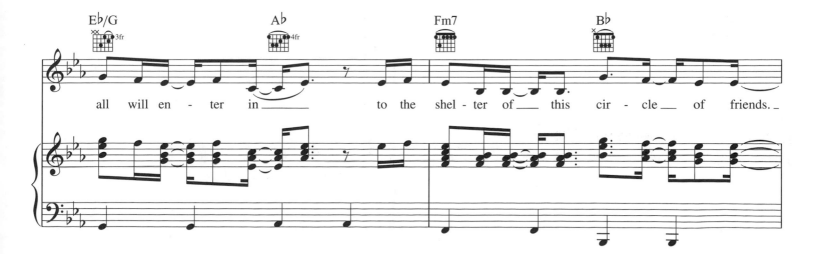

all will en - ter in _ to the shel - ter of _ this cir - cle _ of friends. _

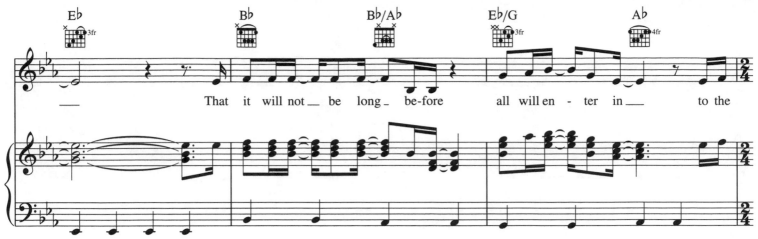

That it will not — be long — be-fore all will en - ter in — to the

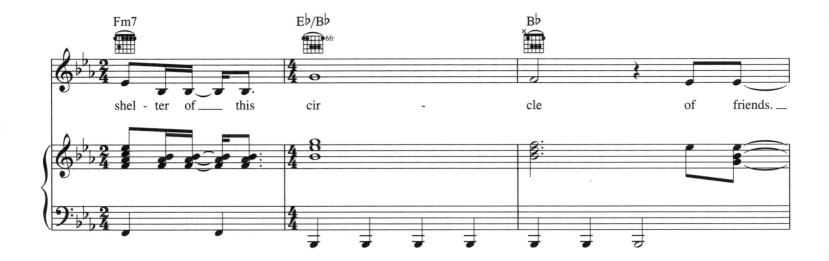

shel - ter of — this cir - cle — of friends. —

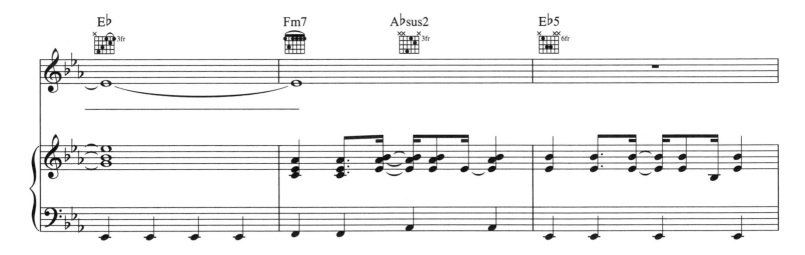

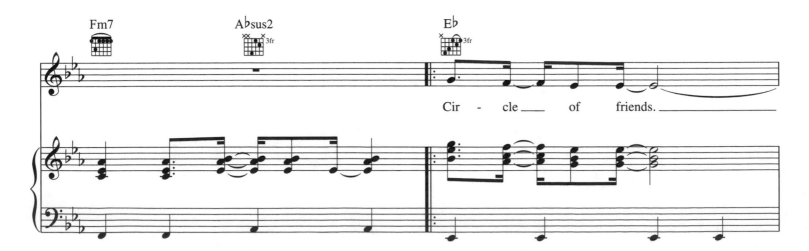

Cir - cle — of friends. —

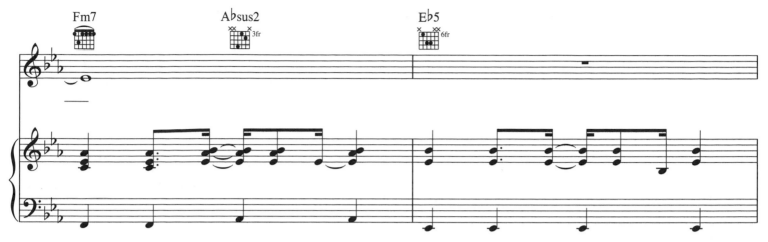

Cir - cle ___ of friends. ___

___ Cir - cle ___ of friends. ___

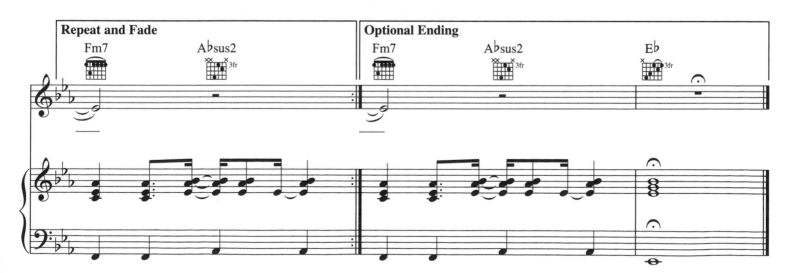

Repeat and Fade

Optional Ending

CLOSER TO MYSELF

Words and Music by RON ANIELLO
and KENDALL PAYNE

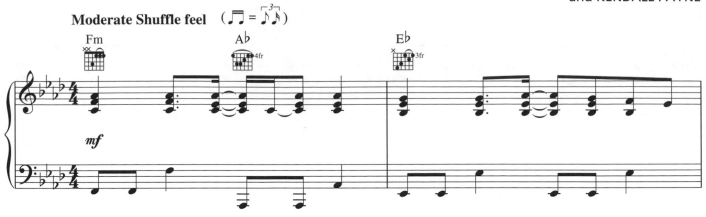

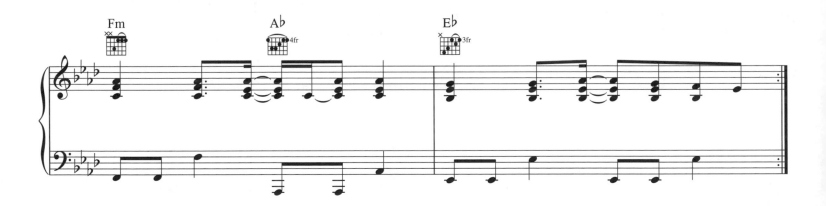

Dig-ging deep, __ I feel my con - science burn. __

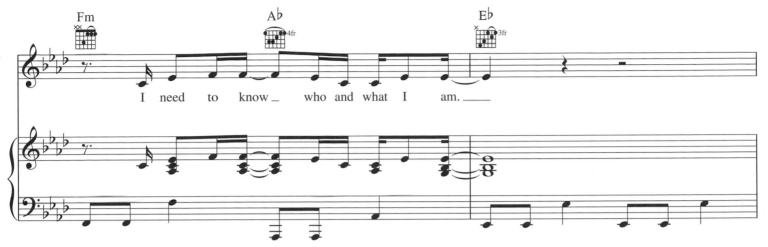

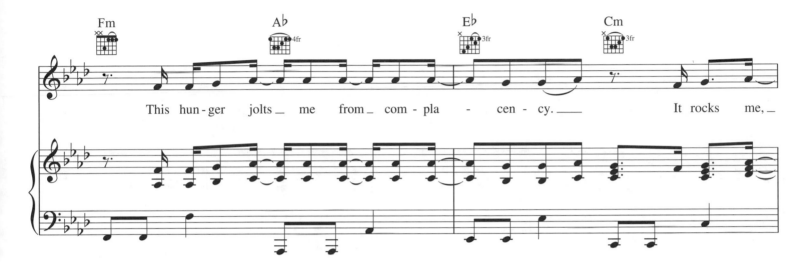

of the great-er gift __ of the great-er One. __

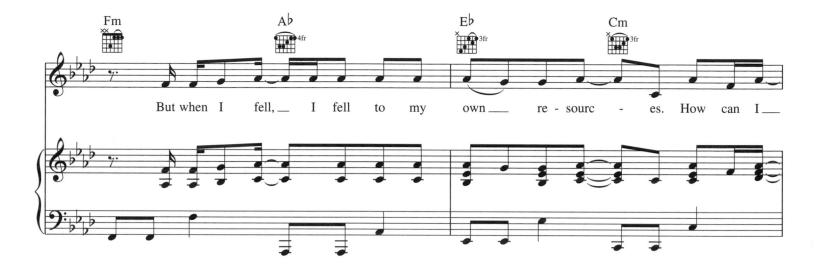

But when I fell, __ I fell to my own __ re-sourc - es. How can I __

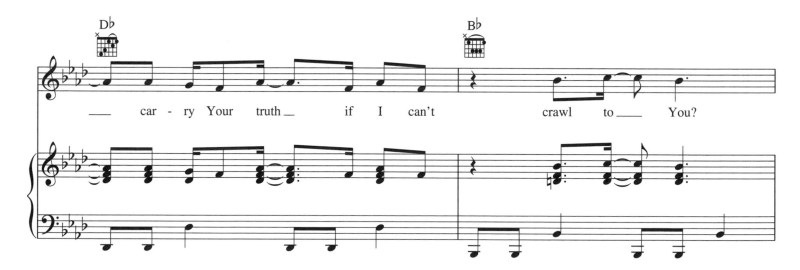

__ car - ry Your truth __ if I can't crawl to __ You?

I wan-na feel __ some-thing sweet - er than __ this sin. __

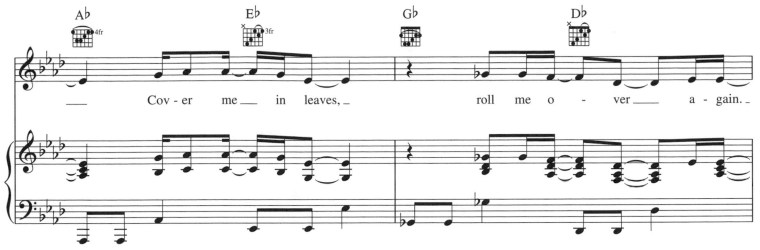

Cov- er me ___ in leaves, ___ roll me o - ver ___ a - gain. ___

___ 'Cause I've been ev - 'ry - bod - y else; ___ now I wan - na be ___ some -

- thing clos- er to ___ my - self.
Da da da ___ da da ___ da da. ___ Da da da ___ da da ___ da da. ___

To Coda ⊕

Da da da ___ da da ___ da da. ___ Da da da ___ da da ___ da da. ___

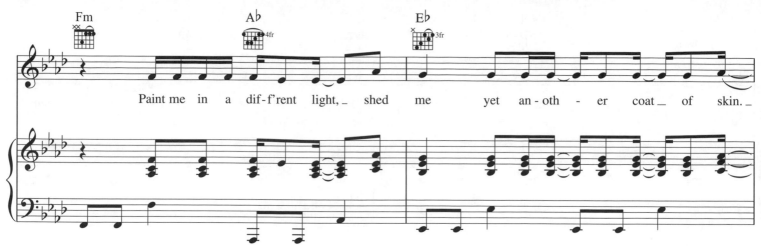

Paint me in a dif-f'rent light, __ shed me yet an-oth - er coat __ of skin. __

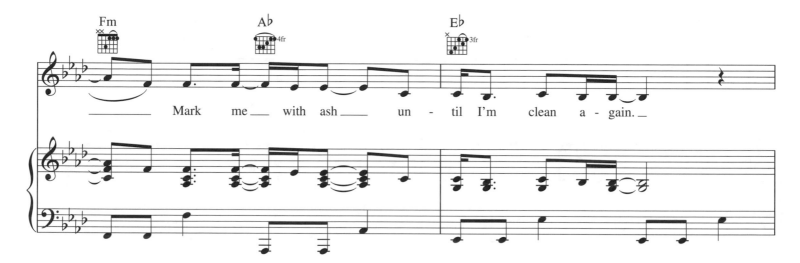

__ Mark me __ with ash __ un - til I'm clean a - gain. __

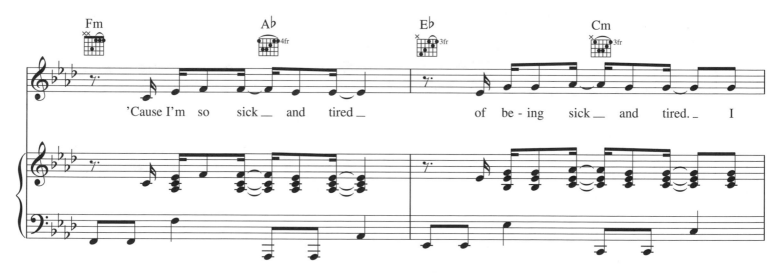

'Cause I'm so sick __ and tired __ of be - ing sick __ and tired. __ I

D.S. al Coda

know I can love __ You. I know __ that I can. __ Hey, __ and

CODA

Da da da___ da da___ da da.___ Da da da___ da da___ da dum.___

Da da da___ da da___ da da.___ Da da da___ da da___ da dum.___

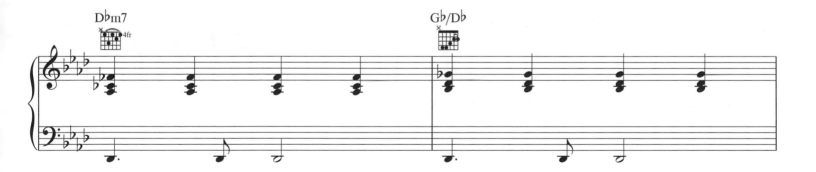

D♭m7   G♭/D♭

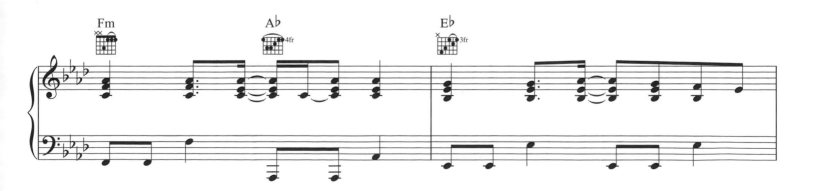

Fm   A♭   E♭

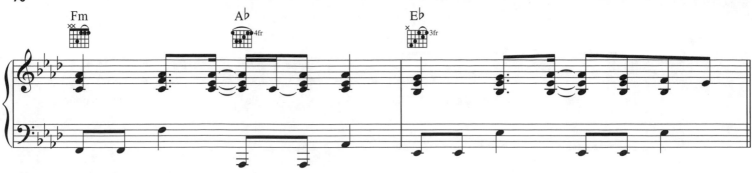

I wan-na feel __ some-thing sweet - er than __ this sin. __

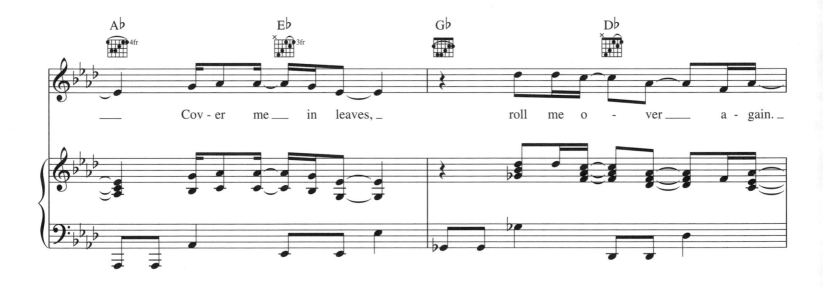

__ Cov - er me __ in leaves, __ roll me o - ver __ a - gain. __

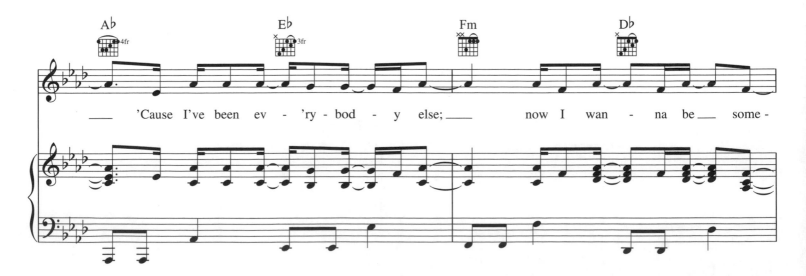

__ 'Cause I've been ev - 'ry - bod - y else; __ now I wan - na be __ some-

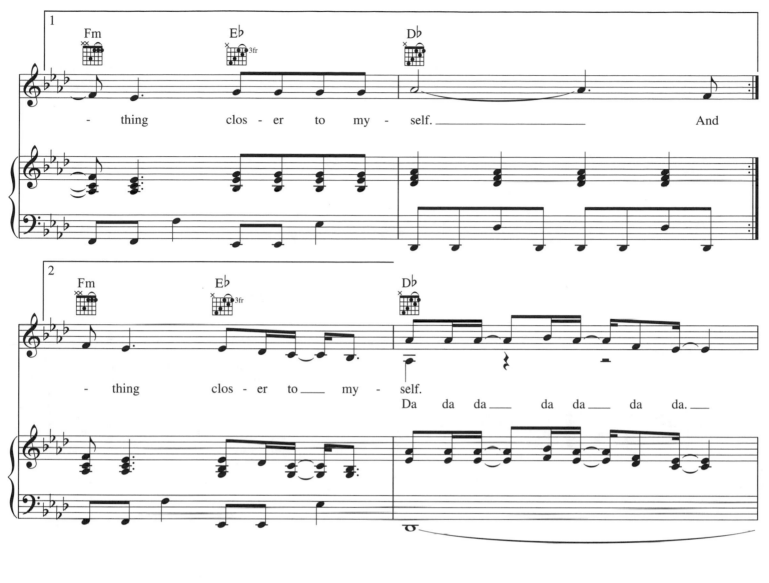

CRAZY

Words and Music by BART MILLARD,
ROBBY HURD, CHAD SIPES
and PETER KIPLEY

Moderately, in 2

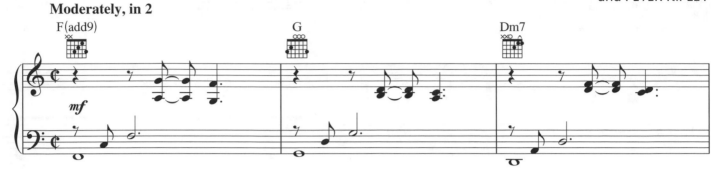

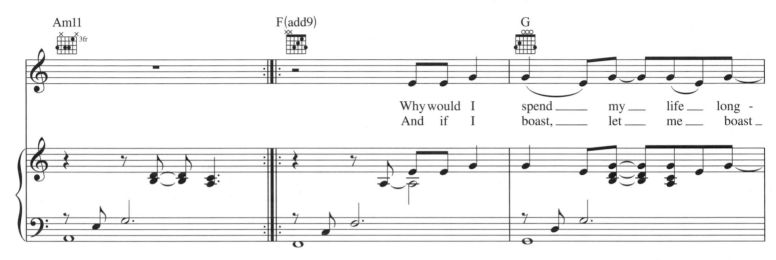

Why would I spend _____ my _____ life _____ long-
And if I boast, _____ let _____ me _____ boast

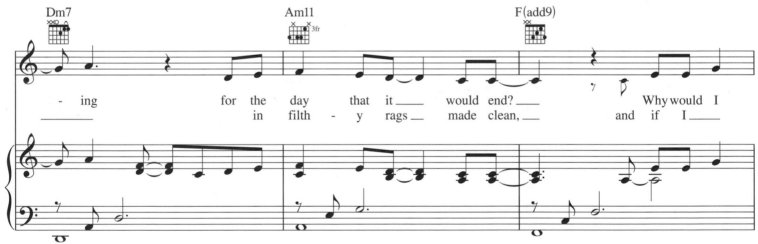

-ing for the day that it _____ would end? _____ Why would I
_____ in filth - y rags _____ made clean, _____ and if I _____

spend _____ my _____ time _____ point - ing to an - oth - er man?
glo - ry, let _____ me glo - ry in my Sav - ior's suf - fer - ing.

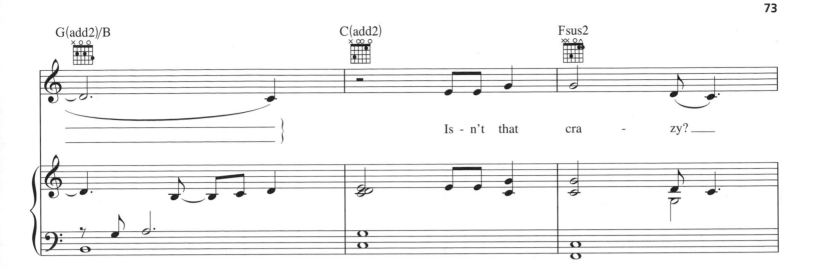

Is - n't that cra - zy? ___

How can I find ___ hope ___ in ___ dy -
And as I live ___ this dai - ly ___ life, _

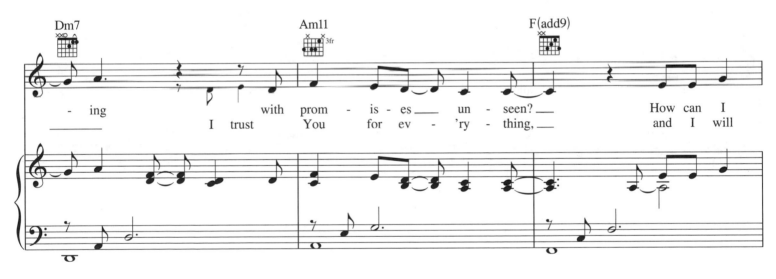

- ing with prom - is - es ___ un - seen? ___ How can I
___ I trust You for ev - 'ry - thing, ___ and I will

learn Your way ___ is bet - ter in ev - 'ry - thing I'm taught to be? _
on - ly take ___ a step ___ when I feel ___ You lead - ing me. _

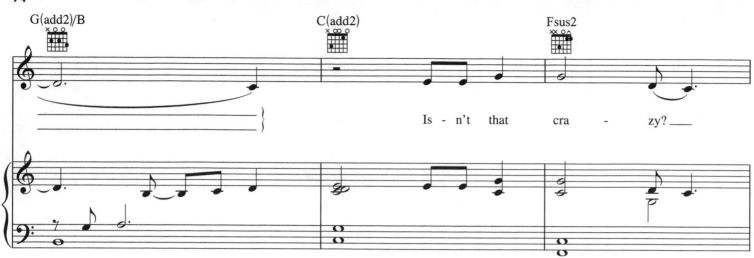

Is - n't that cra - zy? ___

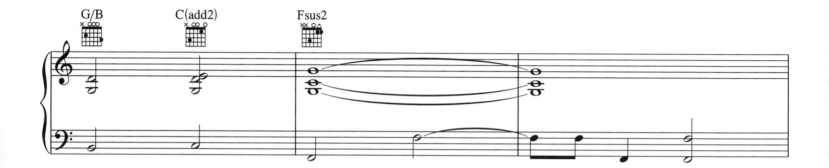

I have not ___ been called ___ to the wis - dom of ___ this world, ___

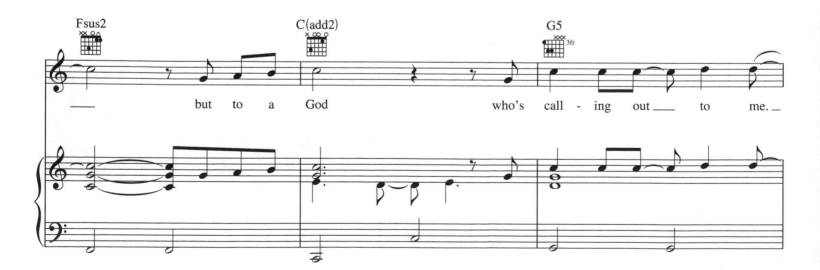

___ but to a God who's call - ing out ___ to me. ___

And e-ven though the world_ may think_

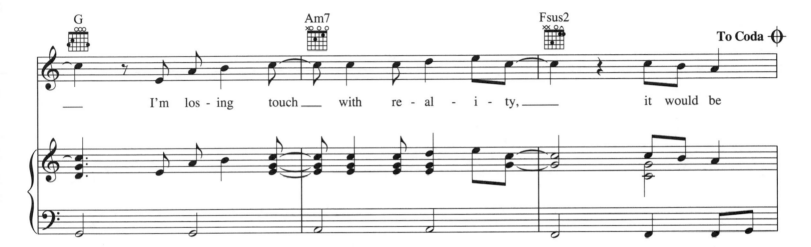

I'm los-ing touch_ with re-al-i-ty,_ it would be

To Coda ⊕

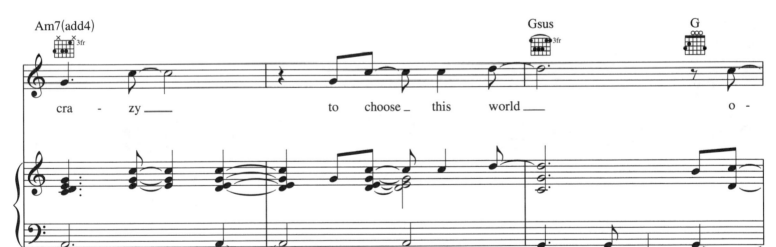

cra-zy_ to choose_ this world_ o-

-ver e-ter-ni-ty._

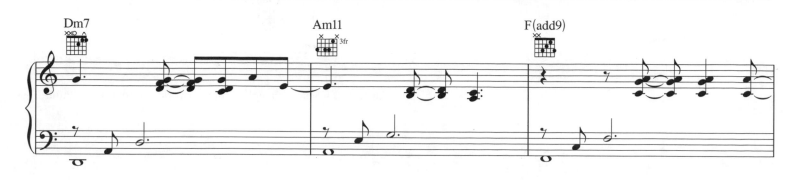

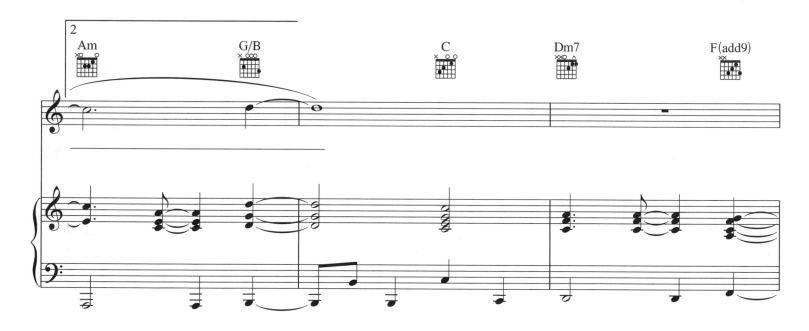

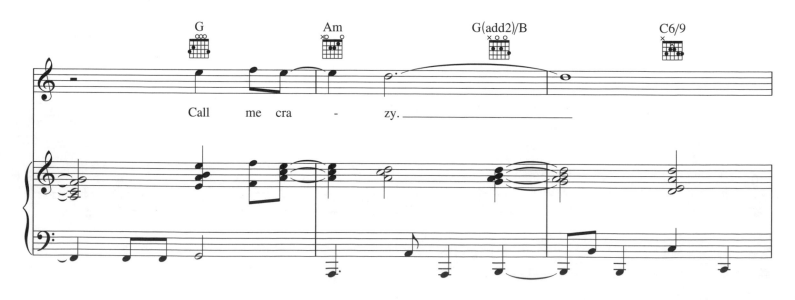

Call me cra - zy. _____

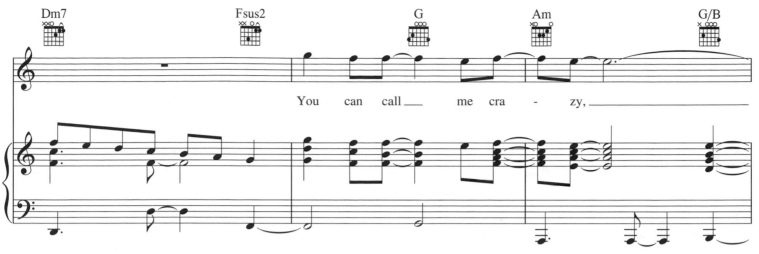

You can call __ me cra - zy, _____

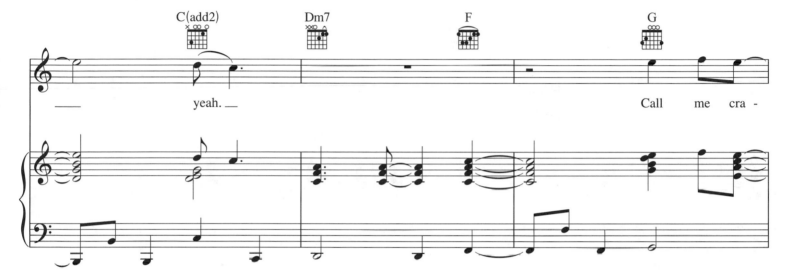

__ yeah. __ Call me cra -

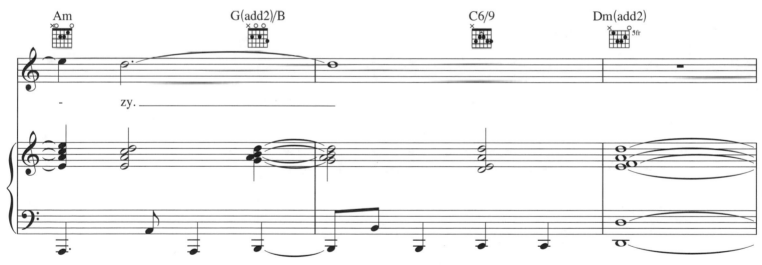

- zy. _____

CODA

D.S. al Coda

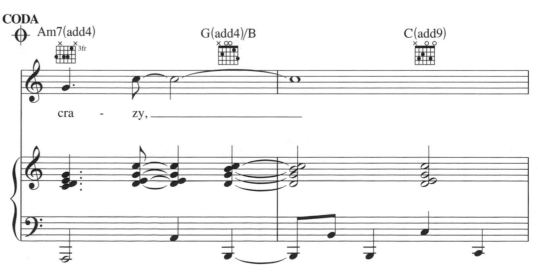

cra - zy, _____

it would be cra - zy, _____ yeah, _____ it would be cra - zy ____ to choose ___ this world ____ o -

- ver e - ter - ni - ty. _____

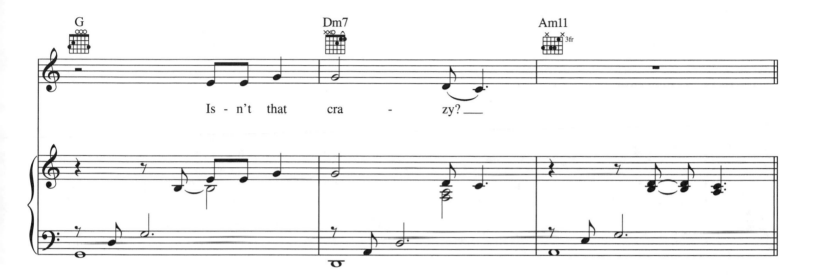

Is - n't that cra - zy? ___

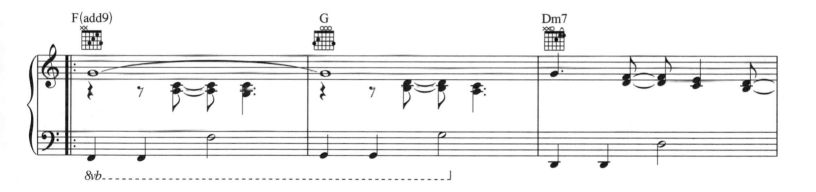

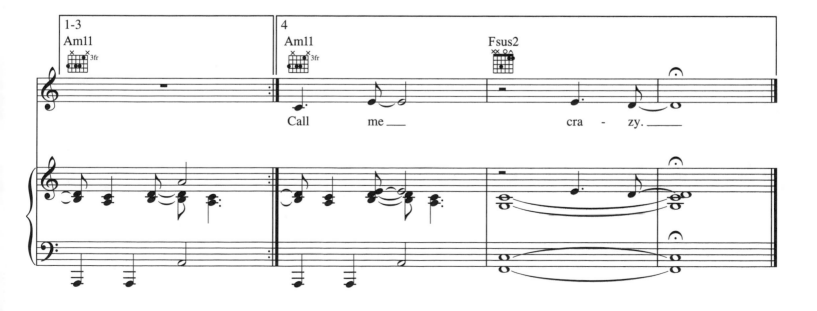

Call me ___ cra - zy. ___

DOWN ON MY KNEES

Words and Music by
WAYNE KIRKPATRICK

Rhythmically

I've got a

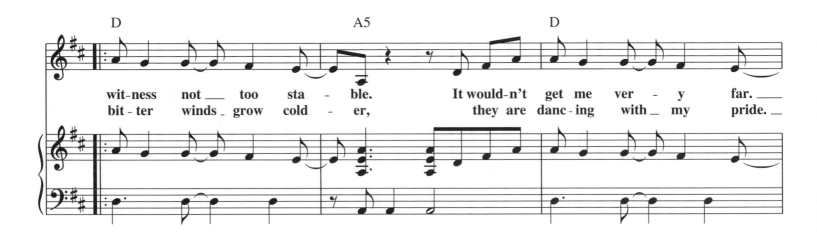

wit-ness not __ too sta - ble. It would-n't get me ver - y far. __
bit - ter winds __ grow cold - er, they are danc-ing with __ my pride. __

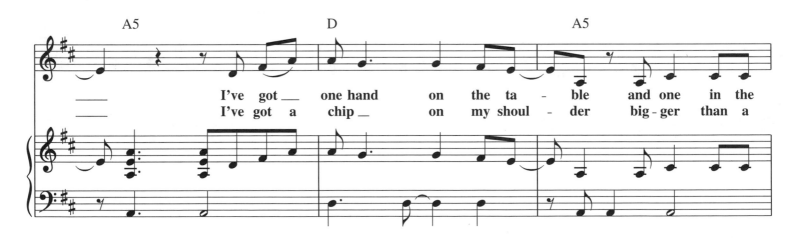

__ I've got __ one hand on the ta - ble and one in the
__ I've got a chip __ on my shoul - der big - ger than a

cook - ie jar. __ I've got sins that need __ e - vic -
moun - tain - side. __ And these claws of hu - man na -

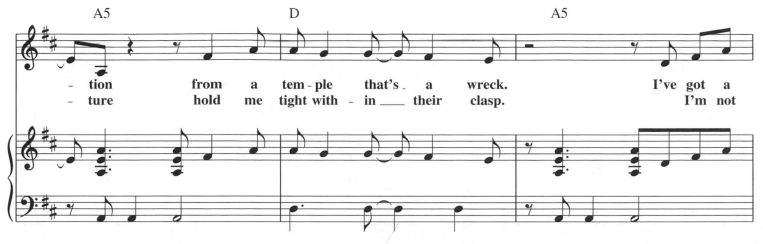

-tion / -ture from a tem-ple that's a wreck. / hold me tight with-in their clasp. I've got a / I'm not

chain of con-tra-dic -tion hang-ing a-round my neck. / worth-y of for-give -ness, but I just have to ask.

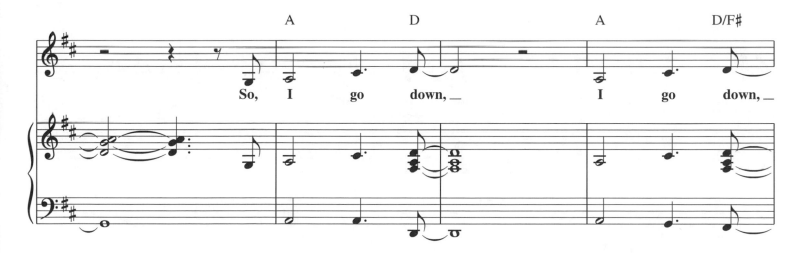

So, I go down, I go down,

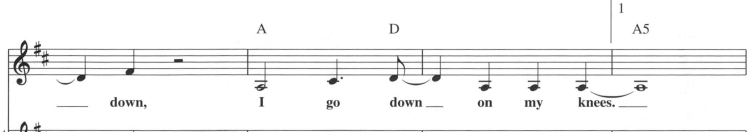

1

down, I go down on my knees.

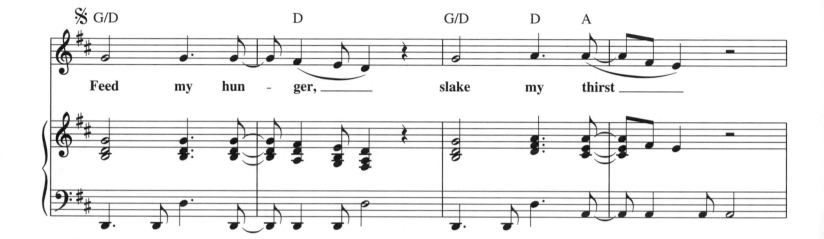

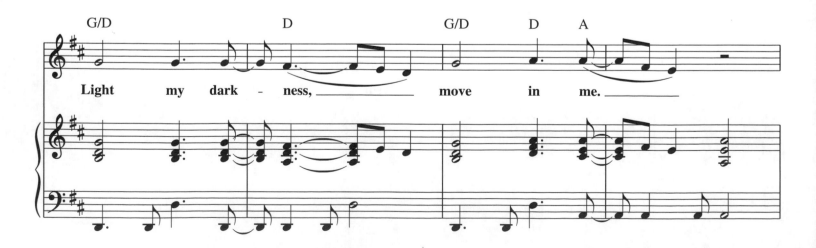

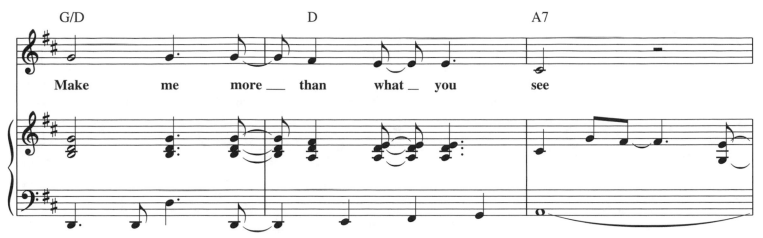

Make me more ___ than what ___ you see

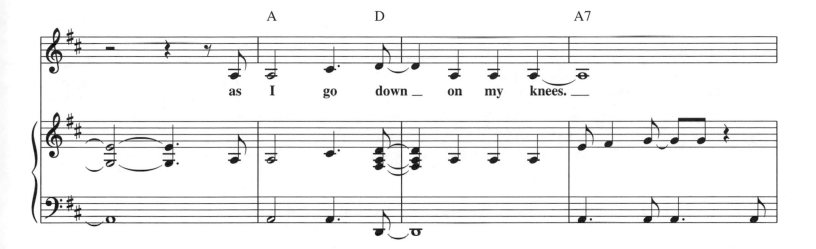

as I go down ___ on my knees. ___

To Coda ⊕

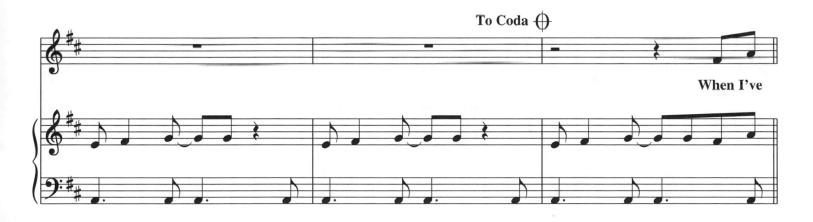

When I've

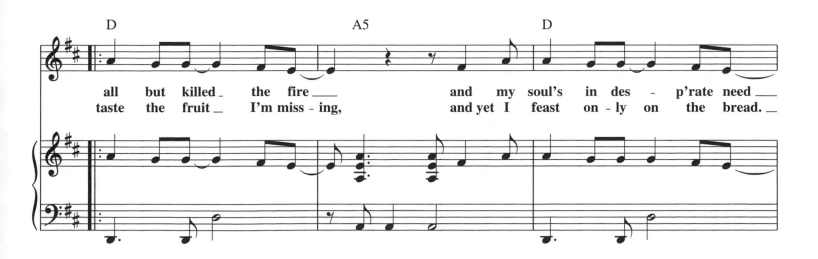

all but killed ___ the fire ___ and my soul's in des - p'rate need ___
taste the fruit ___ I'm miss - ing, and yet I feast on - ly on the bread. ___

but I wal - low in ___ the mire of com - pla -
My de - sire's a - live and kick - ing, but my drive ___

- cen - cy, ___ that's when
___ is dead. ___ So, I go down ___ on my knees. ___

1
A

2
A
D.S. al Coda

Yeah, I want to

CODA

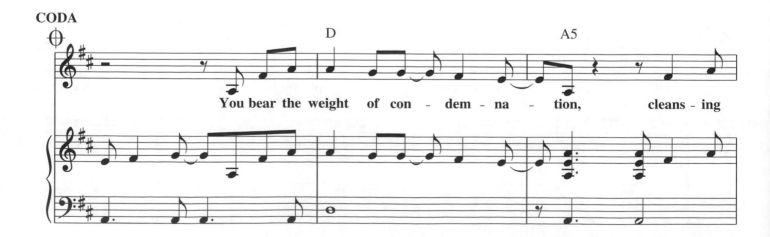

You bear the weight of con - dem - na - tion, cleans - ing

with the blood of truth. __ So, with my hum - ble ac - - cla - ma -

- tion I want to give my - self __ to you. __ So,

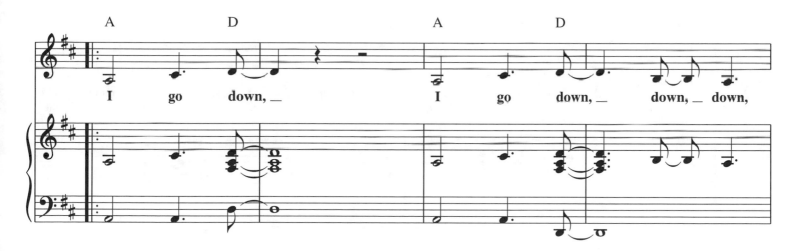

I go down, __ I go down, __ down, __ down,

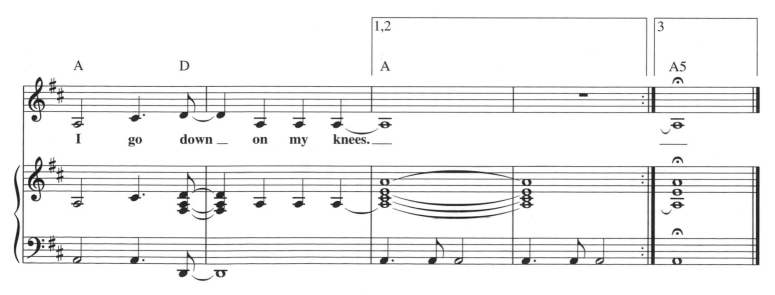

I go down __ on my knees. __

FAVORITE SONG OF ALL

Words and Music by
DAN DEAN

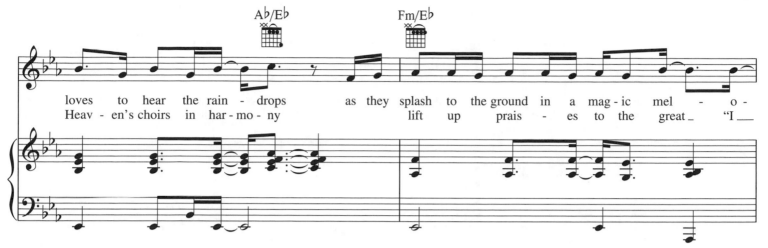

loves to hear the rain - drops   as they splash to the ground in a mag - ic mel - o -
Heav - en's choirs in har - mo - ny   lift up prais - es to the great   "I

- dy. _____
_____ Am." _____

He
But He

smiles in _____ sweet ap - prov - al   as the waves crash ___ to the rocks ___ in har - mo - ny. ___
lifts His hands ___ for si - lence   when the weak - est saved by grace ___ be - gins to sing, ___

_____
_____

Cre - a -
and a

-tion joins __ in __ u - ni - ty __ to sing to Him __ ma - jes - tic sym -
mil - lion an - gels lis - ten __ as a new-born soul __ sings, "I __ have been __

- pho - nies. __
__ re - deemed." __

But
'Cause } His fav - 'rite song of

all __

is the song __ of the __ re - deemed __

when lost sin - ners now __ made clean __

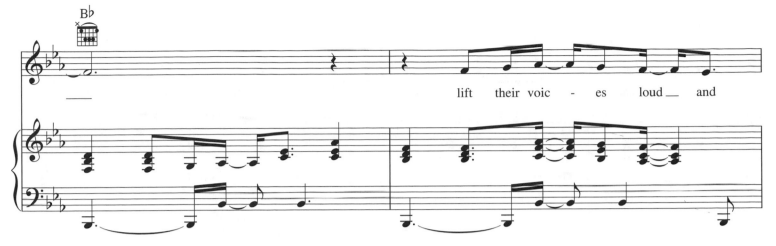

lift their voic - es loud __ and

strong; _____ when those pur - chased by __ His blood __

lift to Him __ a song __ of love. __

There's noth-ing more __ He'd rath - er hear, __

nor so pleas - ing to His ear as His fav - 'rite song

of all. And He

of all. It's not just

mel - o - dies and har - mo - nies that catch - es His at - ten - tion. It's not just

clev - er lines ___ and phras - es that caus - es ___ Him to stop ___ and lis - ten but when

an - y heart ___ set free, ___ washed and bought ___ by Cal - va - ry, ___ be - gins ___ to sing. ___

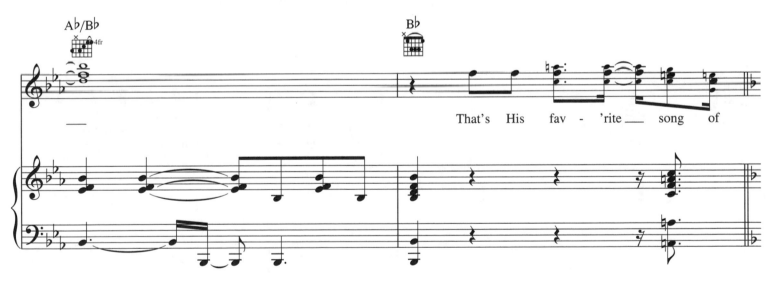

___ That's His fav - 'rite ___ song of

all is the song ___ of the ___ re - deemed ___

when lost sin-ners now __ made clean __

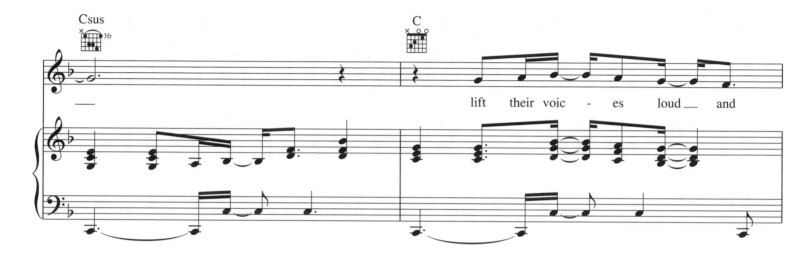

__ lift their voic - es loud __ and

strong; _____ when those pur - chased by __ His blood __

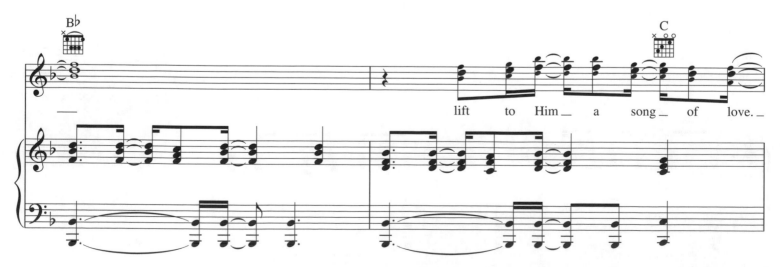

__ lift to Him __ a song __ of love. __

There's noth-ing more _ He'd rath-er hear, _ nor so pleas- ing to _ His ear _

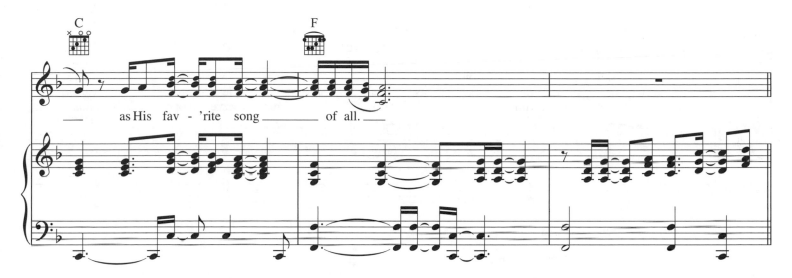

_ as His fav - 'rite song _____ of all. _

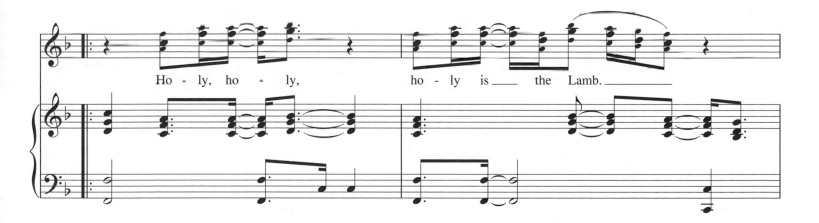

Ho - ly, ho - ly, ho - ly is ____ the Lamb. _____

Hal - le - lu - jah, hal - le - lu - jah. _____

FOR FUTURE GENERATIONS

Words and Music by MARK HARRIS,
DAVE CLARK and DON KOCH

With conviction

The signs _____ are ob - vi - ous; _____ they are ev - 'ry - where. _____
So na - ture has its needs; _____ that's a les - son learned. _____
If we _____ could find a way _____ to pre - serve our faith, _____

All that we hear _____ a - bout _____ is the
But it ap - pears _____ to me _____ there are
so those who fol - low us _____ see the

gloom and de - spair. _____
great - er con - cerns. _____
price that was paid, _____

Too man - y would - be proph -
'Cause we can save _____ the plan
then may - be when _____ they ques -

faith. I won't com - pro - mise__ in a world of des - per - a -

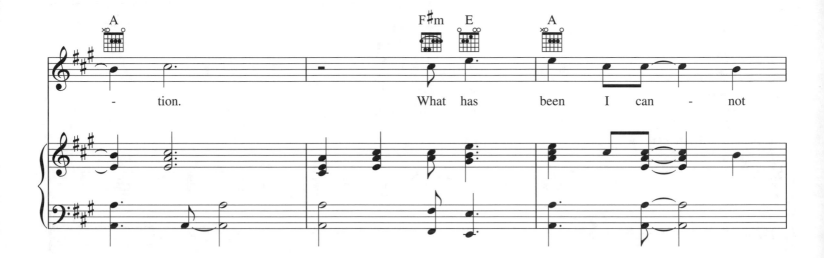

- tion. What has been I can - not

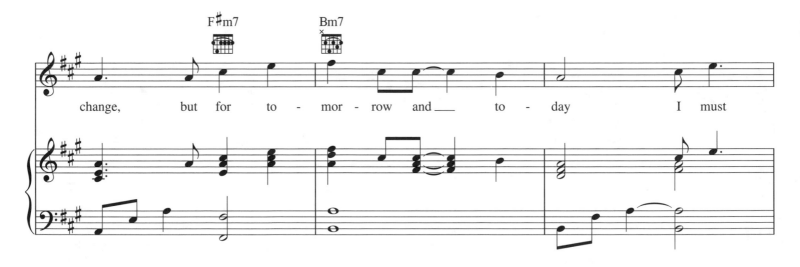

change, but for to - mor - row and __ to - day I must

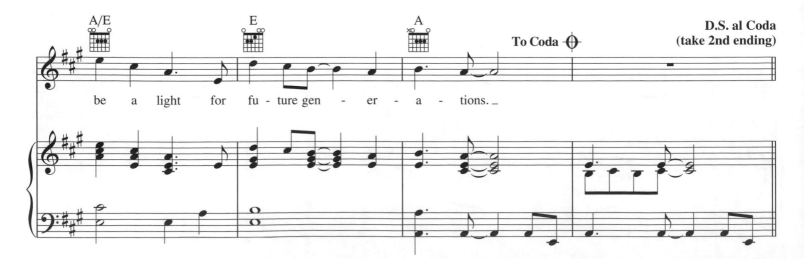

be a light for fu - ture gen - er - a - tions. __

D.S. al Coda
(take 2nd ending)

To Coda ⊕

CODA

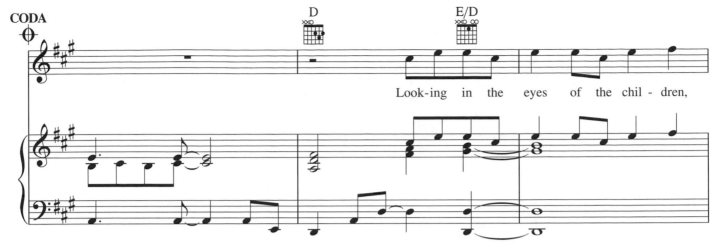

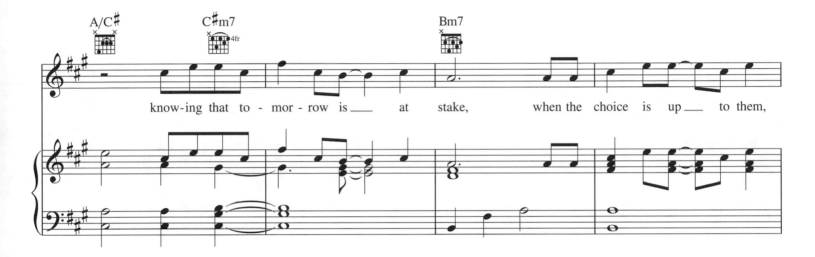

Look-ing in the eyes of the chil - dren,

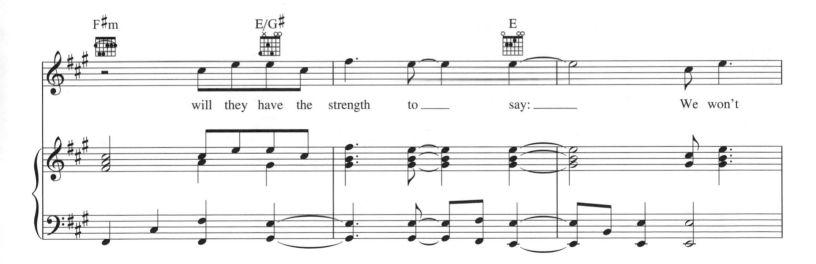

know-ing that to - mor - row is ___ at stake, when the choice is up ___ to them,

will they have the strength to ___ say: ___ We won't

bend and we ___ won't break. We won't wa - ter down ___ our

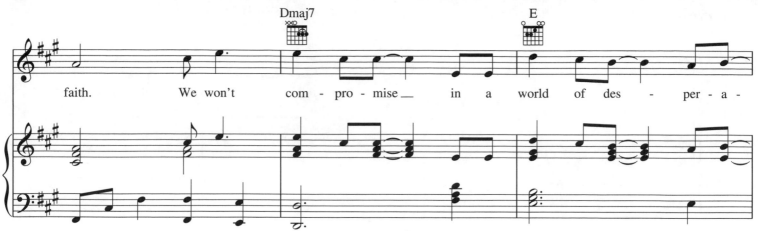

faith. We won't com - pro - mise __ in a world of des - per - a -

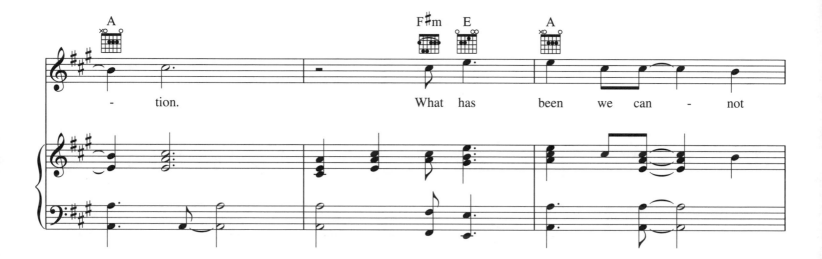

\- tion. What has been we can - not

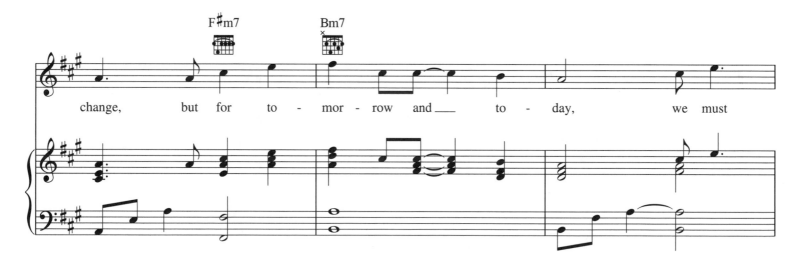

change, but for to - mor - row and __ to - day, we must

be a light for fu - ture gen - er - a - tions. __

CROSS OF GOLD

Words and Music by MICHAEL W. SMITH
and WAYNE KIRKPATRICK

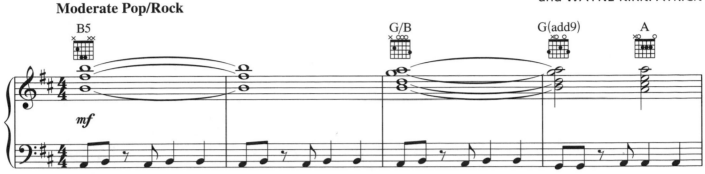

Where do you stand? __ What is your state - ment? What is it you're __ try - in' to
Is it a flame? __ Is it a pas - sion, a sym - bol of love ___ liv - ing in

say? __ What's in your hand? __ What's in your base - ment?
you? __ Or is it a game, __ re - li - gion in fash - ion,

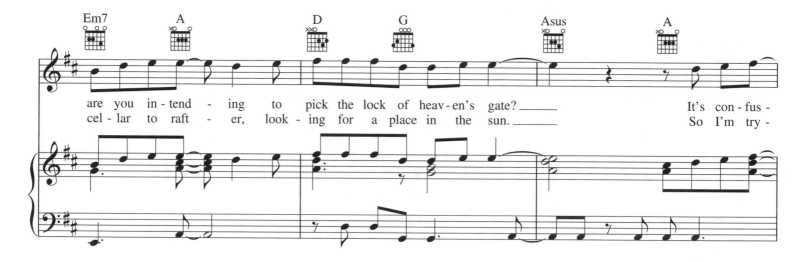

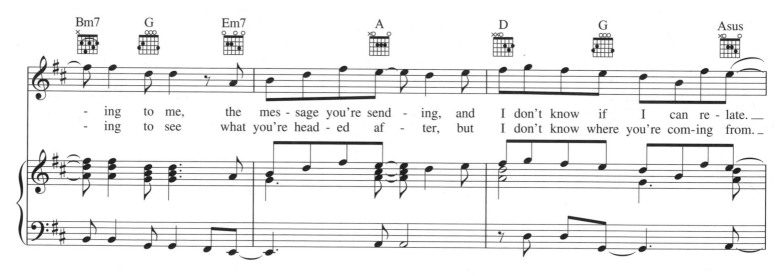

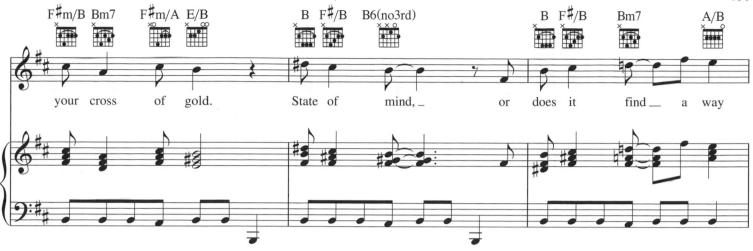

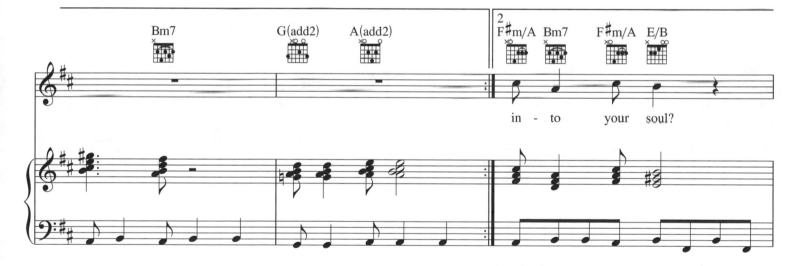

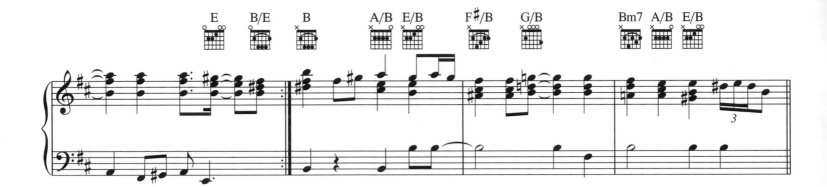

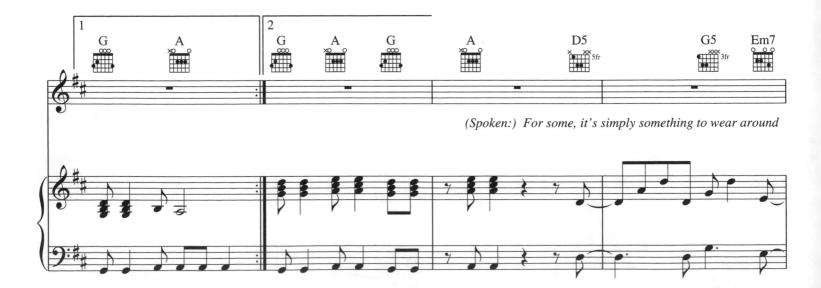

(Spoken:) For some, it's simply something to wear around

FOR THE FIRST TIME

Words and Music by MARK HARRIS
and PETE KIPLEY

Steady four

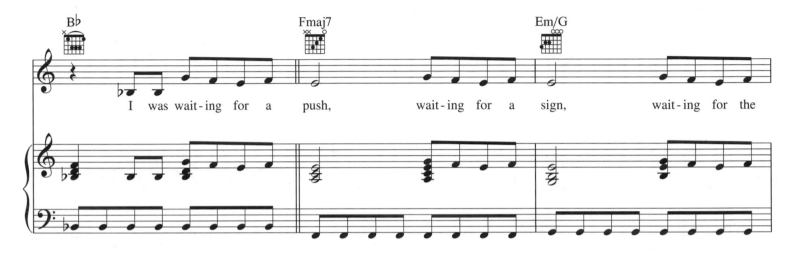

I was wait-ing for a push, wait-ing for a sign, wait-ing for the per-fect mo-ment to ar-rive. Stead-y as a clock, caught be-tween the

lines, liv-ing for my-self un-til I re-al-ized there's too _

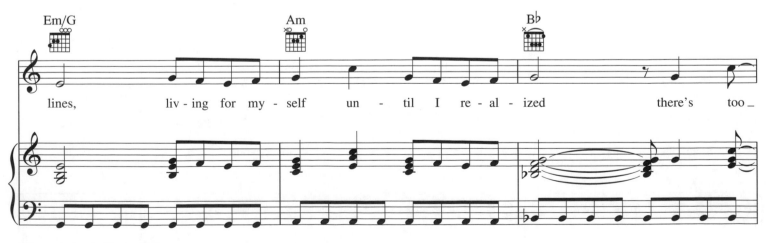

*Recorded a half step higher.

much life ___ You've giv-en me   to let ___ it slip a-way.

I'm read-y to live, ___   read-y to breathe, _   read-y to take _

___ in ev-'ry-thing. ___   I'm read-y to love, ___   read-y to shine, _

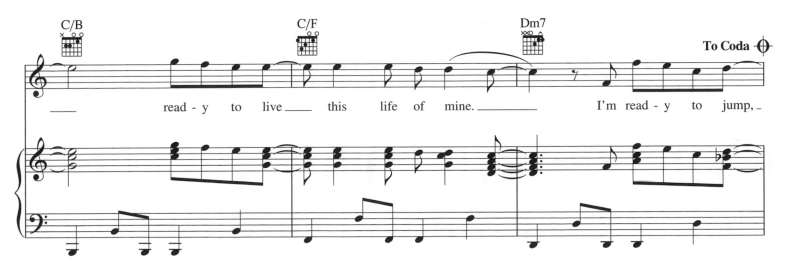

___ read-y to live ___ this life of mine. ___   I'm read-y to jump, _

To Coda

I'm read-y to fly ___ for the first ___ time. ___

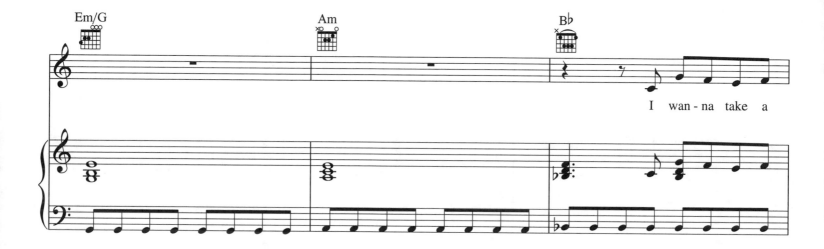

I wan-na take a

dive, I wan-na take a chance, I wan-na make the most of ___ ev-'ry day I

have. I wan-na be a-live, I wan-na be a man, 'cause be-ing wild at

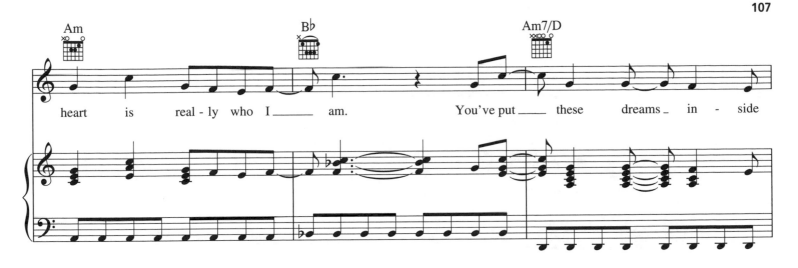

heart is real-ly who I _____ am. You've put _____ these dreams ___ in - side

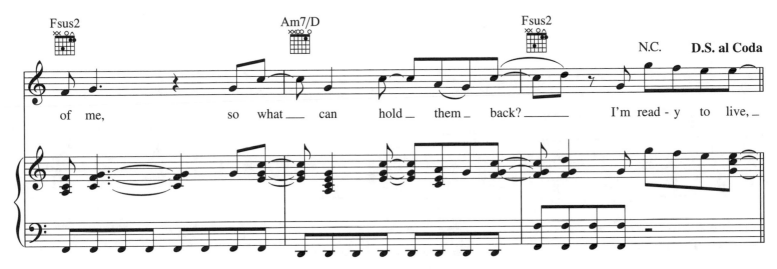

of me, so what ___ can hold ___ them ___ back? _____ I'm read - y to live, ___

___ I'm read - y to fly _____ for the first ___ time. _____

I can feel ___

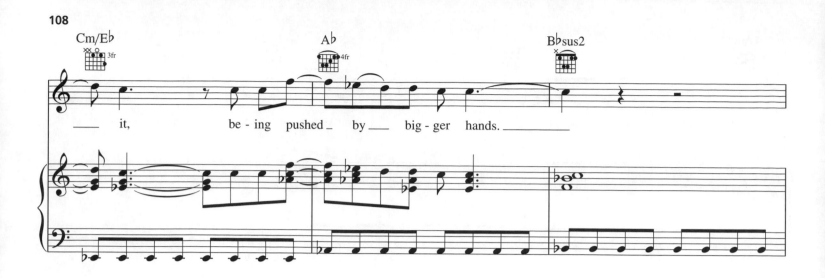

ready to live____ this life of mine._____ I'm read - y to live, _

I'm read - y to jump, ___ read - y to fly _____

for the first ___ time, _____

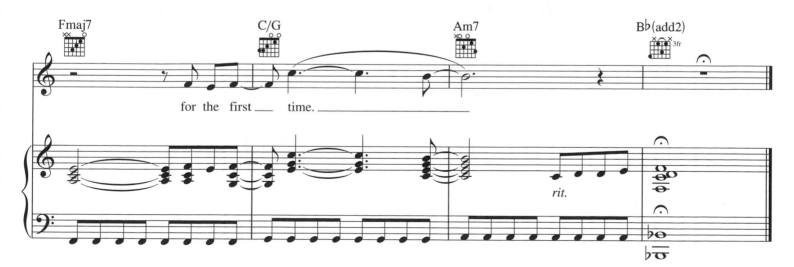

for the first ___ time. _____

FOR THE SAKE OF THE CALL

Words and Music by
STEVEN CURTIS CHAPMAN

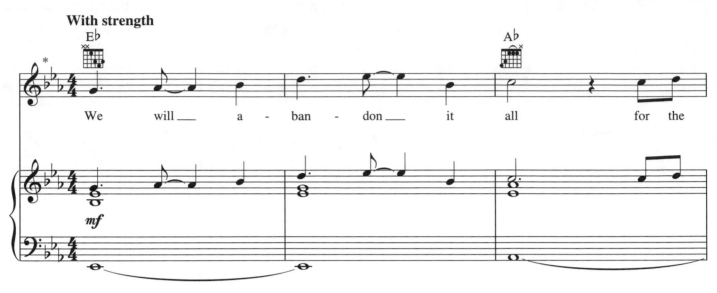

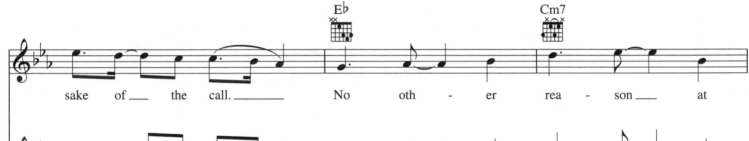

*Recorded a half step higher.

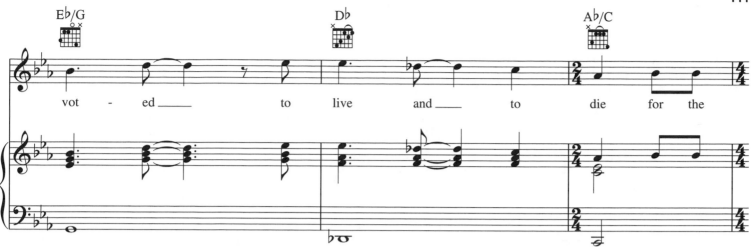

voted ___ to live and ___ to die for the

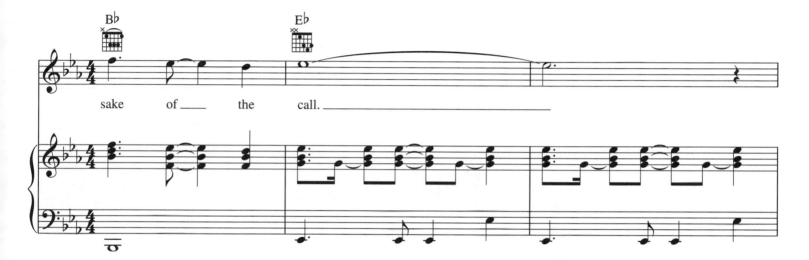

sake of ___ the call. _____

Emp - ty

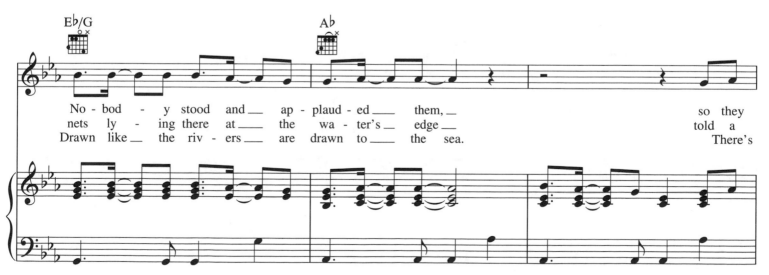

No - bod - y stood and ___ ap - plaud - ed ___ them, ___ so they
nets ly - ing there at ___ the wa - ter's edge ___ told a
Drawn like ___ the riv - ers ___ are drawn to ___ the sea. There's

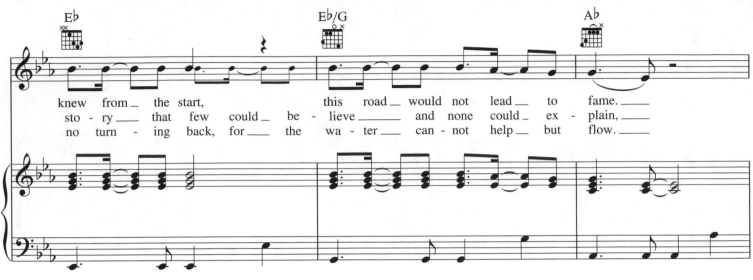

knew from __ the start, this road __ would not lead __ to fame.

sto - ry __ that few could __ be - lieve and none could __ ex - plain, __

no turn - ing back, for __ the wa - ter __ can - not help __ but flow. __

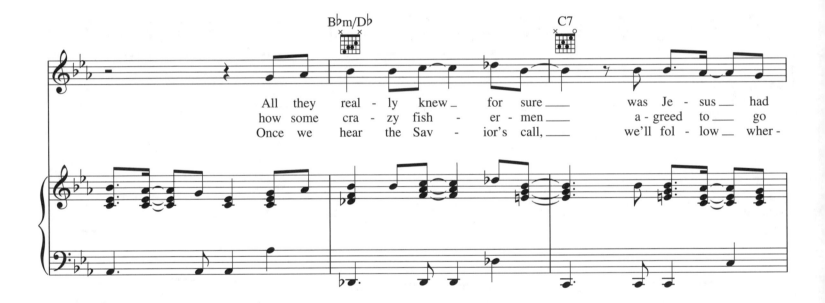

All they real - ly knew __ for sure __ was Je - sus __ had

how some cra - zy fish - er - men __ a - greed to __ go

Once we hear the Sav - ior's call, __ we'll fol - low __ wher -

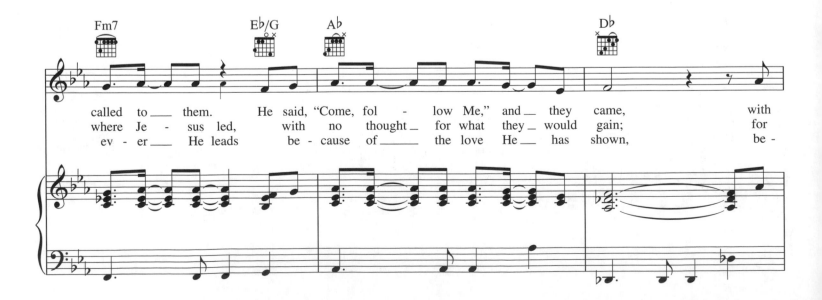

called to __ them. He said, "Come, fol - low Me," and __ they came, with

where Je - sus led, with no thought __ for what they __ would gain; for

ev - er __ He leads be - cause of __ the love He __ has shown, be -

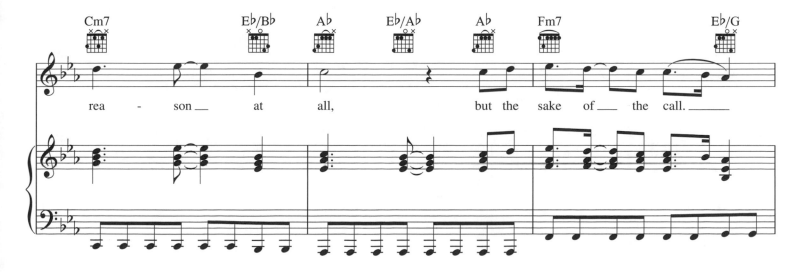

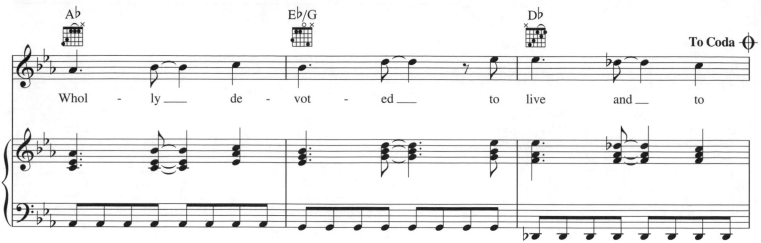

Whol - ly ____ de - vot - ed ____ to live and ____ to

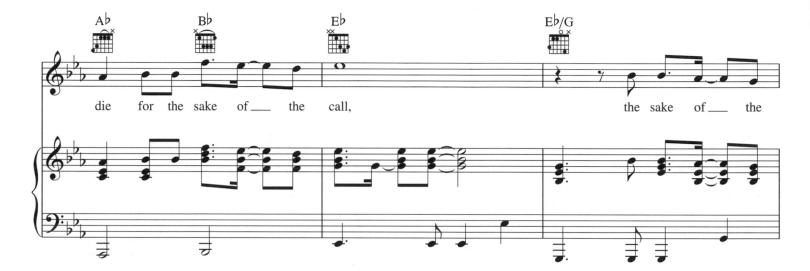

die for the sake of ___ the call, the sake of ___ the

call." _____

D.S. al Coda
(take 2nd ending)

CODA

die.

Not for ___ the sake of ___ a creed or ___ a cause. ___ Not for ___ a dream or a

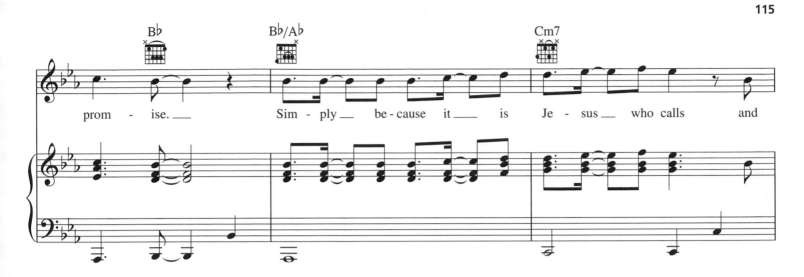

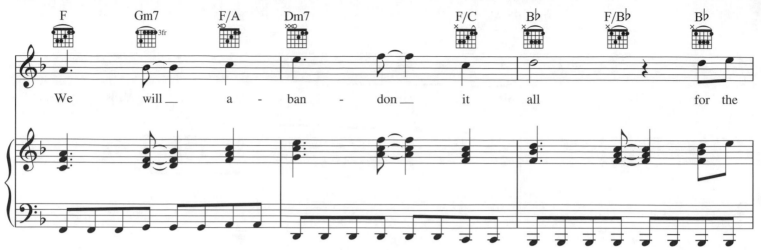

We will __ a - ban - don __ it all   for the

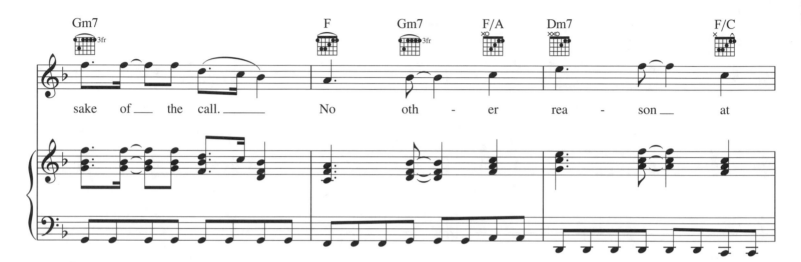

sake of __ the call. _____ No   oth - er   rea - son __ at

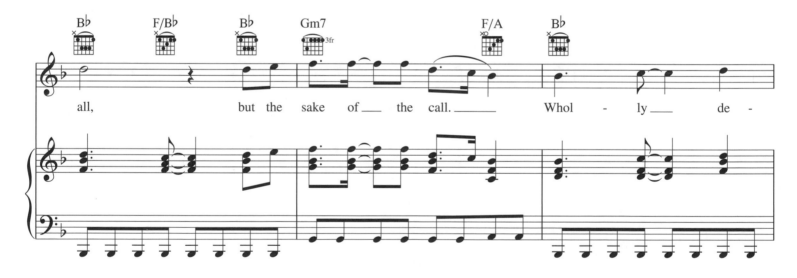

all,   but the sake of __ the call. _____ Whol - ly __ de -

vot - ed __ to __ live   and to die ____   for the sake of __ the

GATHER AT THE RIVER

Words and Music by JOEL LINDSEY
and REGIE HAMM

Moderate Pop feel

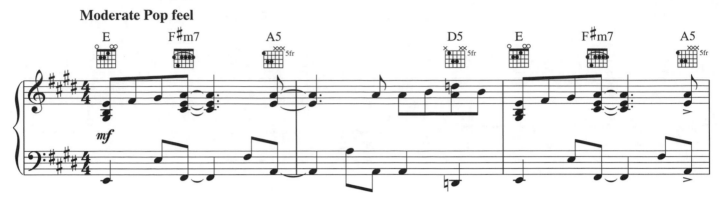

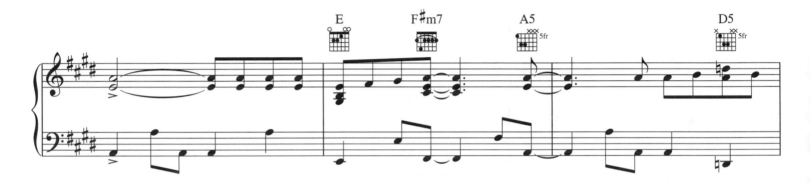

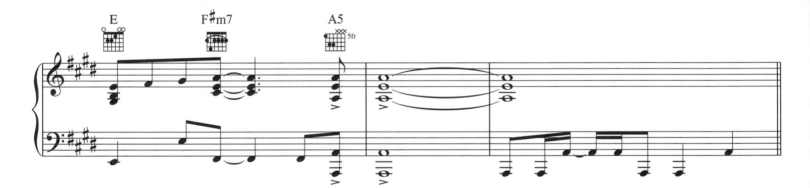

Some - times we don't see _____ eye to eye. _____
We have all made _____ en - e - mies of _____

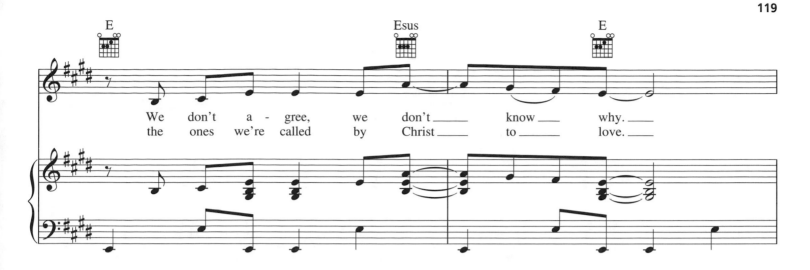

We don't a - gree, we don't ___ know ___ why. ___
the ones we're called by Christ ___ to ___ love. ___

But Je - sus prayed that we'd ___ be ___ one. ___
But there's re - demp - tion at the riv - er - side. ___

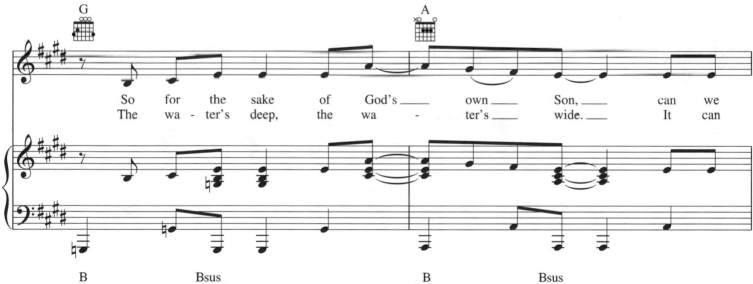

So for the sake of God's ___ own ___ Son, ___ can we
The wa - ter's deep, the wa - ter's ___ wide. ___ It can

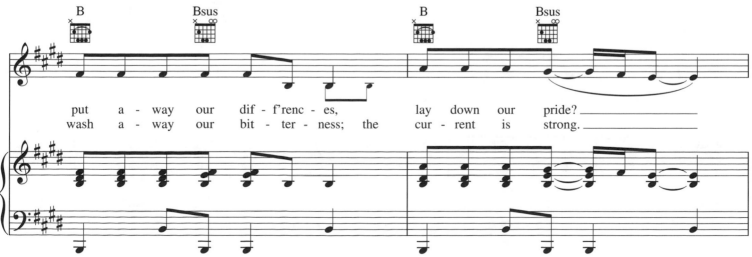

put a - way our dif - f'renc - es, lay down our pride? ___
wash a - way our bit - ter - ness; the cur - rent is strong. ___

I think it's time we start turn-ing the tide. _____
I think we've been out in the des-ert too long. _____

Shall we gath-er at the riv-er of for-give-ness? _ Come to-geth-er at the

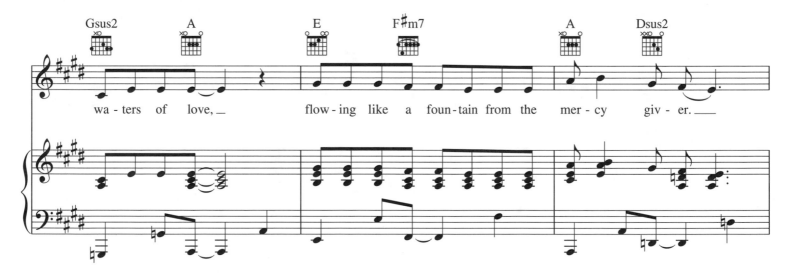

wa-ters of love, _ flow-ing like a foun-tain from the mer-cy giv-er. ___

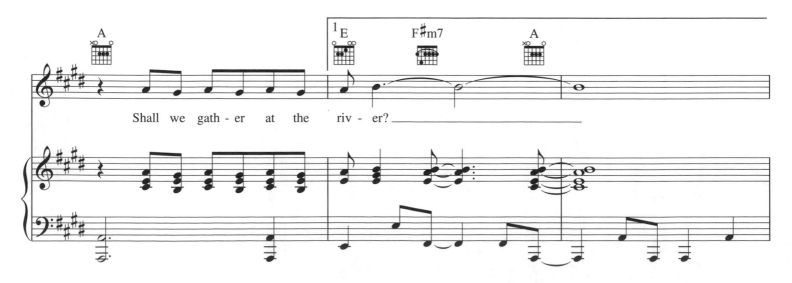

Shall we gath-er at the riv-er? _____

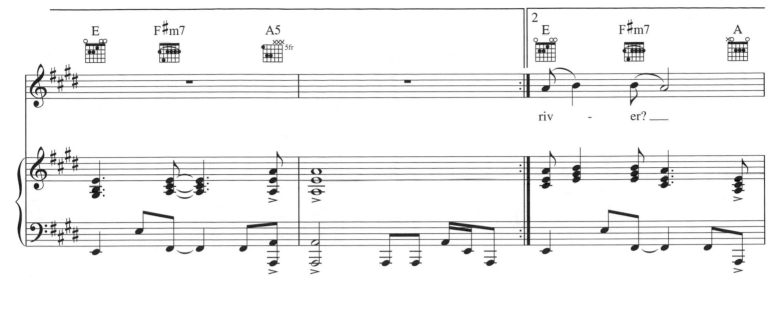

riv - er? ___

N.C.

We can wade in - to the mid - dle where the heal - ing wa - ters flow. It

on - ly takes a lit - tle to heal ___ a wound - ed soul. ___ It will on - ly bring us clos - er than we've

ev - er been be - fore. This is just what Je - sus was pray - in' for. ___

D.S. al Coda

flow - ing like a foun - tain from the mer - cy giv - er.___ Shall we gath - er at the

CODA

Shall we gath - er at the riv - er,_____ gath - er at the

riv - er,_____ gath - er at the riv - er,_____

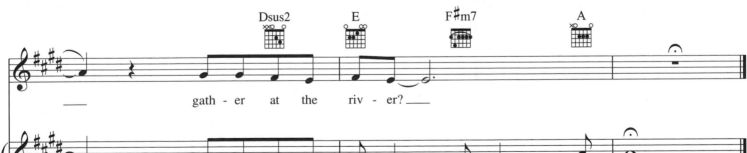

___ gath - er at the riv - er?___

HELPING HAND

Words and Music by TOMMY SIMS,
AMY GRANT and BEVERLY DARNALL

Ev-'ry-bod-y needs a help - ing hand. Take a look at your fel-low man and tell me,

what can I do to-day? _ 'Cause ev-'ry bod-y needs a help - ing out.

If that ain't what it's all a - bout, _ tell me, what, what can I do, _

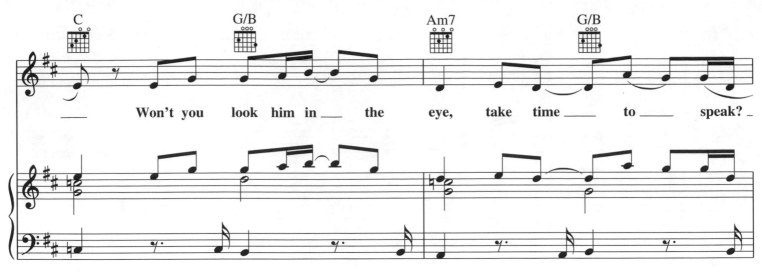

Won't you look him in ___ the eye, take time ___ to ___ speak? _

___ That's mer - cy, ___ yeah. _

D.S. al Coda

CODA

___ what can I ___ do?

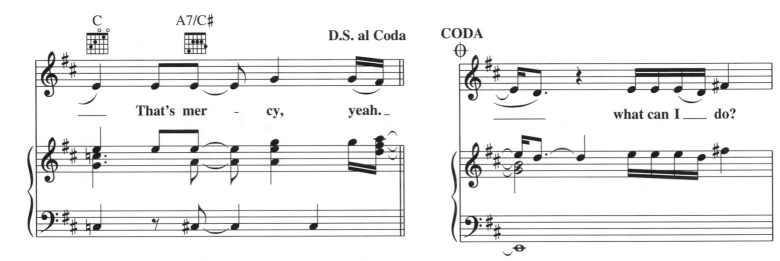

Love ___ one an-oth-er, sis - ter and broth-er.

Love _ is the on - ly way, hey, _ hey, yeah. _____

Ev-'ry-bod-y needs _ a help - ing hand. Take a look at your fel-low man and tell me,

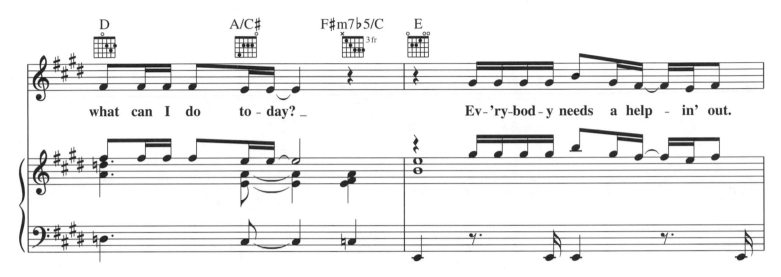

what can I do to - day? _ Ev-'ry-bod-y needs a help - in' out.

If that ain't what it's all a - bout, _ tell me, what, (what) what can I do, _

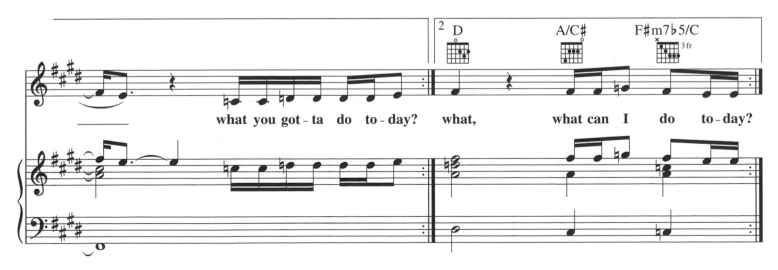

what you got - ta do to - day? what, what can I do to - day?

'ry-bod-y needs a __ help - ing __ hand. _____ Ev -

'ry-bod-y needs it, oh, __ ev - 'ry-bod-y needs it. Ev -

Am7/D

'ry-bod-y needs a help - ing __ hand. _____ Ev -

Repeat and Fade

'ry-bod-y needs it, oh, __ ev - 'ry-bod-y needs it. Ev -

IF THIS WORLD

Words and Music by MICHELLE TUMES, TYLER HAYES,
ERIK SUNDIN and MARK HEIMERMANN

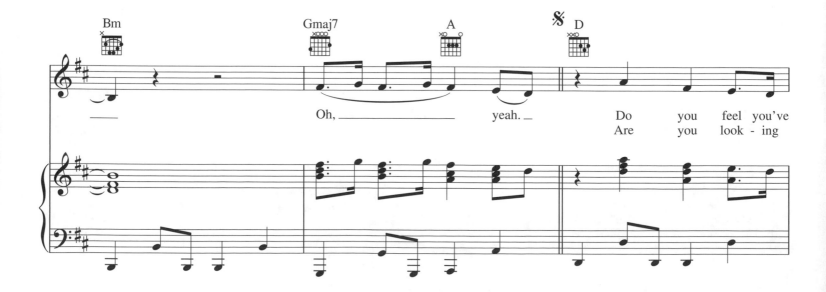

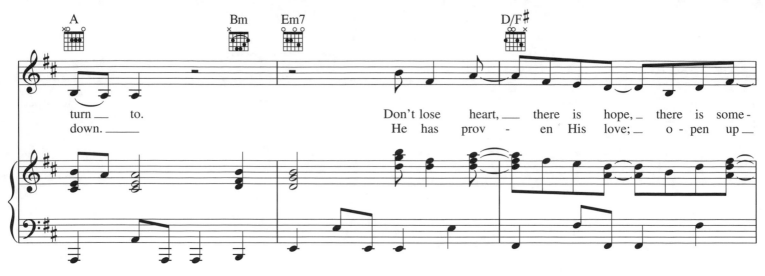

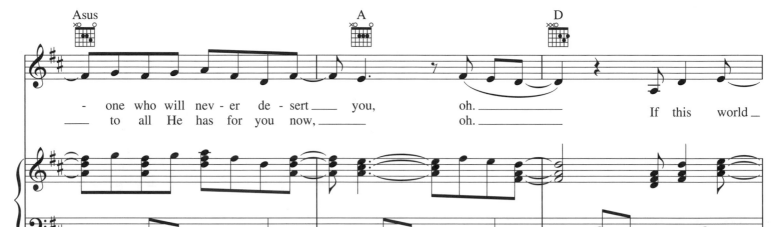

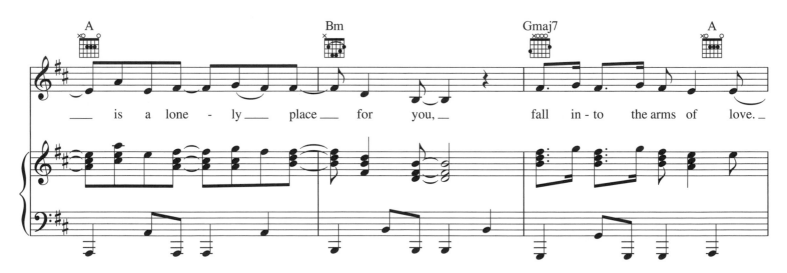

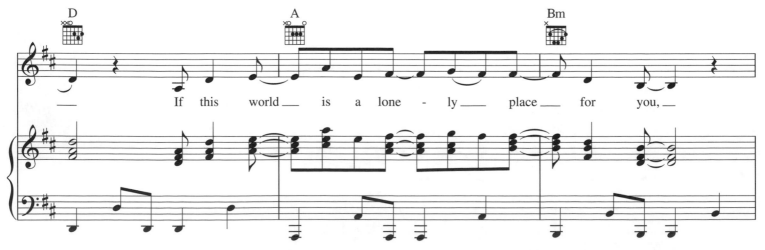

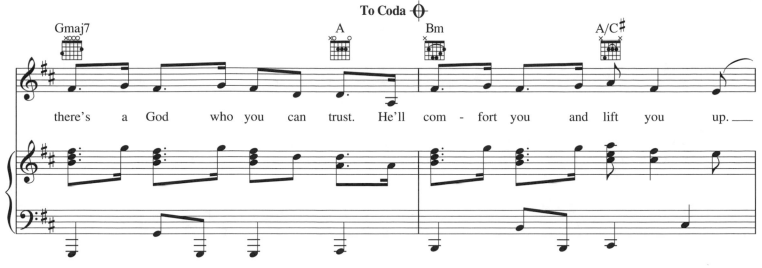

there's a God who you can trust. He'll com-fort you and lift you up.

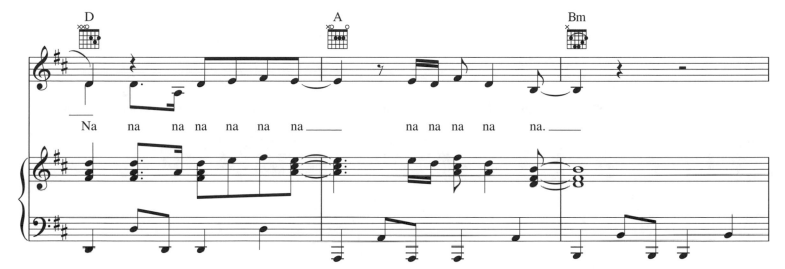

Na na na na na na na na na na na.

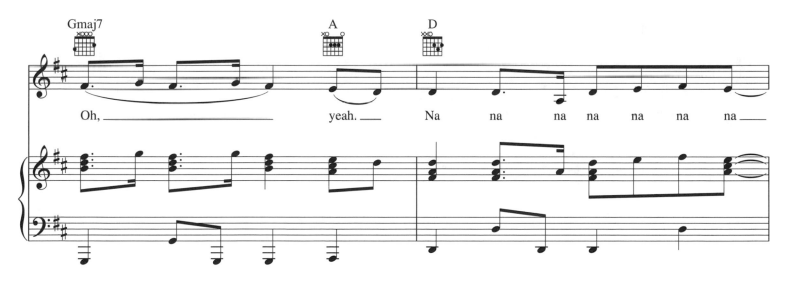

Oh, yeah. Na na na na na na na

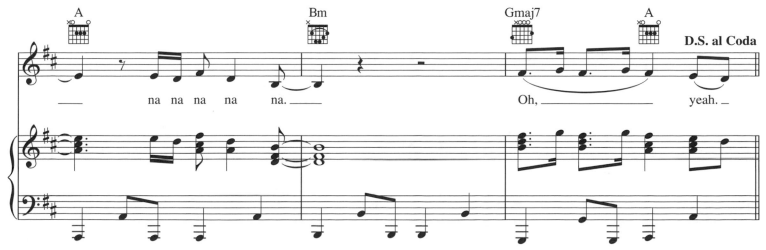

na na na na na. Oh, yeah.

com - fort you and lift you up. ____ He hears your cry, He sees your

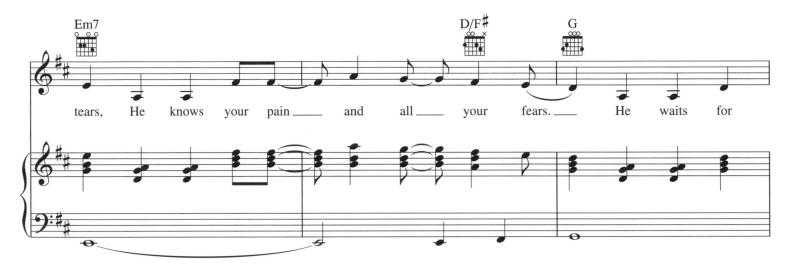

tears, He knows your pain ____ and all ____ your fears. ____ He waits for

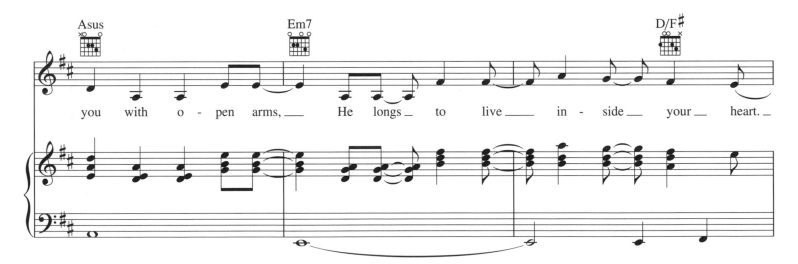

you with o - pen arms, ___ He longs ___ to live ____ in - side ___ your ___ heart.

____ You'll nev - er be a - lone ___ a - gain. _____ If this world ___

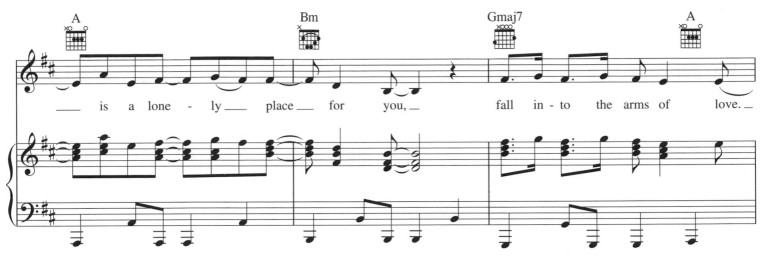

is a lone - ly____ place____ for you, ____ fall in - to the arms of love. ____

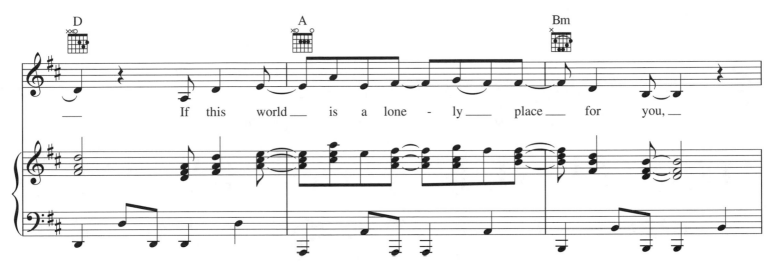

____ If this world____ is a lone - ly____ place____ for you, ____

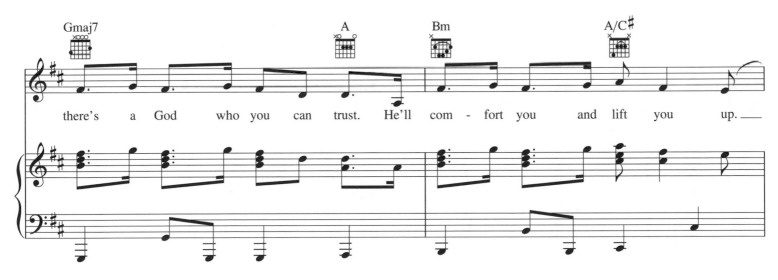

there's a God who you can trust. He'll com - fort you and lift you up. ____

Na na na na na na na na ____ na na na na na. ____

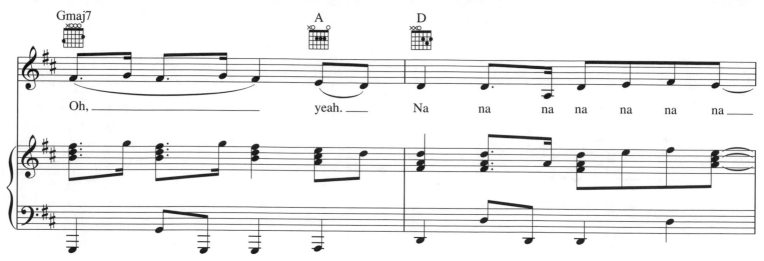

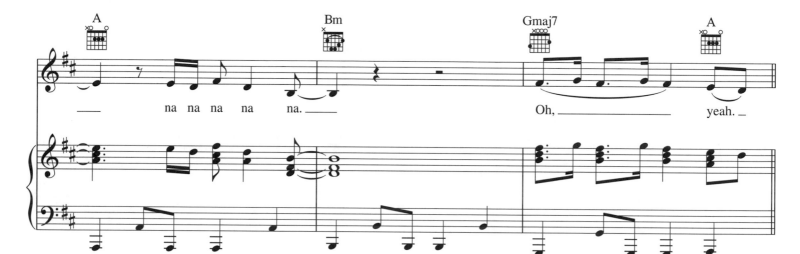

FOR YOU

Words by WAYNE KIRKPATRICK
Music by MICHAEL W. SMITH and BILL OWSLEY

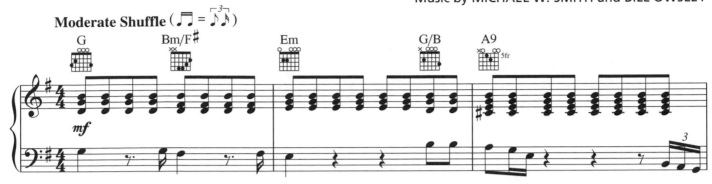

throw you a line. ___ Rest as - sured that I ___ won't ev - er let you drown. ___
car - ry the load, ___ e - ven if we don't ___ quite _ un - der - stand ___

it. } 'Cause when you're up ___ a - gainst _ the wall, __ you know ___

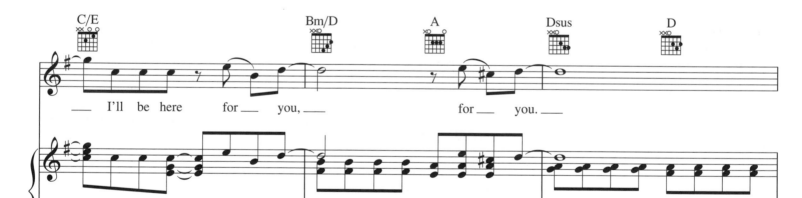

__ I'll be here for __ you, ___ for __ you. ___

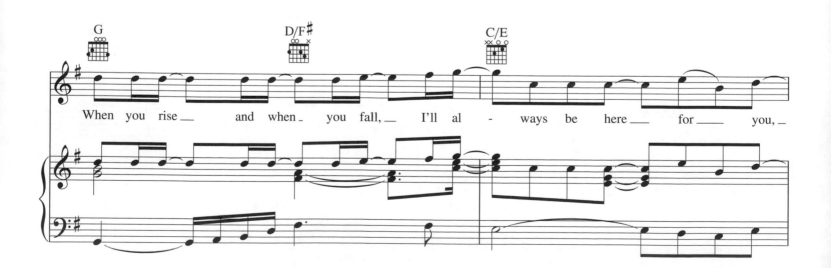

When you rise ___ and when _ you fall, __ I'll al - ways be here ___ for ___ you, __

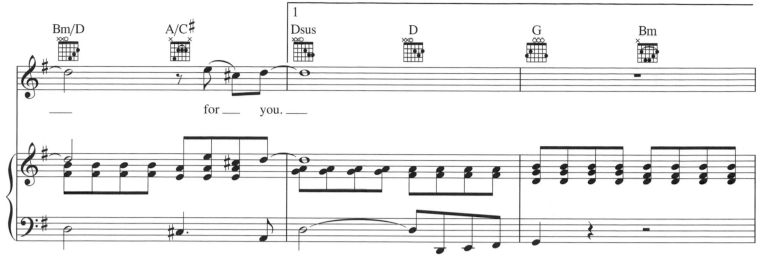

for you.

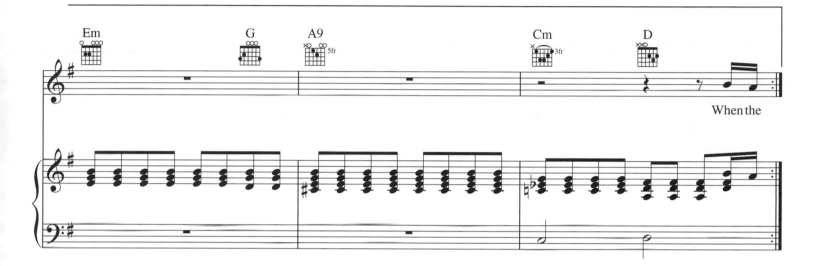

When the

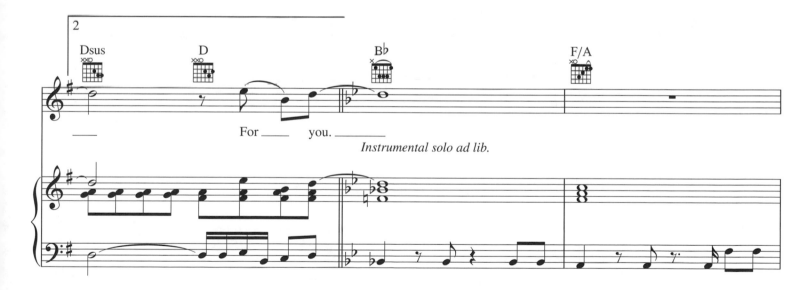

For you.

Instrumental solo ad lib.

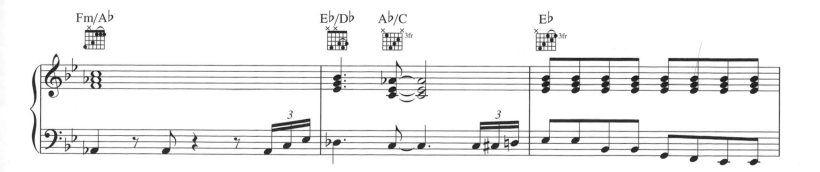

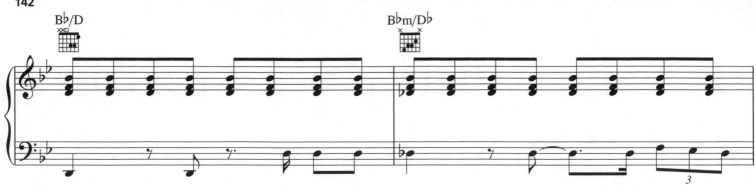

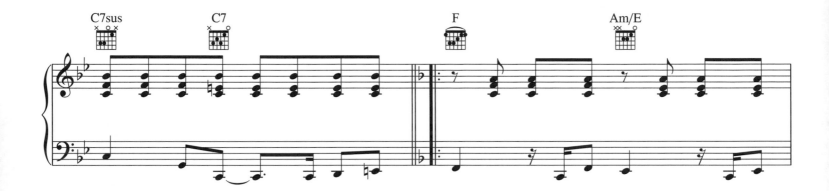

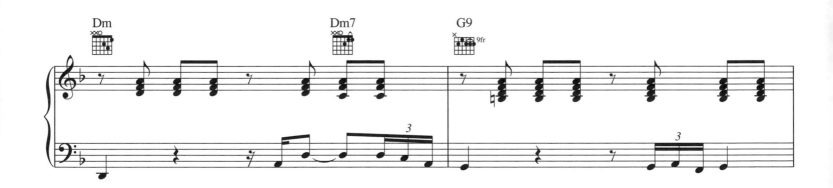

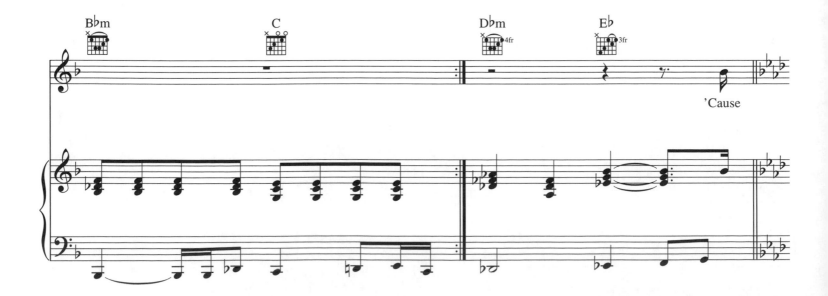

'Cause

when you're up ___ a - gainst ___ the wall, ___ you know ___ I'll be here for ___ you, ___

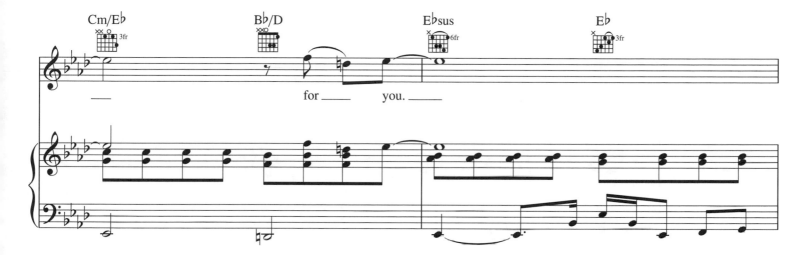

___ for ___ you. ___

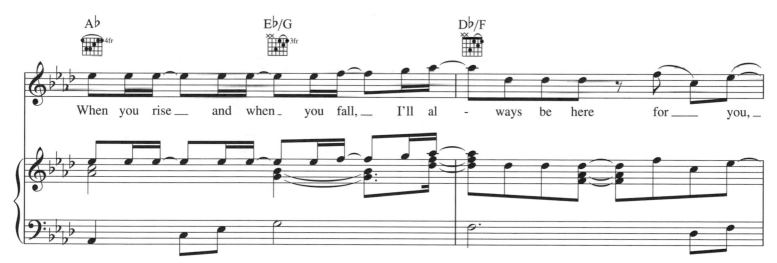

When you rise ___ and when ___ you fall, ___ I'll al - ways be here for ___ you, ___

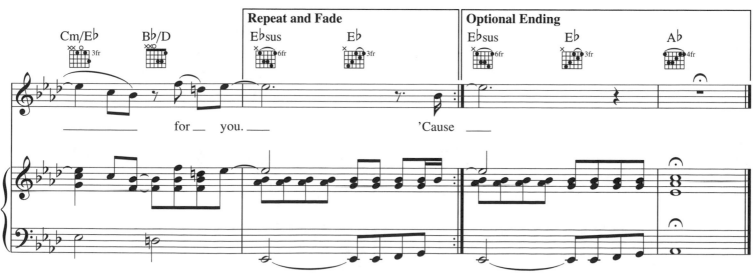

Repeat and Fade   **Optional Ending**

___ for ___ you. ___   'Cause ___

IF WE ARE THE BODY

Words and Music by
MARK HALL

Moderately fast

It's
A

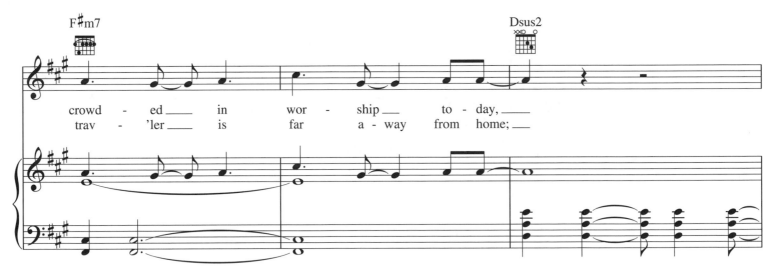

crowd - ed ___ in wor - ship ___ to - day, ___
trav - 'ler ___ is far a - way from home; ___

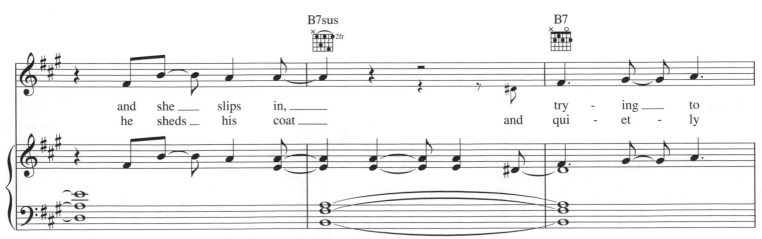

and she ___ slips in, ___ try - ing ___ to
he sheds ___ his coat ___ and qui - et - ly

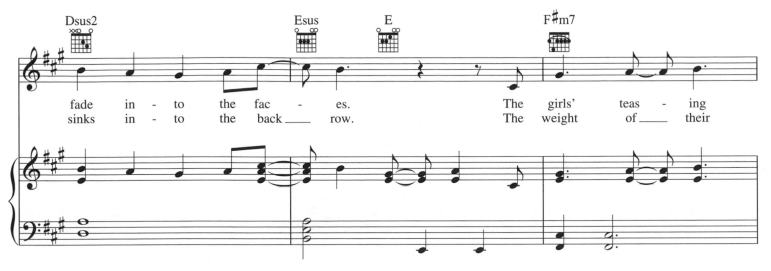

fade in - to the fac - es.
sinks in - to the back ___ row.
The girls' teas - ing
The weight of ___ their

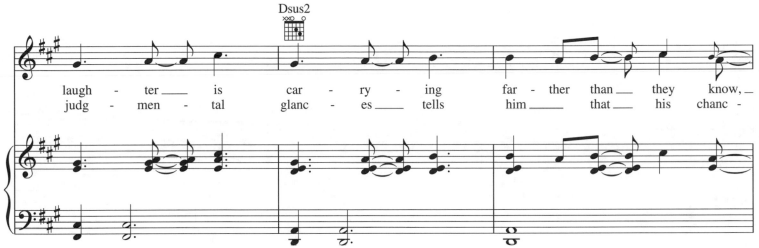

laugh - ter ___ is car - ry - ing far - ther than __ they know, __
judg - men - tal glanc - es ___ tells him ___ that ___ his chanc -

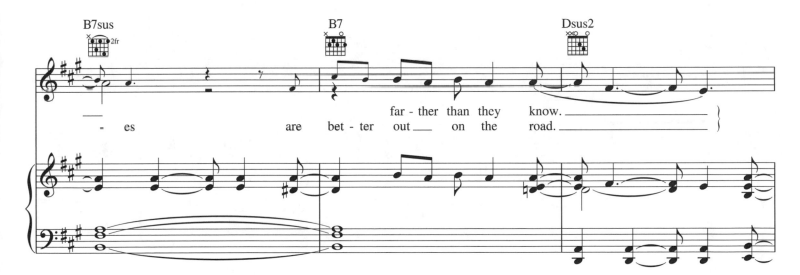

_ - es are bet - ter out __ on the road. ___
far - ther than they know. ___

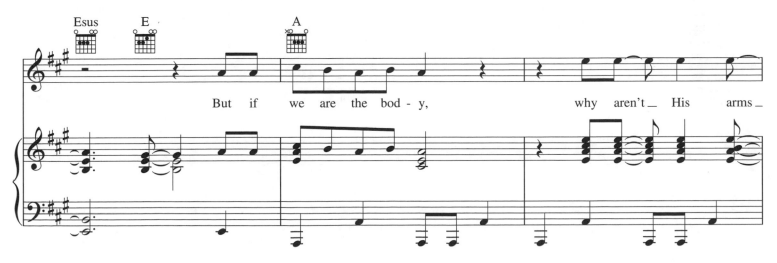

But if we are the bod - y, why aren't __ His arms __

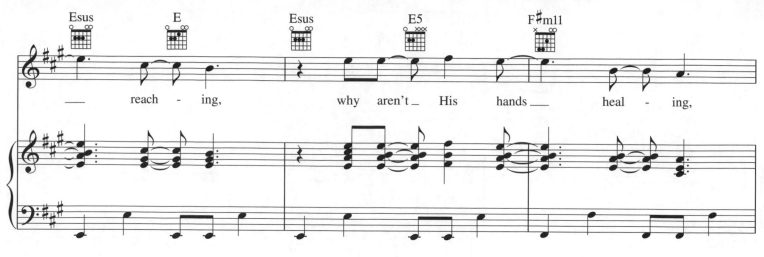

reach - ing, why aren't __ His hands __ heal - ing,

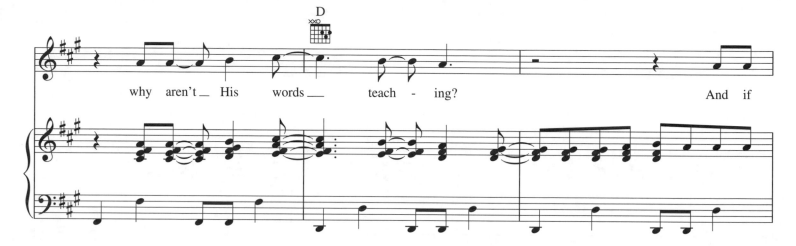

why aren't __ His words __ teach - ing? And if

we are the bod - y, why aren't __ His feet ___ go - ing,

why is ___ His love ___ not show-ing them ___ there is ___ a way. __

There is ___ a way. ___

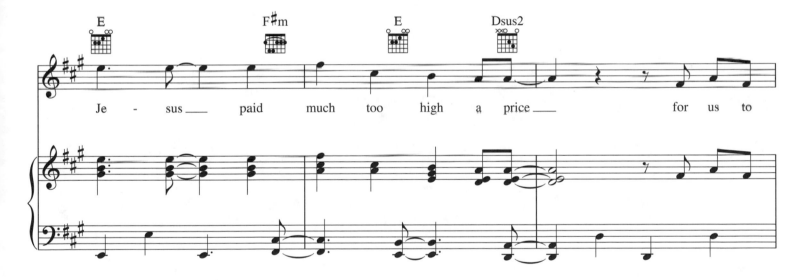

Je - sus ___ paid much too high a price ___ for us to

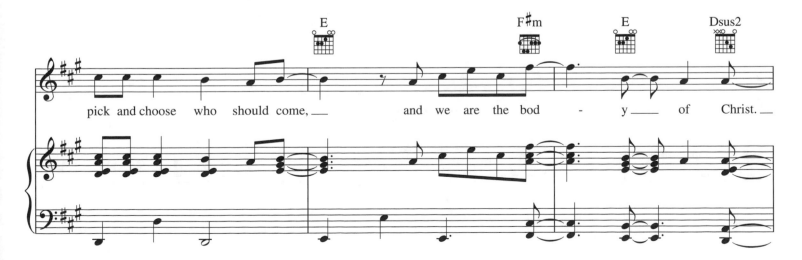

pick and choose who should come, ___ and we are the bod - y ___ of Christ. ___

If we are the bod - y,

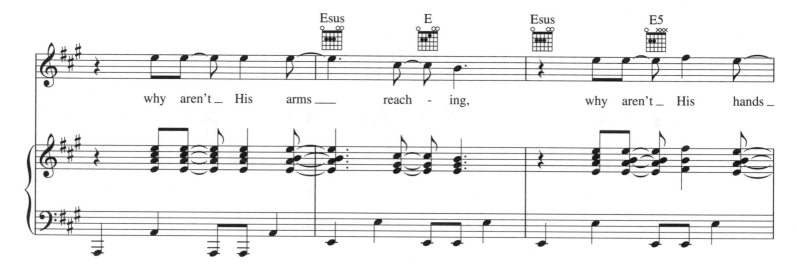

why aren't __ His arms __ reach - ing, why aren't __ His hands __

F#m11

__ heal - ing, why aren't __ His words __ teach - ing?

A

And if we are the bod - y, why aren't __ His feet __

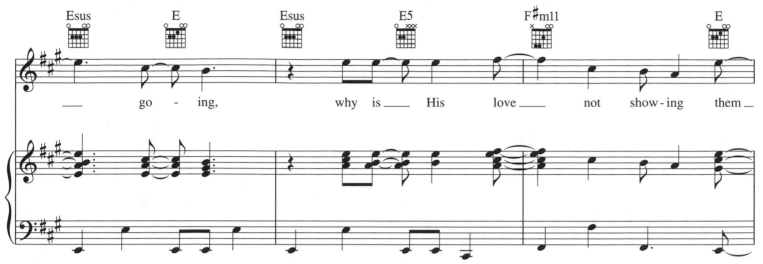

there is __ a way. __ If

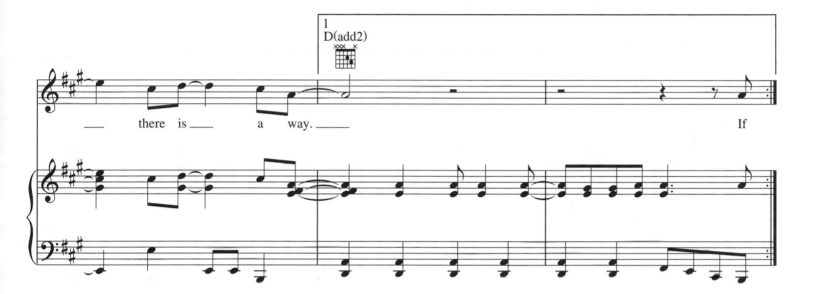

Je - sus is __ the way. __

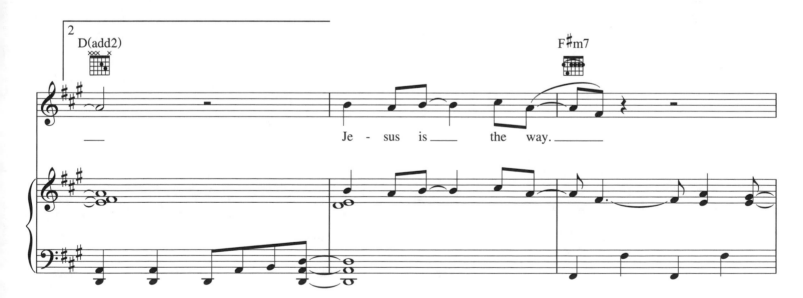

IMAGINE ME WITHOUT YOU

Words and Music by RUDY PEREZ
and MARK PORTMANN

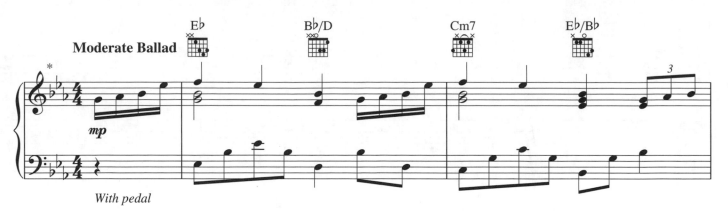

Moderate Ballad

With pedal

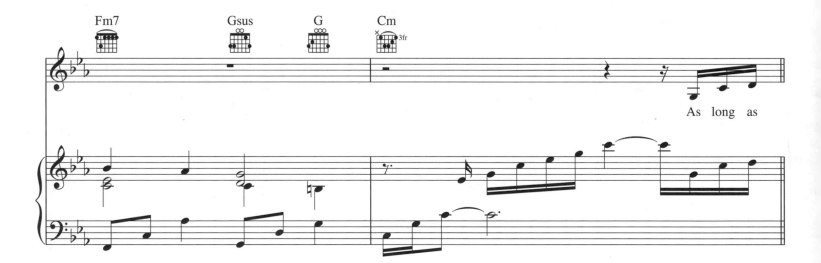

As long as

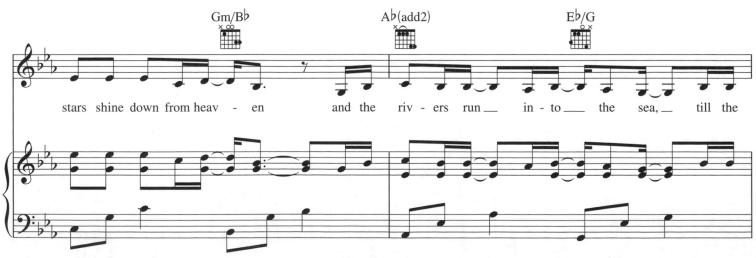

stars shine down from heav - en and the riv - ers run ___ in - to ___ the sea, ___ till the

* Recorded a half step lower.

end of time _ for - ev - er, You're the on - ly love _ I'll need. _ In my

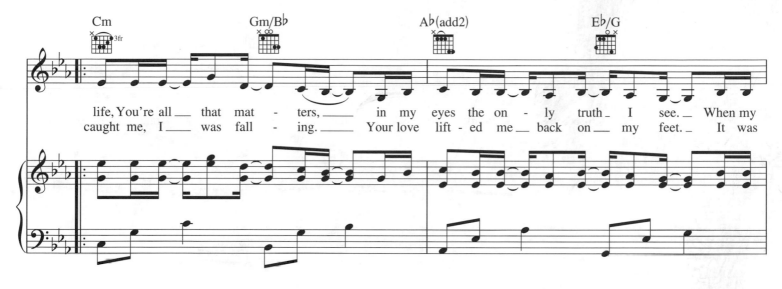

life, You're all _ that mat - ters, _ in my eyes the on - ly truth _ I see. _ When my
caught me, I _ was fall - ing. _ Your love lift - ed me _ back on _ my feet. _ It was

hopes and dreams _ have shat - tered, You're the one that's there _ for me. _
like You heard _ my call - ing, and You rushed to set _ me free. _

When I found You,

I _ was blessed, _ and I will nev - er leave You. I need _____ You. _

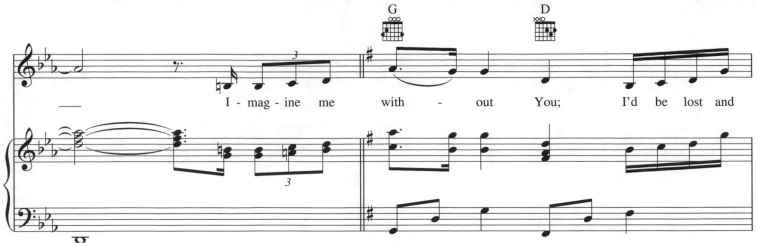

I - mag - ine me with - out You; I'd be lost and

so con - fused. I would-n't last a day, __ I'd __ be a - fraid __ with-out You

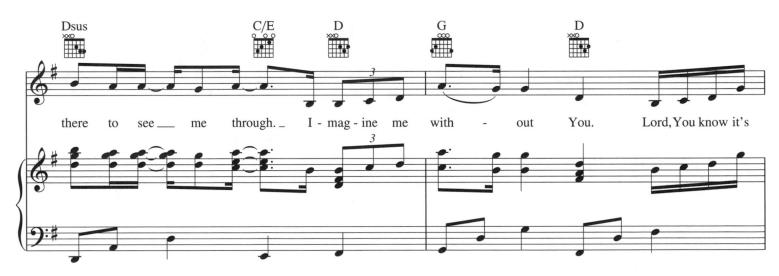

there to see __ me through. __ I - mag - ine me with - out You. Lord, You know it's

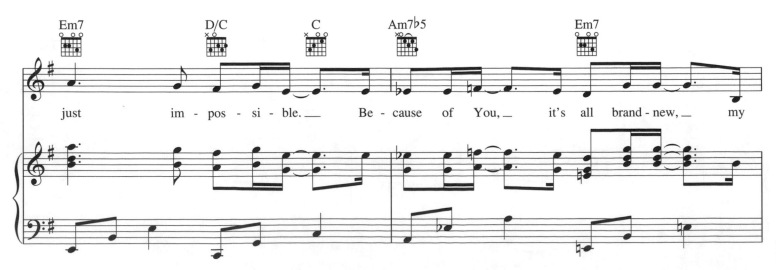

just im - pos - si - ble. __ Be - cause of You, __ it's all brand - new, __ my

with - out You; I'd be lost and so con - fused. I would-n't
(Vocal ad lib.)

last a day, __ I'd __ be a - fraid __ with-out You there to see __ me through. __ I - mag-ine me

with - out You. Lord, You know it's just im - pos - si - ble. __ Be -

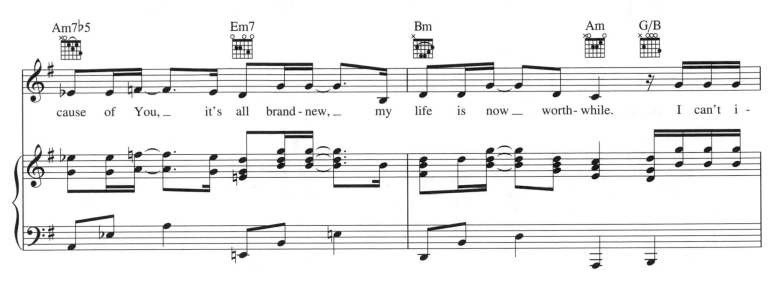

cause of You, ___ it's all brand-new, ___ my life is now ___ worth-while. I can't i-

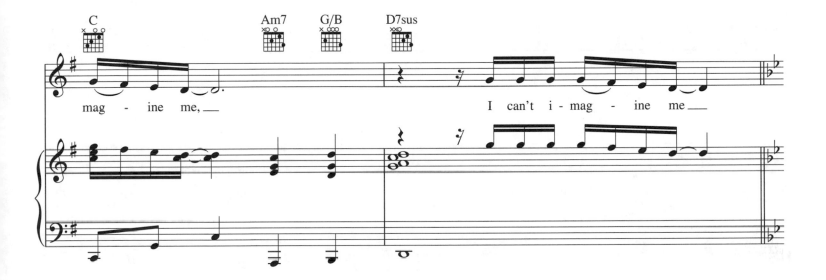

mag - ine me, ___ I can't i-mag - ine me ___

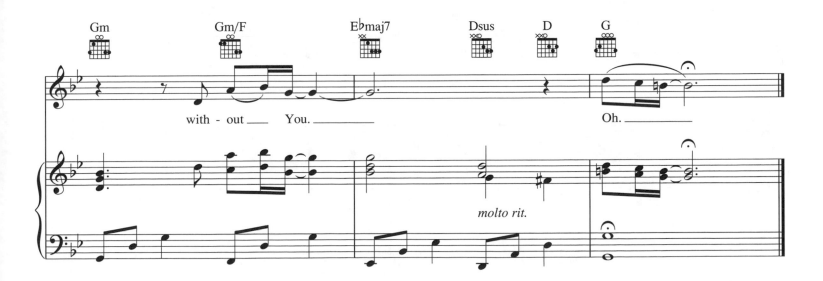

with - out ___ You. _____ Oh. _____

molto rit.

KEEP THE CANDLE BURNING

Words and Music by JEFF BORDERS,
GAYLA BORDERS and LOWELL ALEXANDER

Moderately

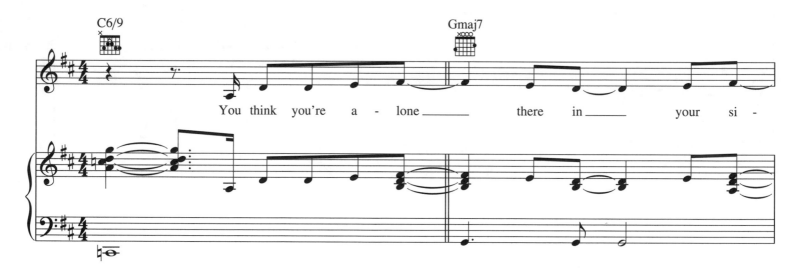

You think you're a - lone _____ there in _____ your si -

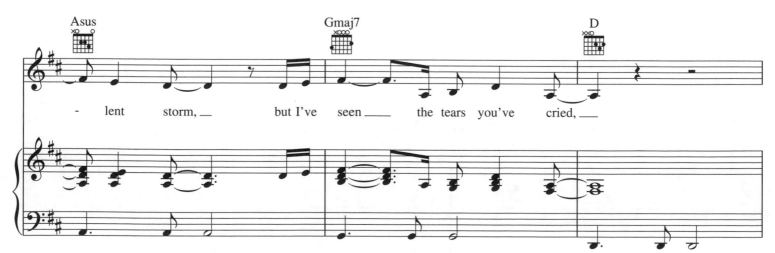

- lent storm, _____ but I've seen _____ the tears you've cried, _____

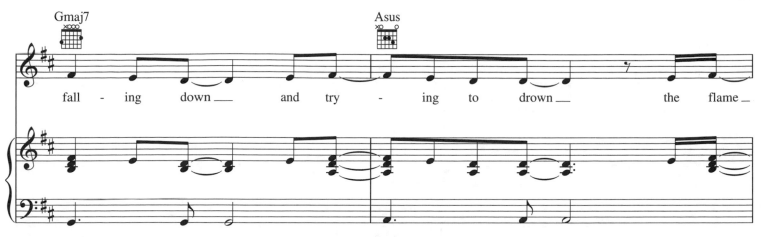

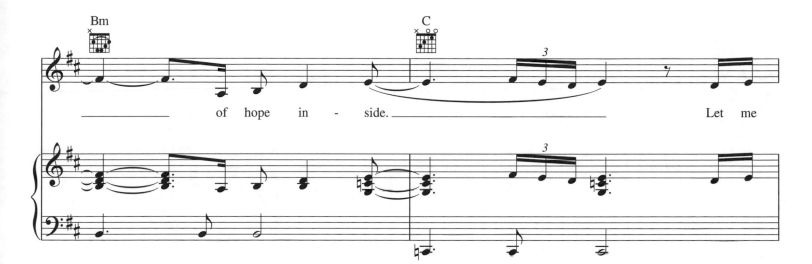

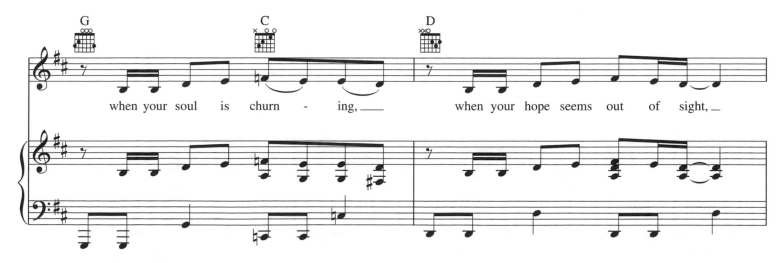

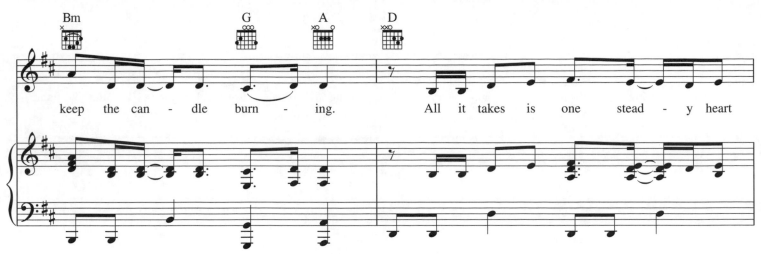

keep the can - dle burn - ing. All it takes is one stead - y heart

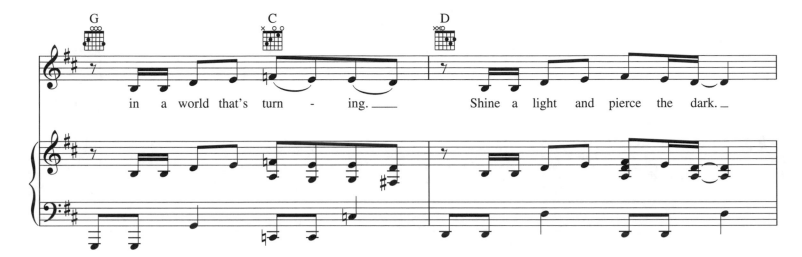

in a world that's turn - ing. _____ Shine a light and pierce the dark. __

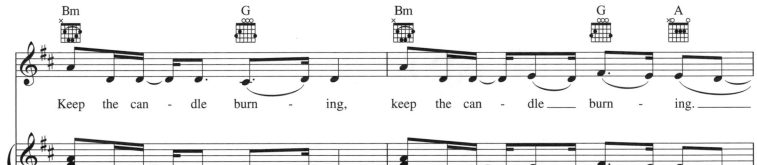

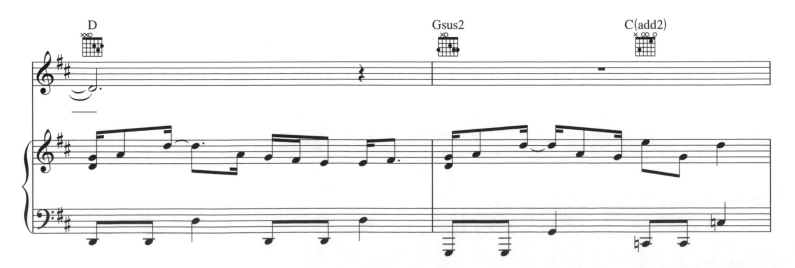

Keep the can - dle burn - ing, keep the can - dle _____ burn - ing. _____

When you're

down and you're dis - cour - aged, _____ when the dark -

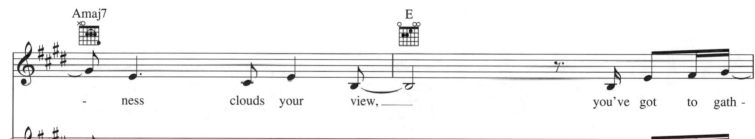

- ness clouds your view, _____ you've got to gath -

- er up _____ your cour - age; you know the Lord _____

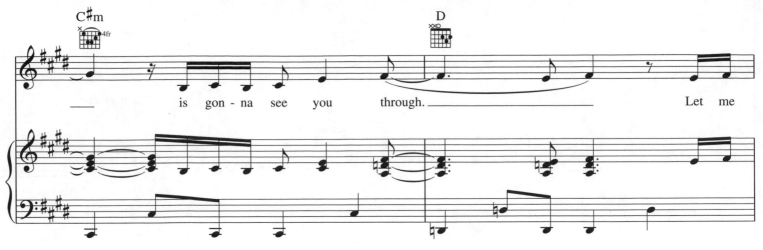

is gon - na see you through. _____ Let me

tell you now, __ tell you now. _____ When you're walk - ing in the dead __ of night,

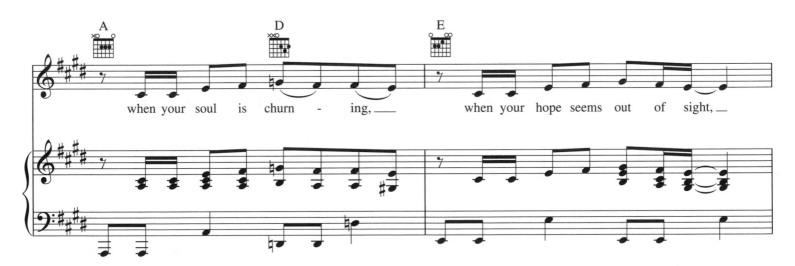

when your soul is churn - ing, ___ when your hope seems out of sight, __

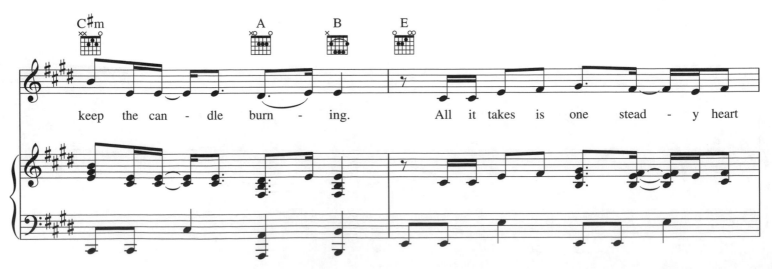

keep the can - dle burn - ing. All it takes is one stead - y heart

To Coda ⊕

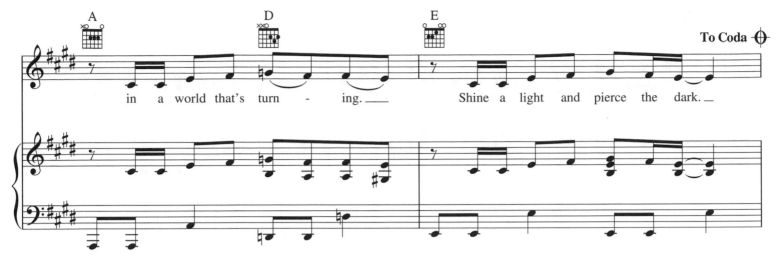

in a world that's turn - ing. ___ Shine a light and pierce the dark. ___

Keep the can - dle burn - ing, keep the can - dle ___ burn - ing. ___

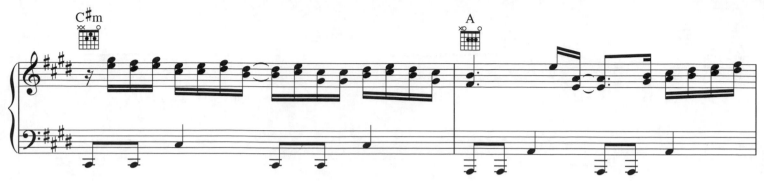

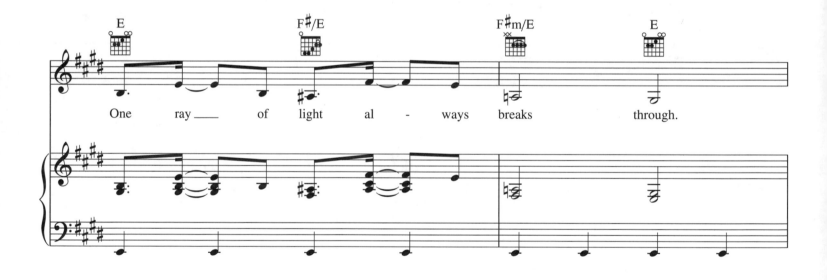

One ray ___ of light al - ways breaks through.

D.S. al Coda

Fol - low ___ wher-ev - er ___ He takes _____ you, wher-ev - er He takes you. ___

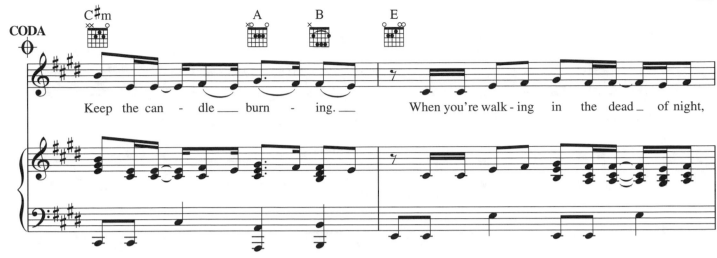

CODA

Keep the can - dle ___ burn - ing. ___ When you're walk - ing in the dead ___ of night,

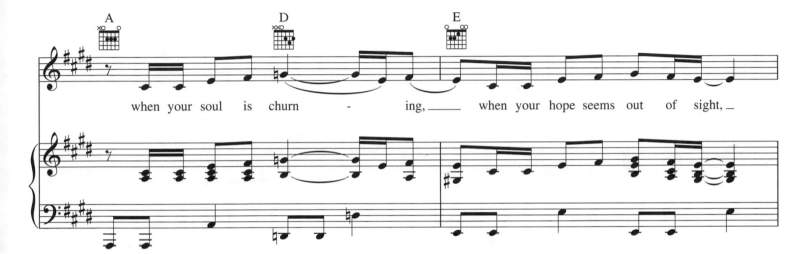

when your soul is churn ___ ing, ___ when your hope seems out of sight, ___

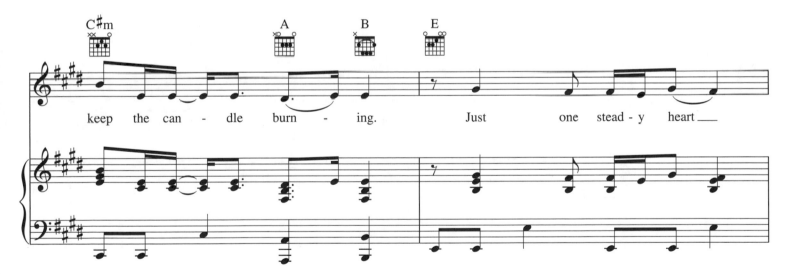

keep the can - dle burn ___ ing. Just one stead - y heart ___

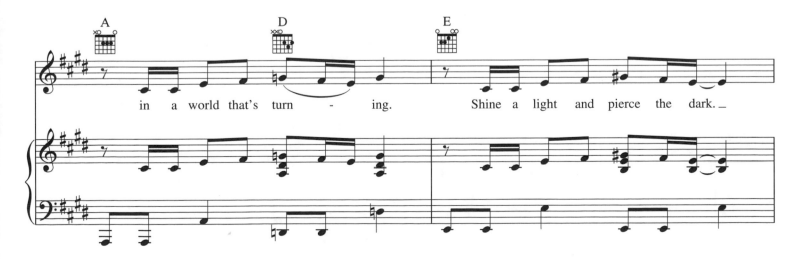

in a world that's turn ___ ing. Shine a light and pierce the dark. ___

Keep the can - dle burn - ing, keep the can - dle ___ burn - ing. ___

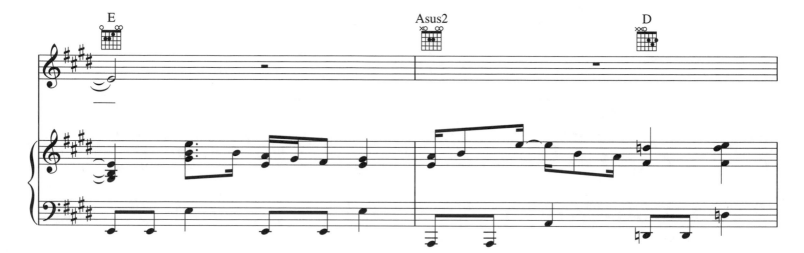

Keep the can - dle ___ burn - ing. ___

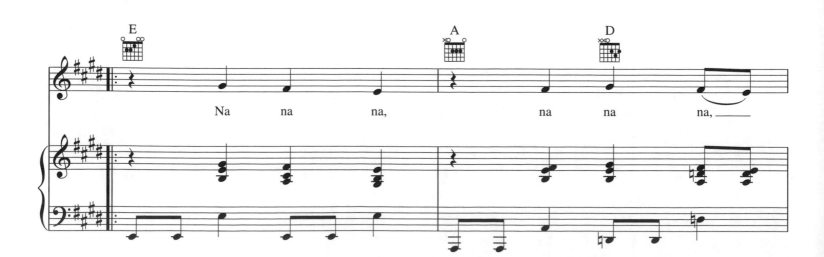

Na na na, na na na, ___

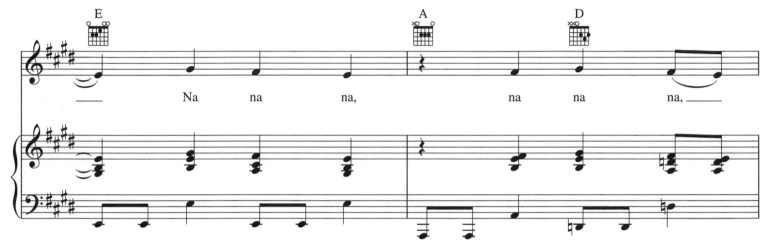

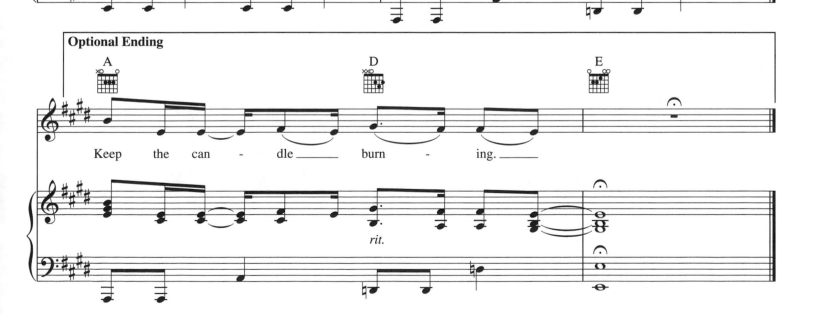

LET YOUR LIGHT SHINE

Words and Music by BETHANY DILLON
and ED CASH

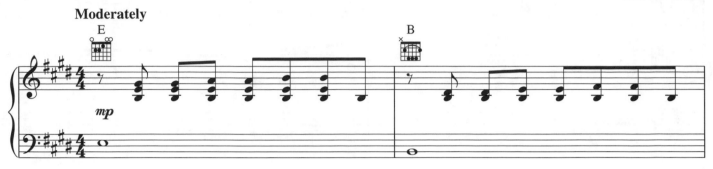

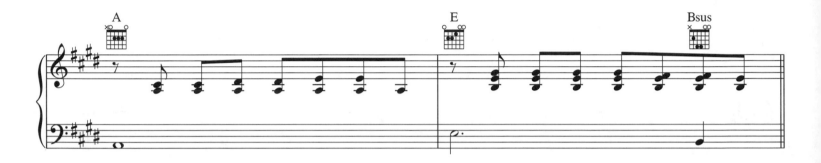

The calm-er of the sea, here in this room with me,
Oh, Je-sus, You be-came what was my deep-est shame,

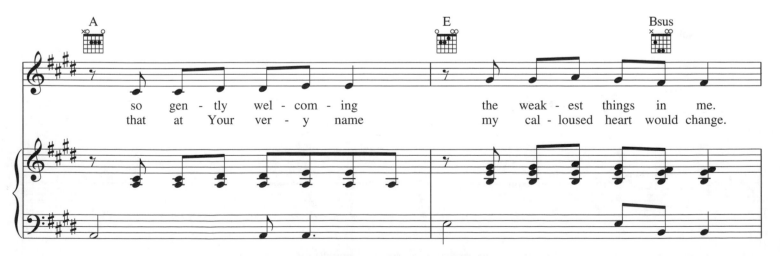

so gen-tly wel-com-ing the weak-est things in me.
that at Your ver-y name my cal-loused heart would change.

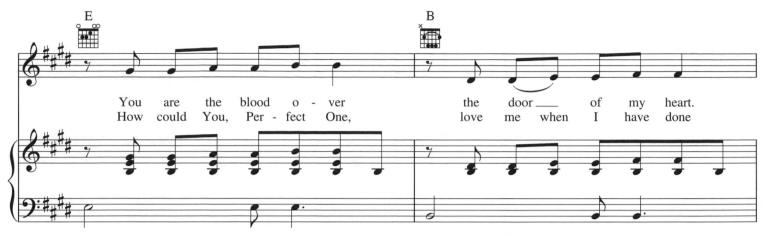

You are the blood o - ver / the door ___ of my heart.
How could You, Per - fect One, / love me when I have done

What pain You spared me from, / how could I know it all? ___
noth - ing that's wor - thy of / my free - dom You have won? ___

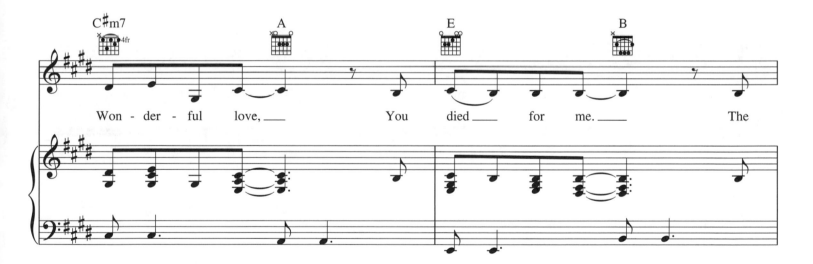

Won - der - ful love, ___ You died ___ for me. ___ The

pow - er of ___ Your life is in me. ___ Fa - ther, let Your

cresc.

sing _____ har - mo - ny. _____ Hold _____ me, _____ God. ____

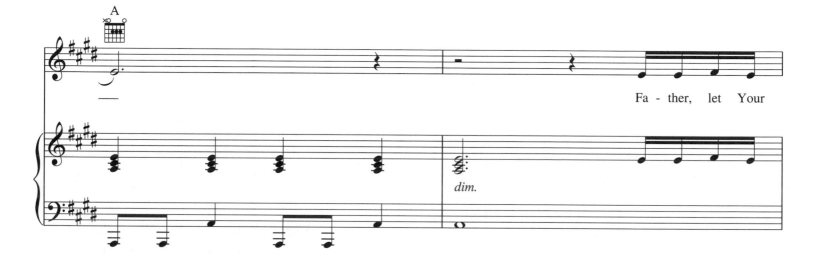

_____ Fa - ther, let Your

dim.

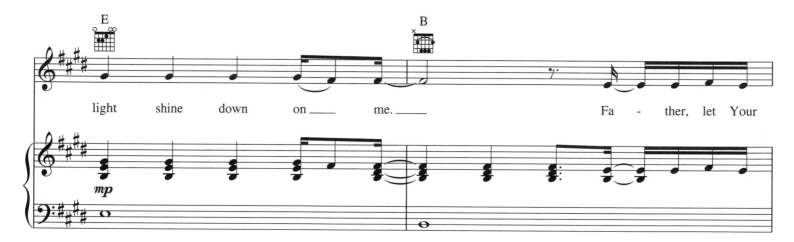

light shine down on _____ me. _____ Fa - ther, let Your

mp

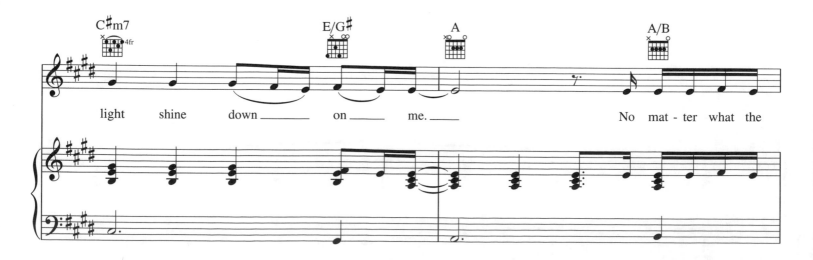

light shine down _____ on _____ me. _____ No mat - ter what the

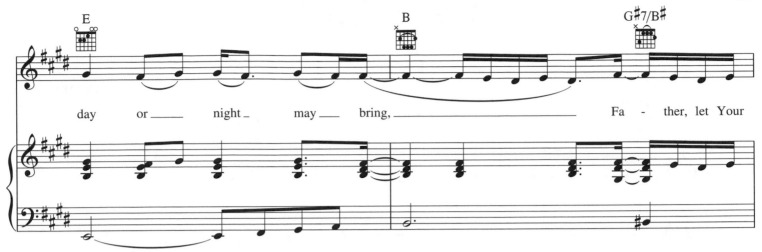

day or ___ night ___ may ___ bring, _____ Fa - ther, let Your

light _____ shine _ down, let ___ your light _____ shine _ down. Fa - ther, let Your

D.S. al Coda

cresc.

CODA

___ Let it shine _ on ___ me. ___ Let it shine _ on ___ me. _

rit.

LIFESONG

Words and Music by
MARK HALL

Recorded a half step higher.

life, _____ I sing in vain ___ to - night. }
need, _____ to be Your hands ___ and feet. }

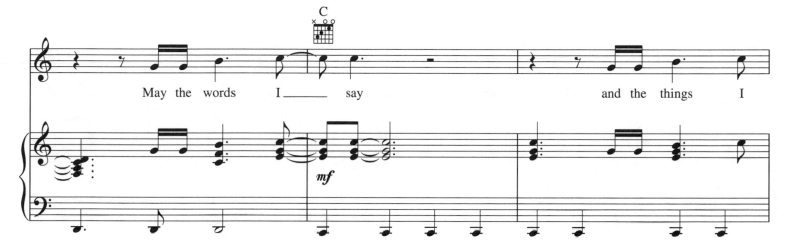

May the words I ___ say and the things I

do _____ make my life - song ___ sing,

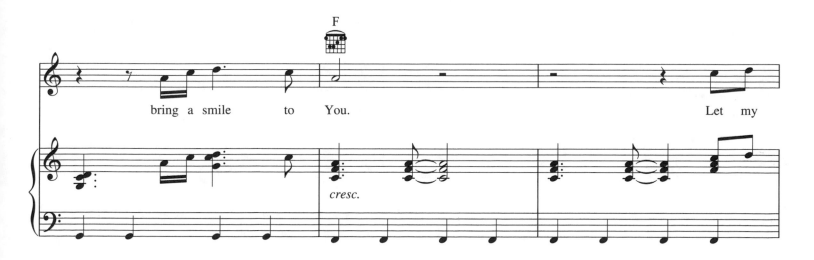

bring a smile to You. Let my

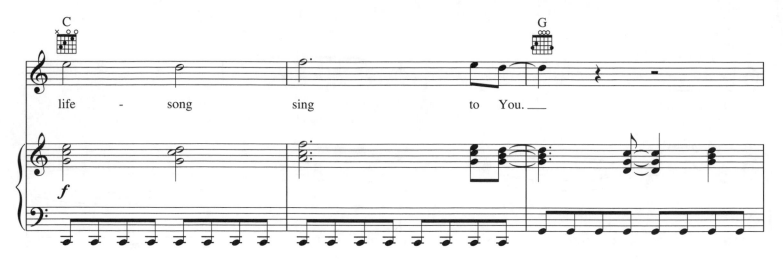

life - song   sing   to You. ___

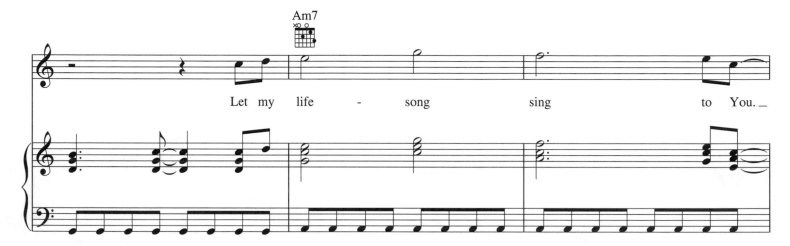

Let my   life - song   sing   to You. __

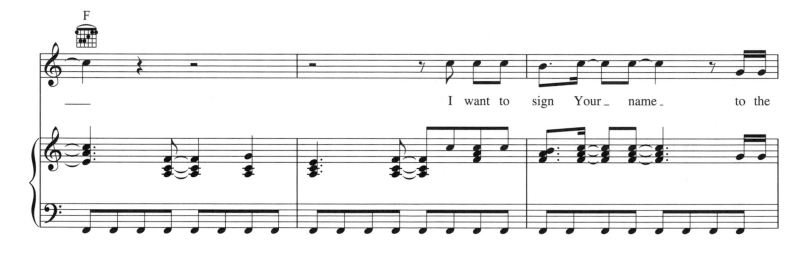

___   I   want to   sign   Your __ name __   to the

end   of ___ this   day,   know-ing   that my   heart ___ was

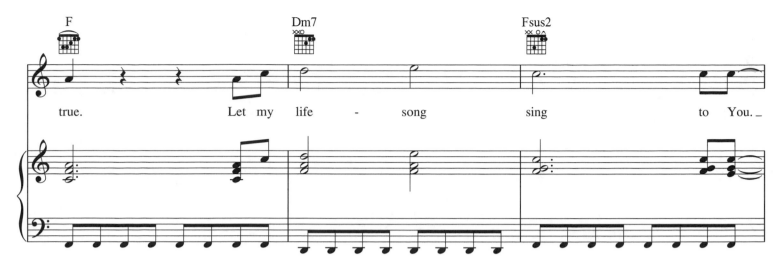

true. Let my life - song sing to You. _

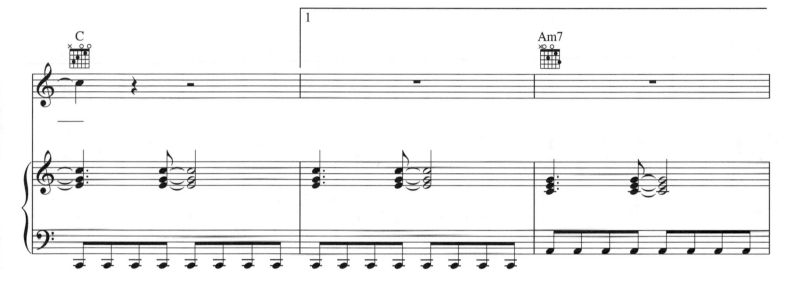

Lord, I give my _ Hal - le -

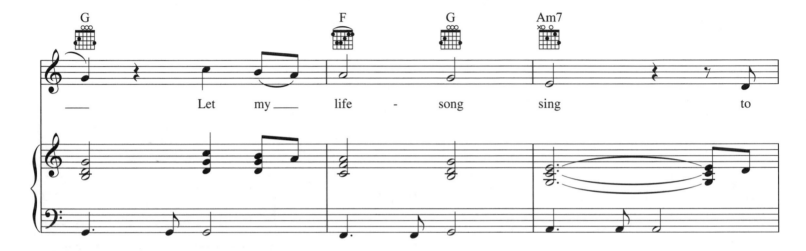

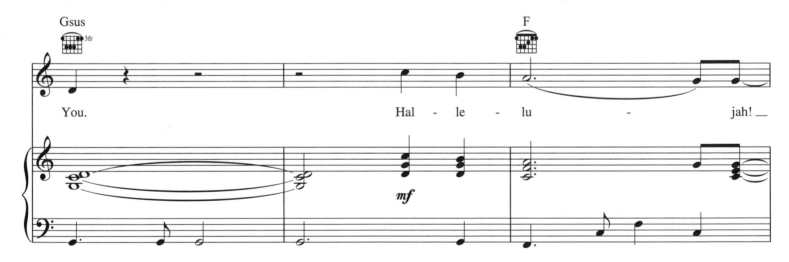

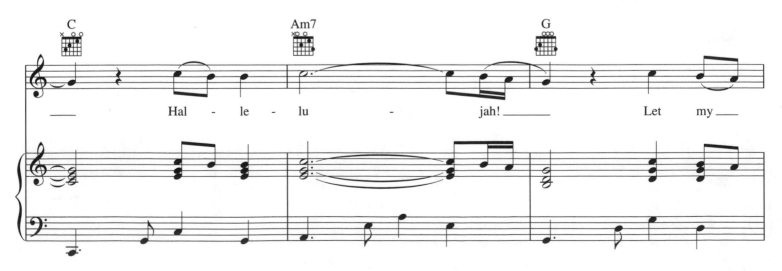

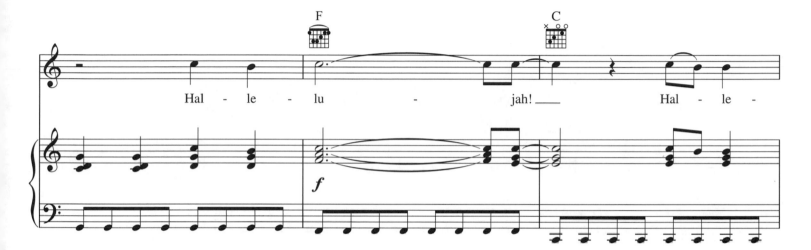

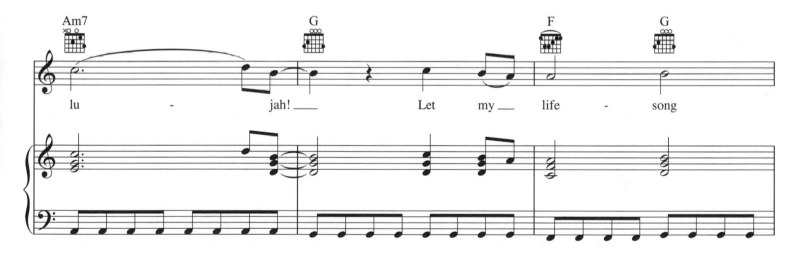

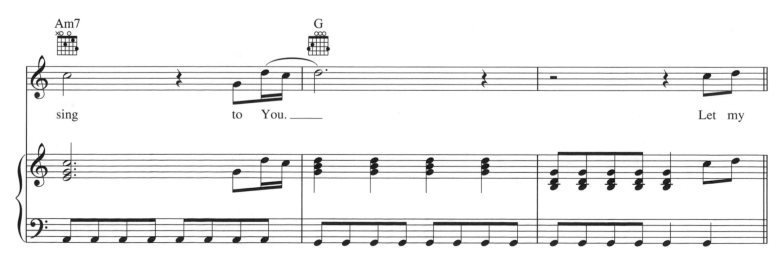

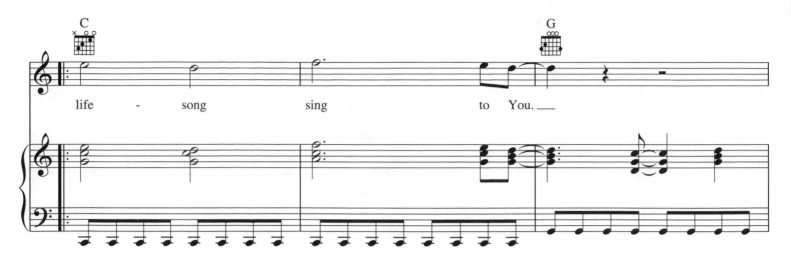

life - song sing to You. __

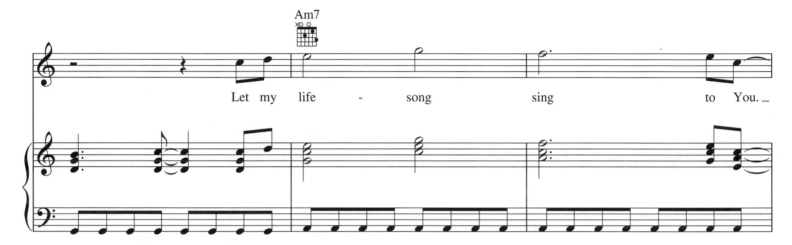

Let my life - song sing to You. __

__ I want to sign Your __ name __ to the

end of __ this day, know-ing that my heart __ was true. Let my

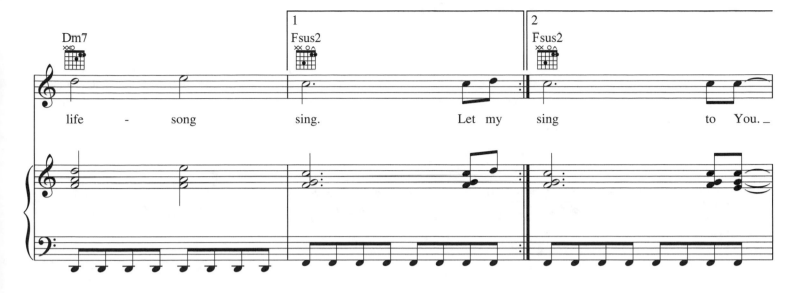

life - song sing. Let my sing to You. __

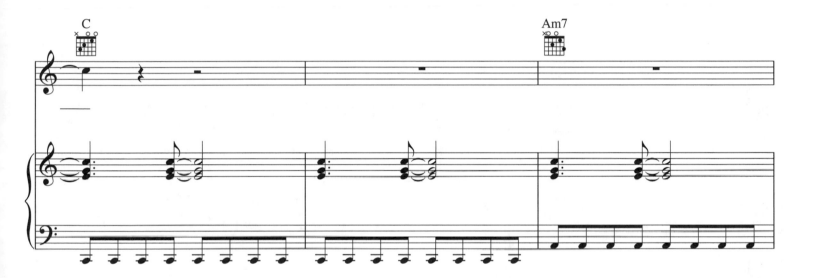

THE MESSAGE

Words and Music by MICHAEL OMARTIAN,
MARK HARRIS and DON KOCH

Moderately slow, in 2

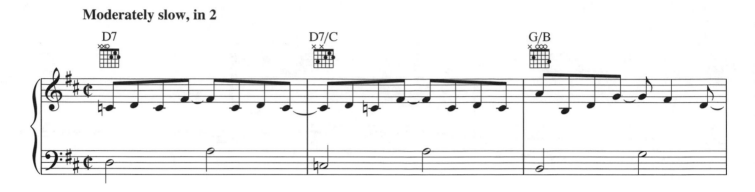

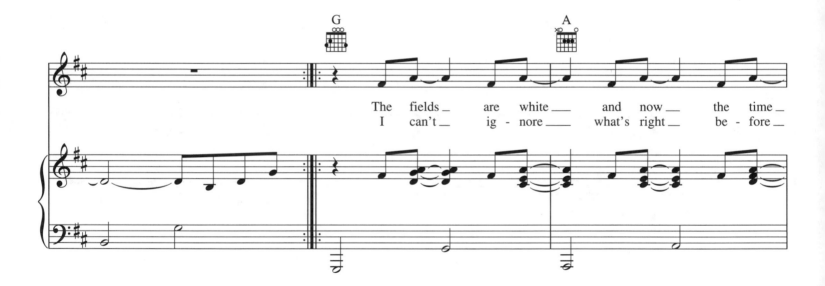

The fields _ are white _ and now _ the time _
I can't _ ig - nore _ what's right _ be - fore _

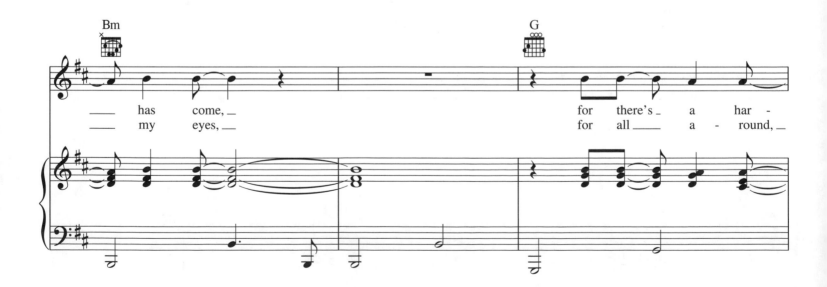

_ has come, _ for there's _ a har -
_ my eyes, _ for all _ a - round,

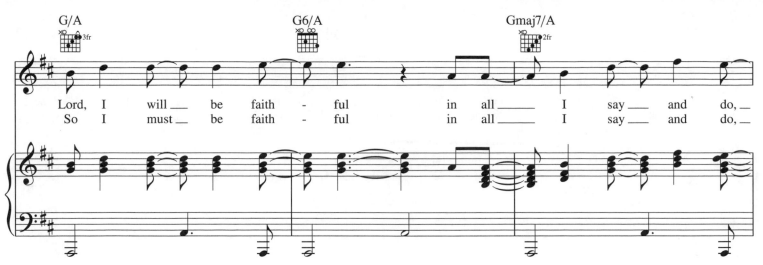

Lord, I will __ be faith - ful in all __ I say __ and do, __
So I must __ be faith - ful in all __ I say __ and do, __

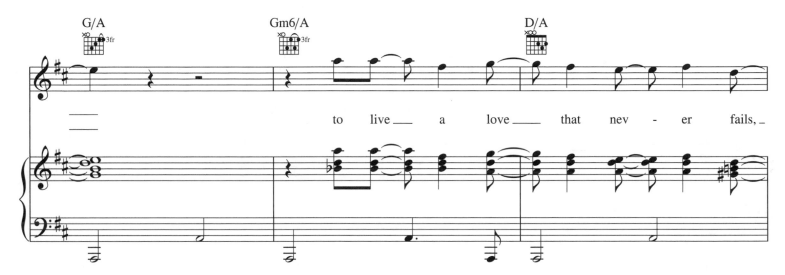

__ to live __ a love __ that nev - er fails, __

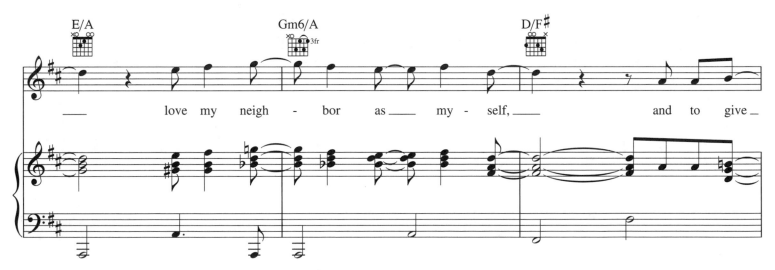

__ love my neigh - bor as __ my - self, __ and to give __

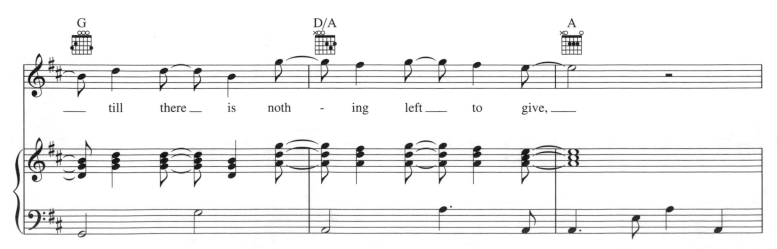

__ till there __ is noth - ing left __ to give, __

to live __ a faith __ that nev - er dies, __ to be cru -

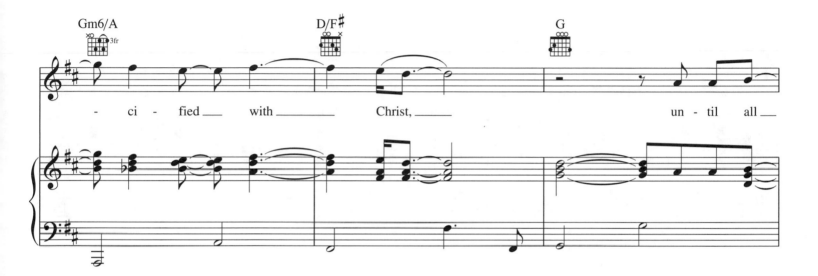

- ci - fied __ with __ Christ, __ un - til all __

__ that lives __ through me __ is the mes - sage. __

If we all ___ will work ___ to - geth - er,

we can make ___ this world ___ a bet - ter place to ___ live. ___

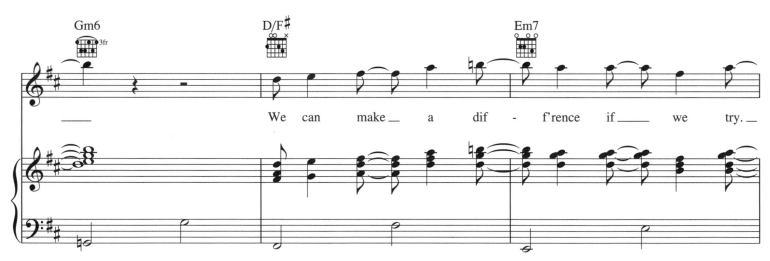

___ We can make ___ a dif - f'rence if ___ we try. __

___ To live ___ a love ___ that nev - er fails, _
- sage. _____

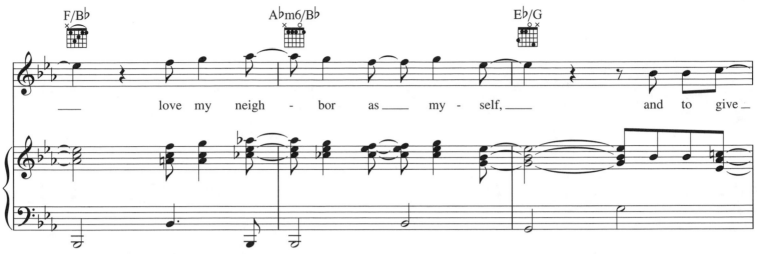

love my neigh - bor as____ my - self, ____ and to give____

____ till there ____ is noth - ing left____ to give, ____

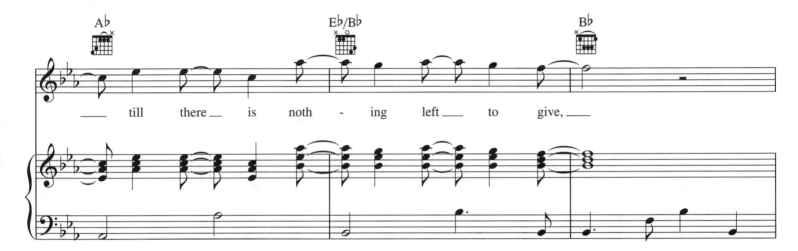

to live ____ a faith____ that nev - er dies, ____ to be cru -

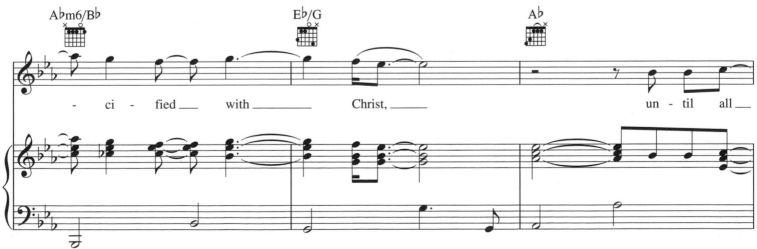

- ci - fied ____ with _____ Christ, _____ un - til all____

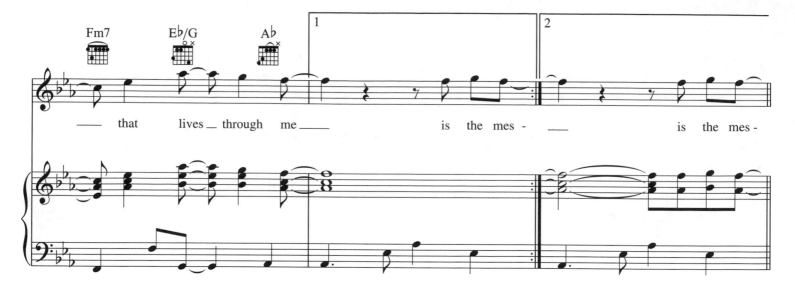

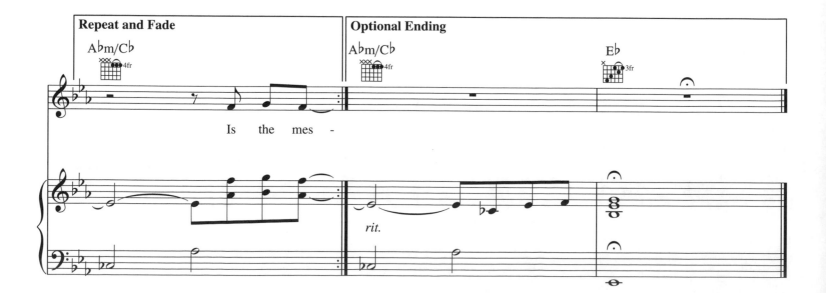

MUCH OF YOU

Words and Music by
STEVEN CURTIS CHAPMAN

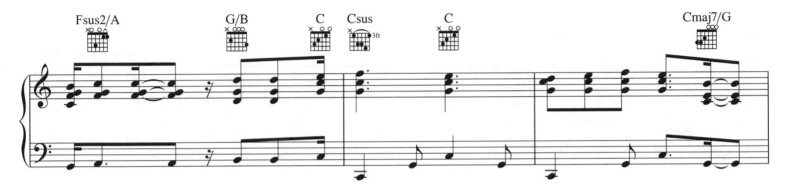

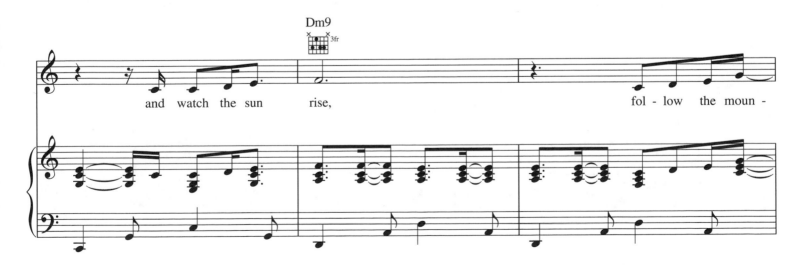

-tains _____ where they touch the sky, _____

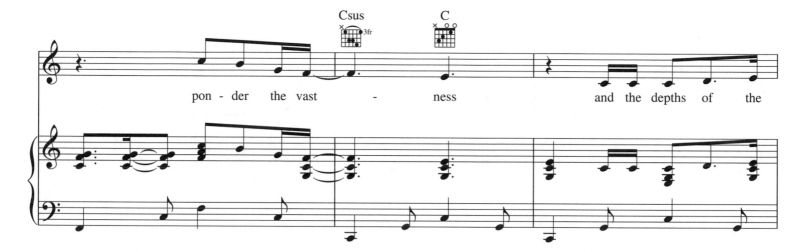

pon - der the vast - ness and the depths of the

sea, and think for a mo - ment the point of it all ___

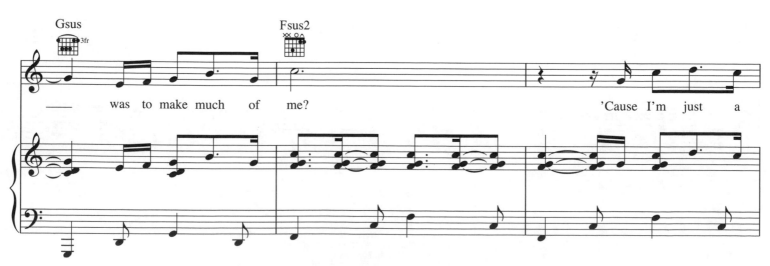

___ was to make much of me? 'Cause I'm just a

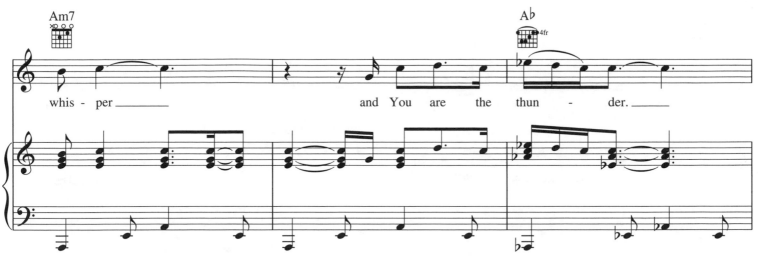

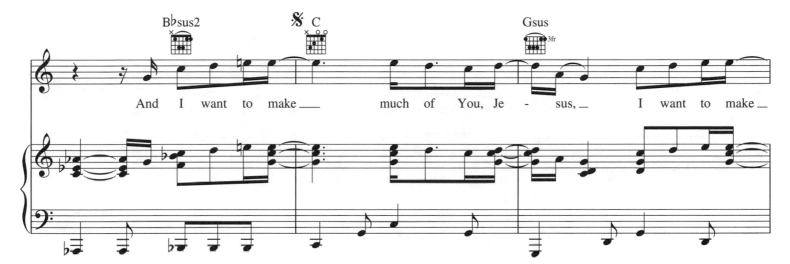

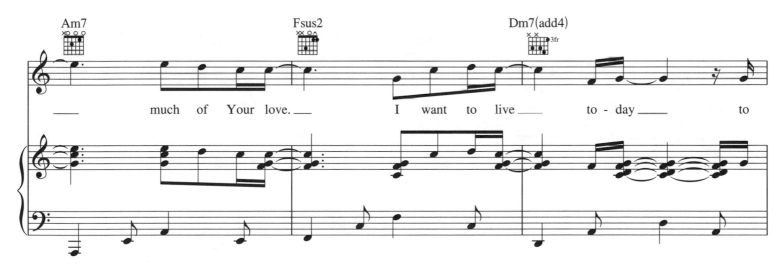

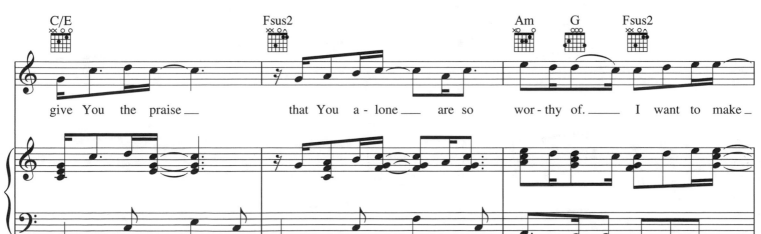

much of Your mer - cy, ___ I want to make ___ much of Your cross. ___

___ I give You my life; ___ take it and let it be

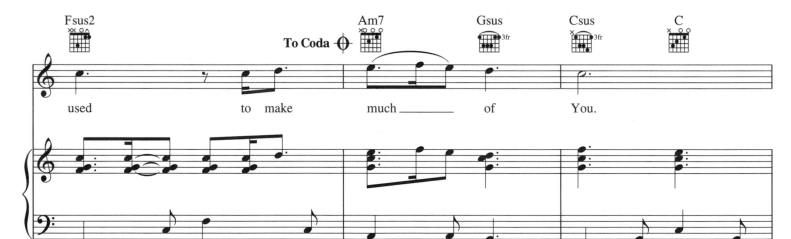

To Coda

used to make much ___ of You.

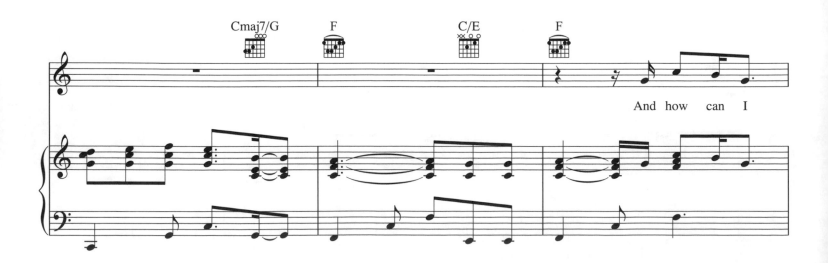

And how can I

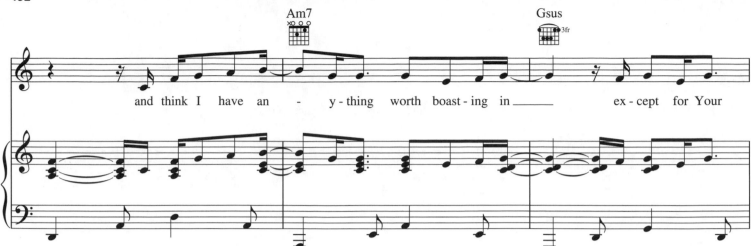

and think I have an - y - thing worth boast - ing in _____ ex - cept for Your

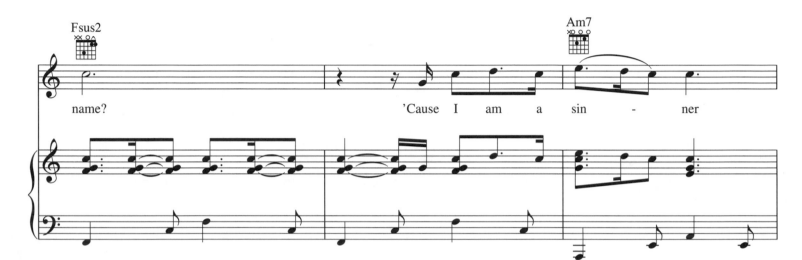

name? 'Cause I am a sin - ner

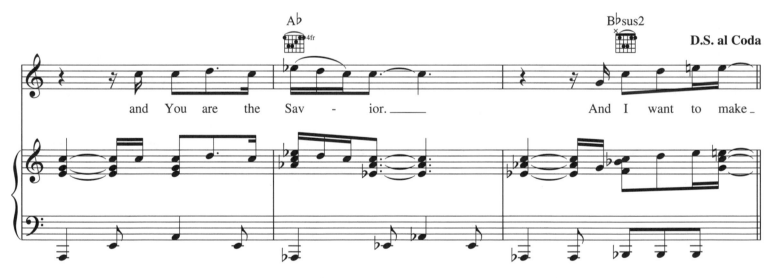

and You are the Sav - ior. _____ And I want to make _

D.S. al Coda

CODA

much _____ of You. This is Your love, ___ oh, ___ God,

not to make ___ much of me, _____ but to send ___

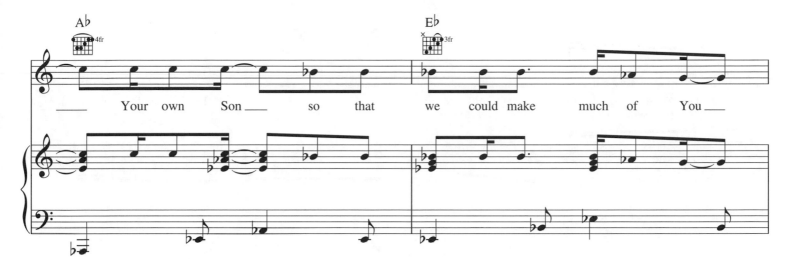

___ Your own Son ___ so that we could make much of You ___

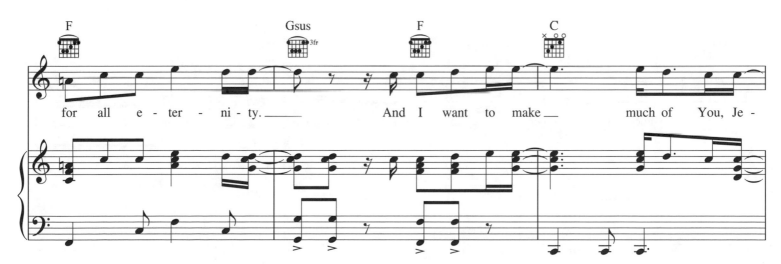

for all e - ter - ni - ty. _____ And I want to make ___ much of You, Je -

- sus, __ I want to make ___ much of Your ___ love. I want to live ___

to - day _____ to give You the praise _____

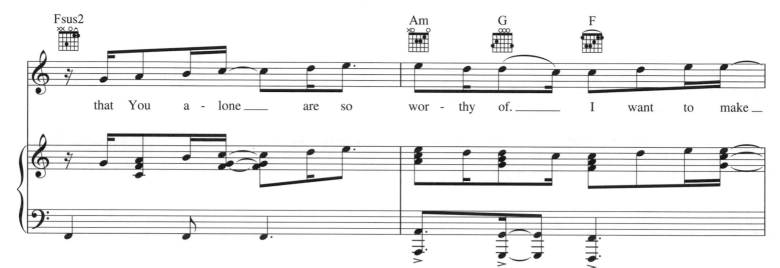

that You a - lone _____ are so wor - thy of. _____ I want to make _____

_____ much of Your mer - cy, _____ I want to make _____ much of Your _____

cross. I give You my life; _____ take it and let it be

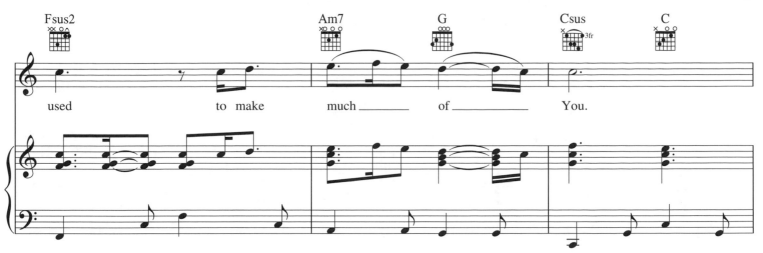

used to make much _____ of _____ You.

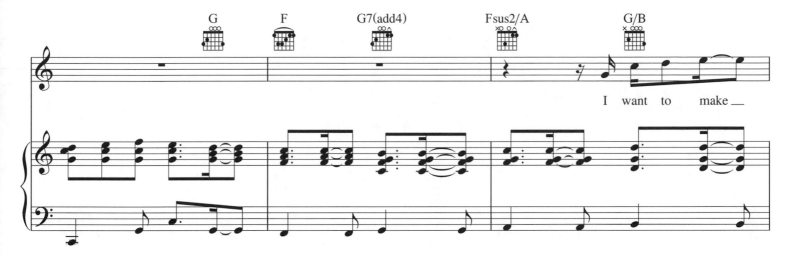

I want to make __

much of You, _____ much of You, Je - sus. ____

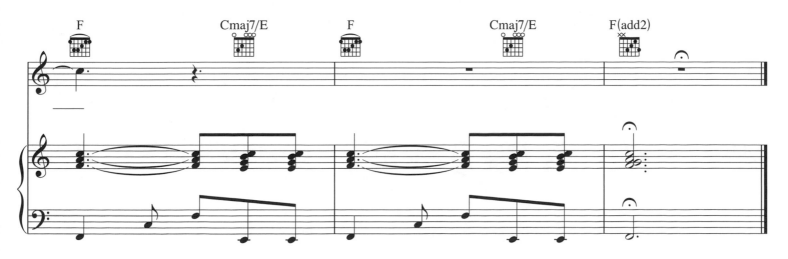

MY FAITH WILL STAY

Words and Music by
CHERI KEAGGY

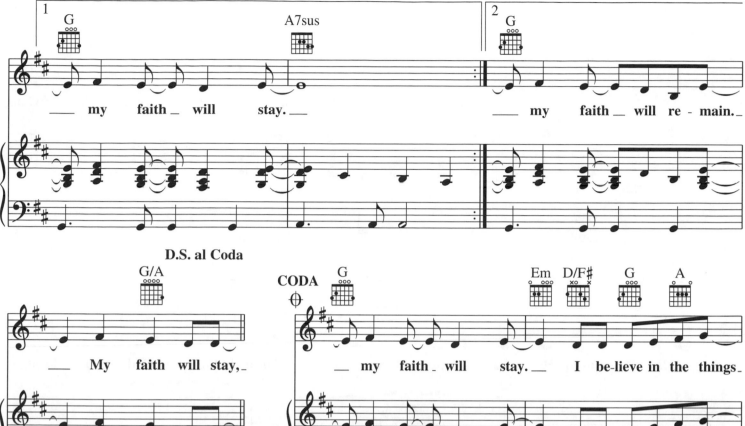

MY PRAISE

Words and Music by DAN DEAN,
DAVE CLARK and DON KOCH

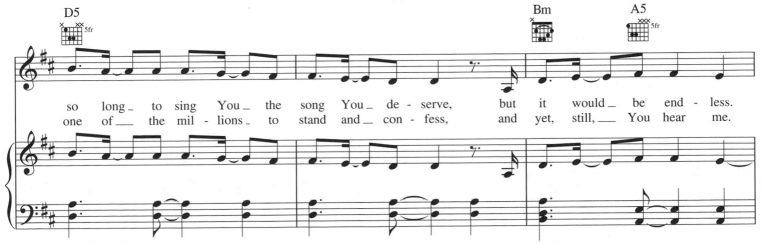

Lord, I wish I ___ could praise You ___ with
thing I ___ could give, You ___ al -

ad - e - quate words, but You leave ___ me speech - less. And I
read - y ___ pos - sess; Lord, I'm so ___ un - worth - y, yeah. ___ I'm just

so long ___ to sing You ___ the song You ___ de - serve, but it would ___ be end - less.
one of ___ the mil - lions ___ to stand and ___ con - fess, and yet, still, ___ You hear me.

I long to move Your heart, I bring You some-thing new, I tell how
Your heart is o-pen wide; You long for what I bring; I pray some-

great You are, till my praise to You is } like an
how You'll find this sim-ple of-fer-ing is } like an

o-cean breeze blow-ing on Your face, like a sum-mer sun with its

warm em-brace. Like a gen-tle rain plays a

sym - pho - ny, that's what I want my praise __ to be. Like a

fra - grant __ rose in the ear - ly __ spring, like an

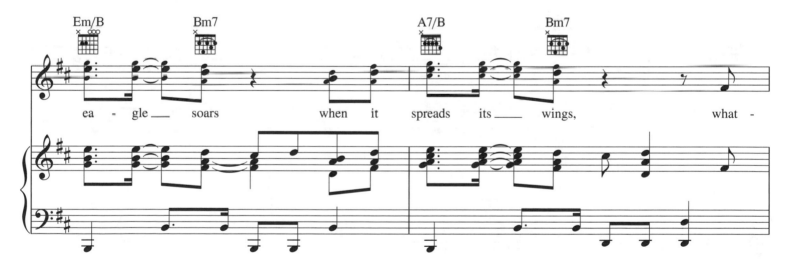

ea - gle __ soars when it spreads its __ wings, what -

ev - er, Lord, You may need __ from me, __ that's what I want my praise __

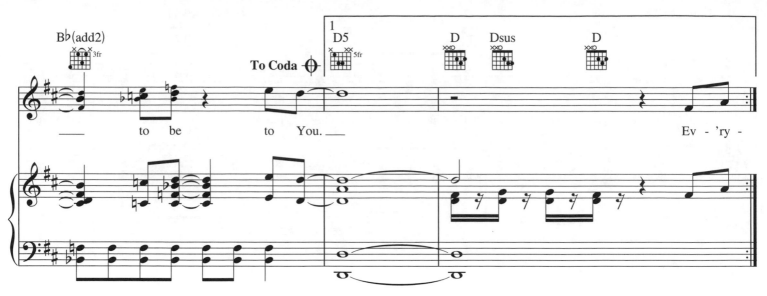

to be to You. Ev - 'ry -

(Yeah, yeah, yeah, yeah, yeah.)
Lord, I want my praise to be like the breeze,
(How I want, how I want.)

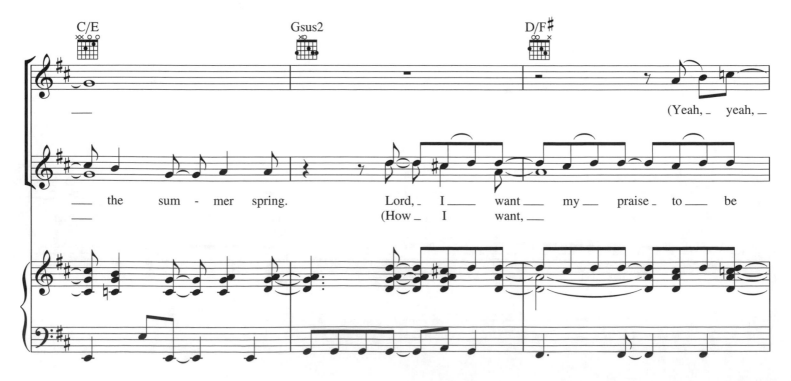

the sum - mer spring. Lord, I want my praise to be
(Yeah, yeah, (How I want,

like __ the ea - gle spreads __ its wings. (Yeah.) __
how __ I want.) __

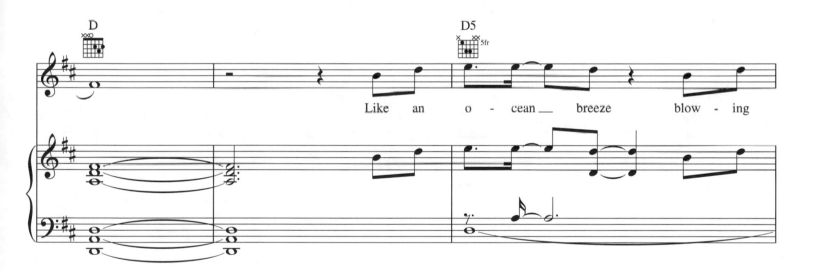

Like an o - cean __ breeze blow - ing

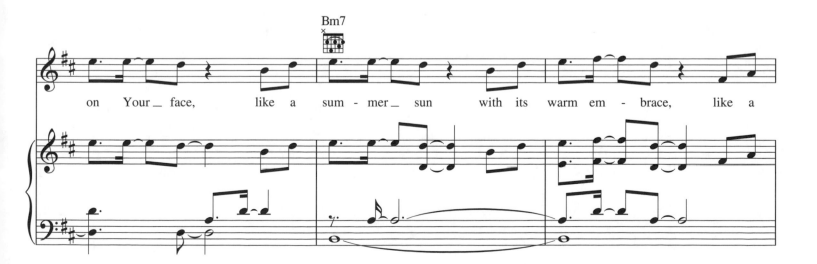

on Your __ face, like a sum - mer __ sun with its warm em - brace, like a

gen - tle __ rain plays a sym - pho - ny. That's what I want my praise __

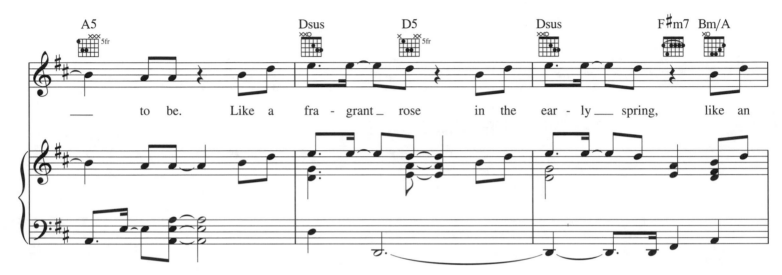

__ to be. Like a fra - grant __ rose in the ear - ly __ spring, like an

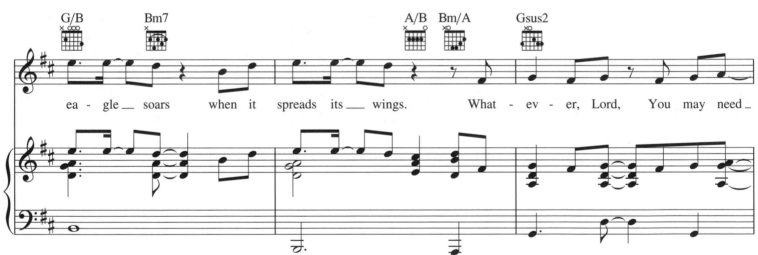

ea - gle __ soars when it spreads its __ wings. What - ev - er, Lord, You may need __

D.S. al Coda

__ from me, that's what I want my praise __ to be. Like an

OPEN MY HEART

Words and Music by
CHERI KEAGGY

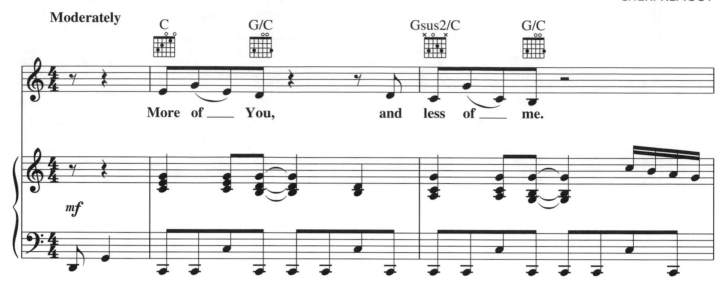

More of ___ You, and less of ___ me.

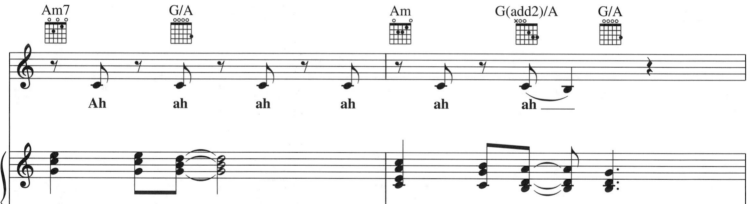

Ah ah ah ah ah ah ___

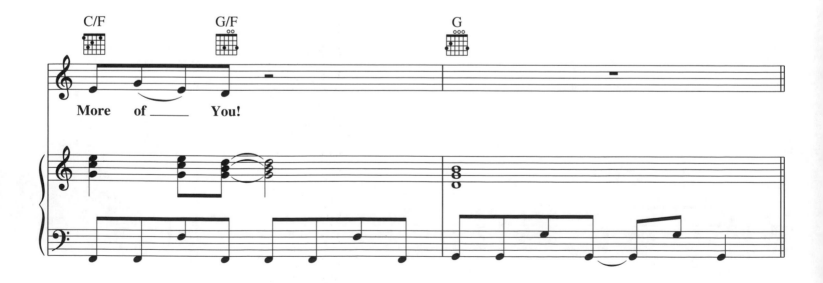

More of ___ You!

O - pen_ my _ heart. _

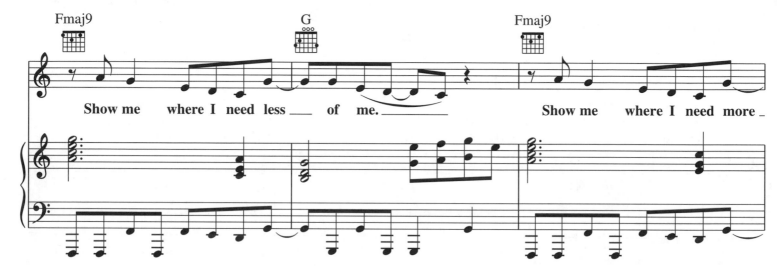

Show me where I need less _ of me. _ Show me where I need more_

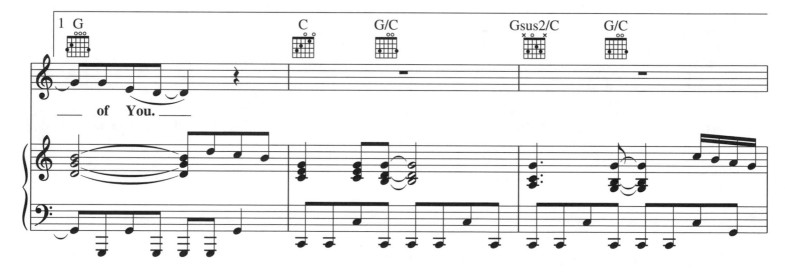

_ of You. _

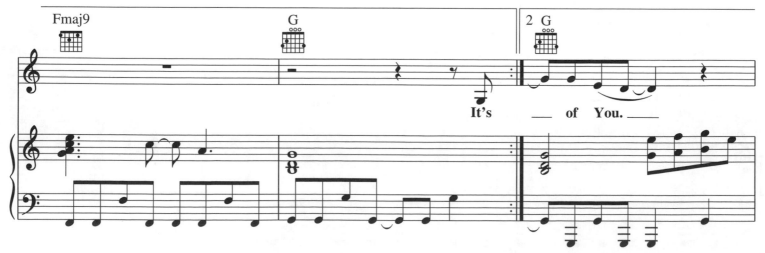

It's _ of You. _

Repeat and Fade

RIGHT HERE

Words and Music by
JEREMY CAMP

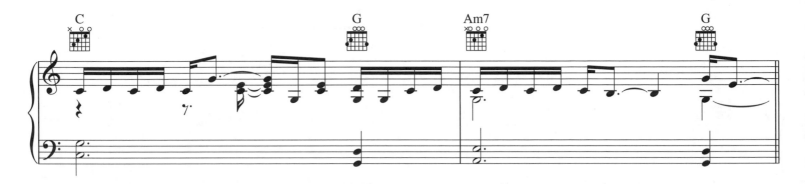

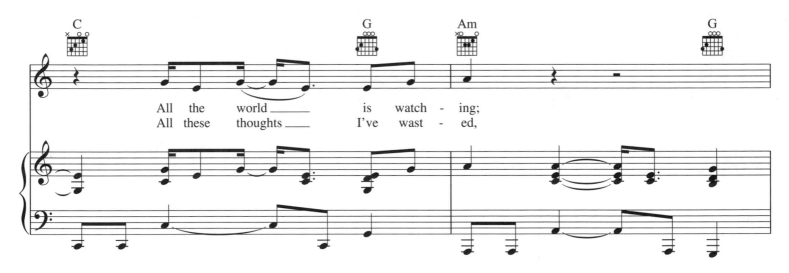

All the world _____ is watch - ing;
All these thoughts _____ I've wast - ed,

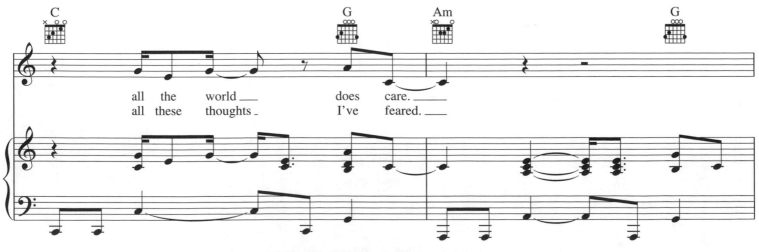

all the world _____ does care. _____
all these thoughts _____ I've feared. _____

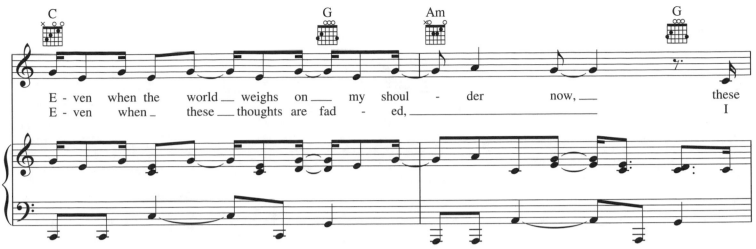

E - ven when the world — weighs on — my shoul - der now, — these
E - ven when — these — thoughts are fad - ed, — I

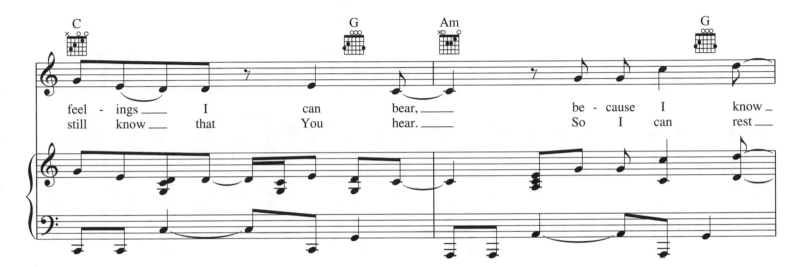

feel - ings — I can bear, — be - cause I know —
still know — that You hear. — So I can rest —

— that You're here. —
my hope in You.

Ev - 'ry-where I go, I know — You're not far a - way. — You're right here, —

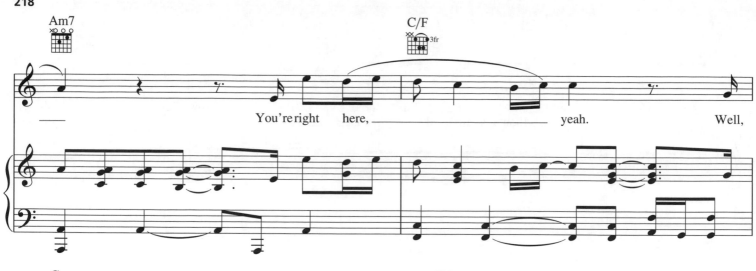

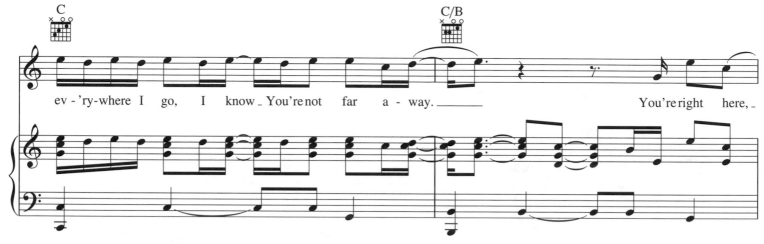

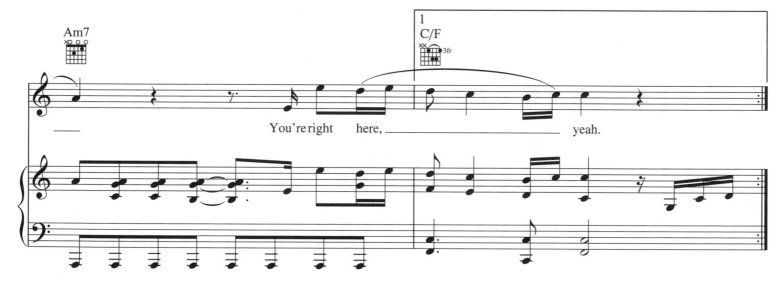

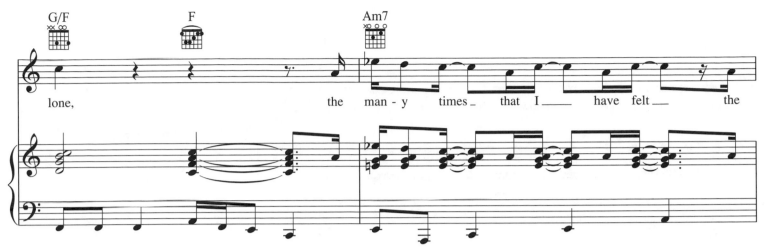

lone,   the man-y times_ that I____ have felt____ the

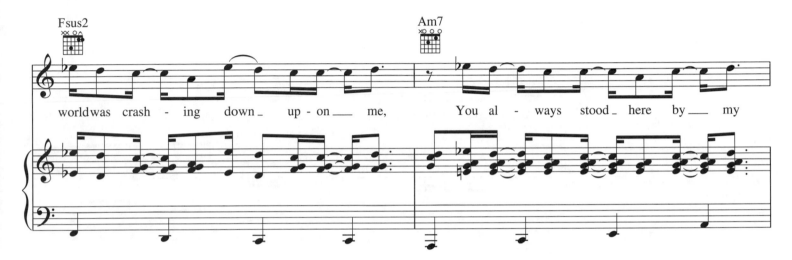

world was crash - ing down_ up-on___ me,   You al - ways stood_ here by___ my

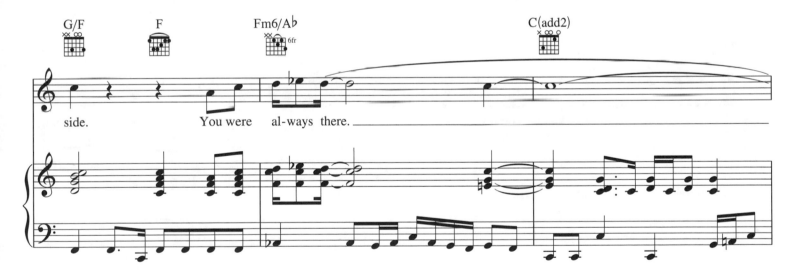

side.   You were al-ways there. _____

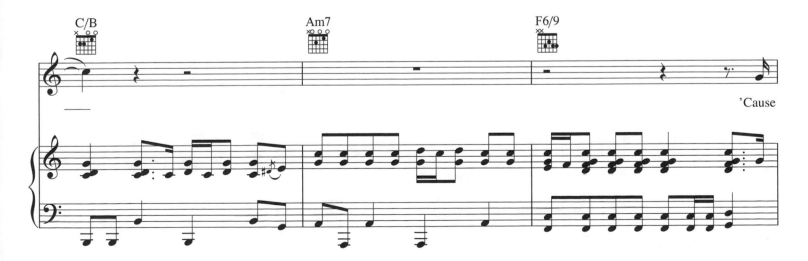

—   'Cause

ev-'ry-where I go, I know _ You're not far a-way. _____ You're right here, _

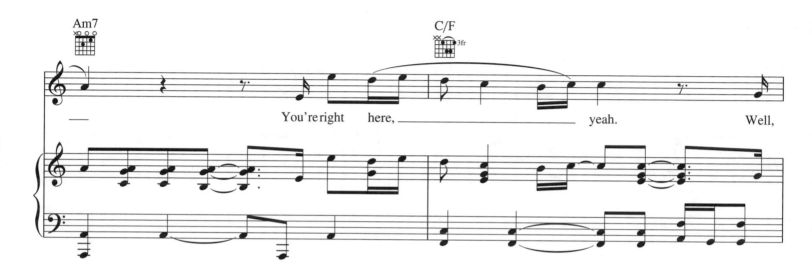

_ You're right here, _____ yeah. Well,

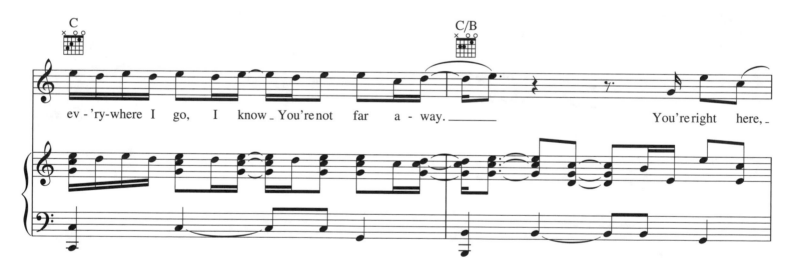

ev-'ry-where I go, I know _ You're not far a-way. _____ You're right here, _

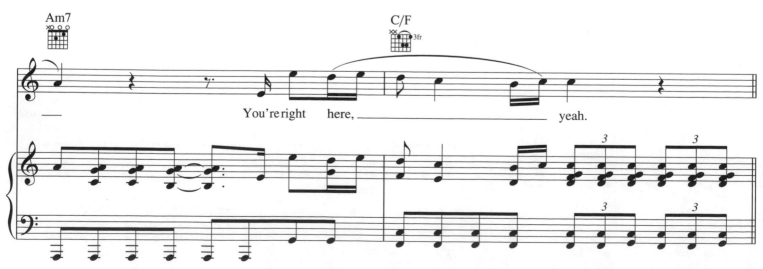

_ You're right here, _____ yeah.

Ev-'ry-where I go, I know __ You're not far a-way. _____ You're right here, ___

__ You're right here. _____

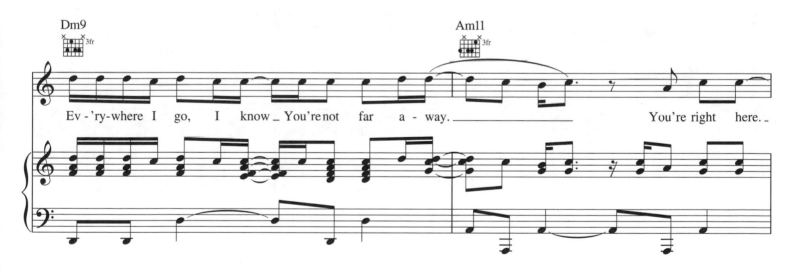

Ev-'ry-where I go, I know __ You're not far a-way. _____ You're right here. _

Optional Ending

Repeat and Fade

You're right here, _____ yeah.

RUN TO YOU

Words and Music by
TWILA PARIS

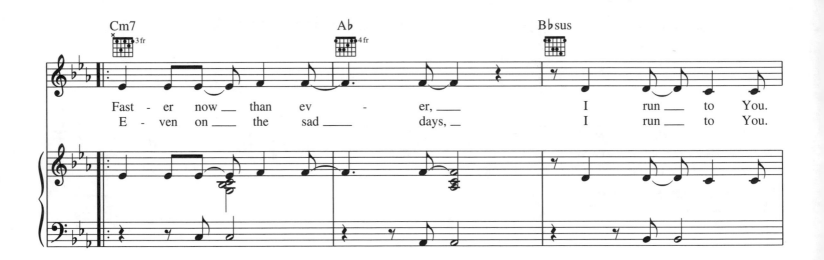

Faster now ___ than ev ___ er, ___ I run ___ to You.
E - ven on ___ the sad ___ days, ___ I run ___ to You.

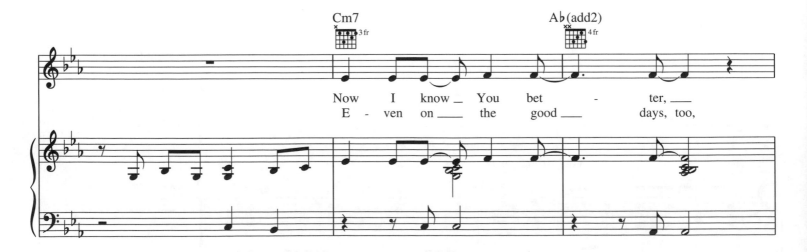

Now I know ___ You bet - ter, ___
E - ven on ___ the good ___ days, too,

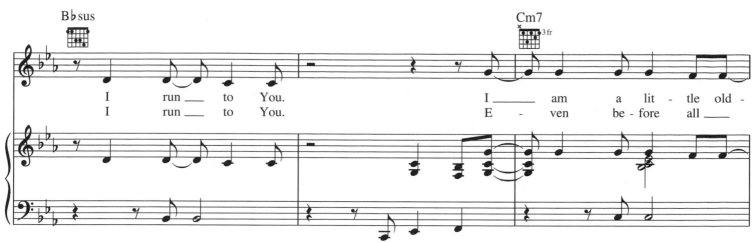

I run ___ to You. I ___ am a lit - tle old -

I run ___ to You. E - ven be - fore all ___

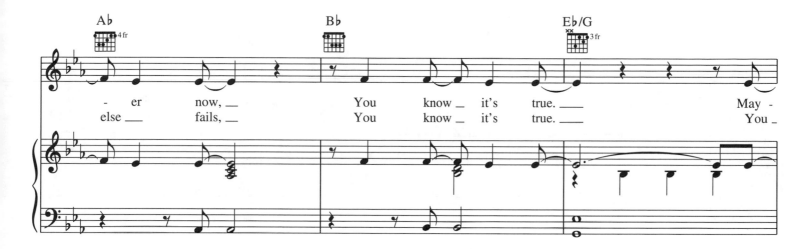

- er now, ___ You know ___ it's true. ___ May -

else ___ fails, ___ You know ___ it's true. ___ You _

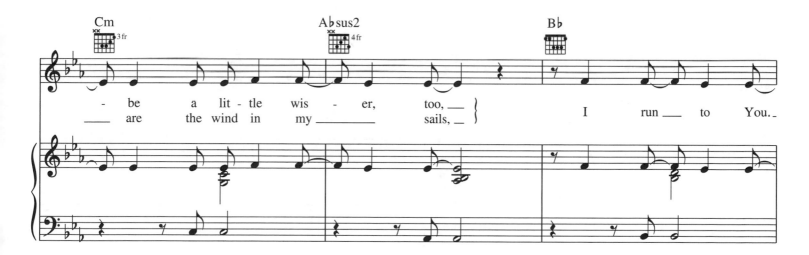

- be a lit - tle wis - er, too, ___ } I run ___ to You. _

___ are the wind in my ___ sails, _

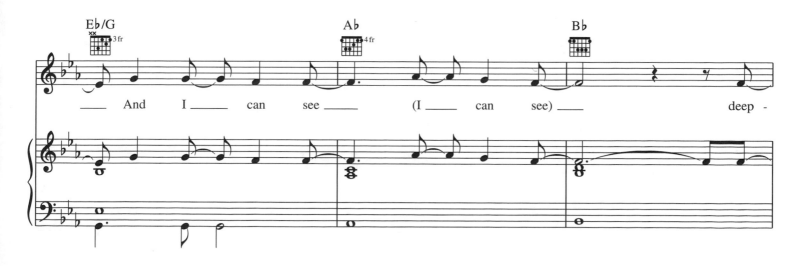

___ And I ___ can see ___ (I ___ can see) ___ deep -

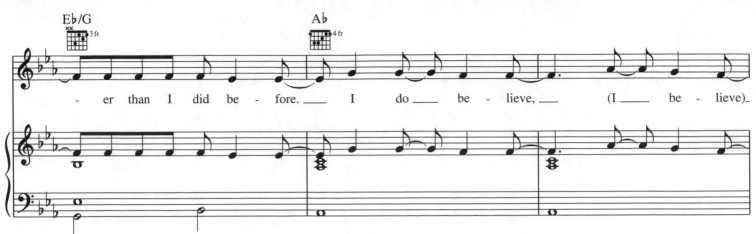

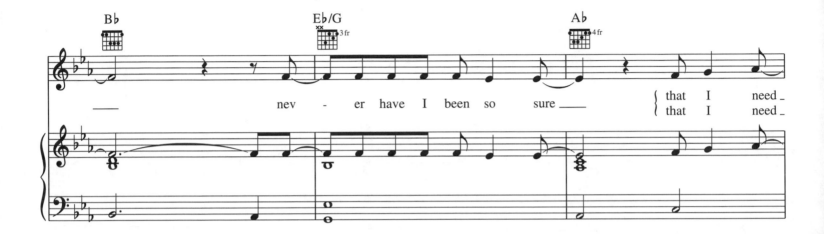

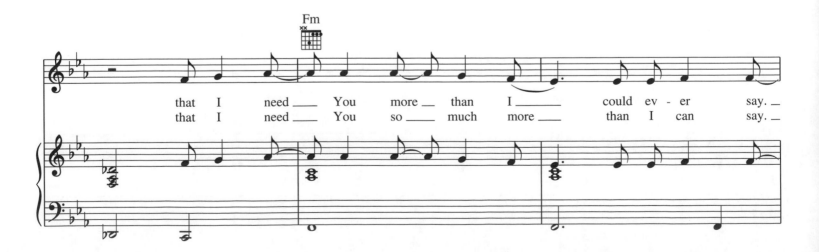

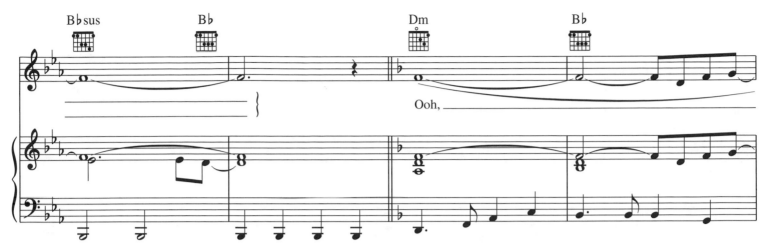

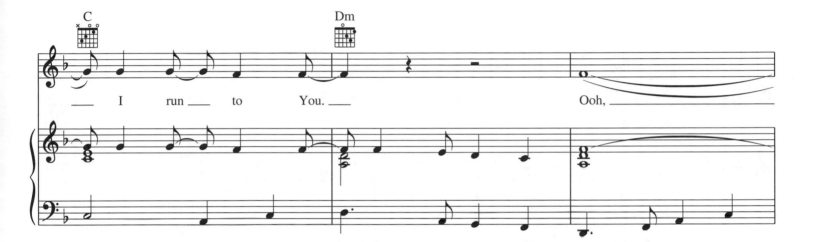

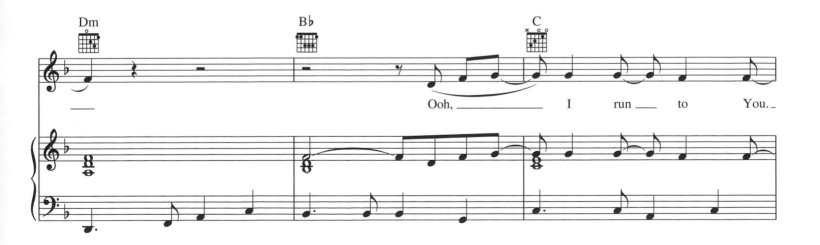

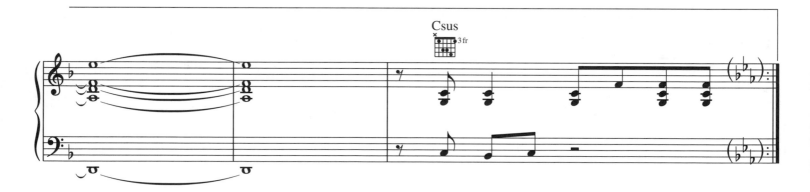

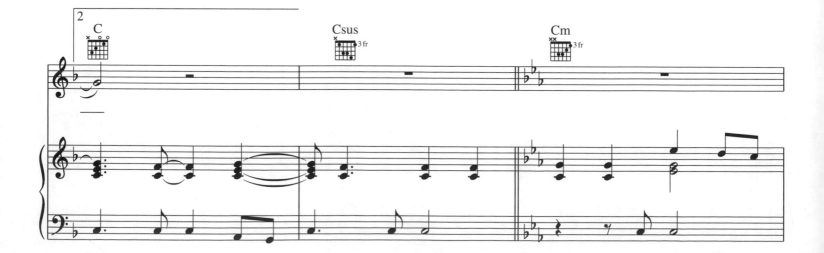

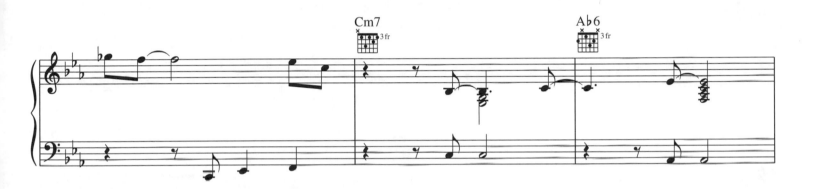

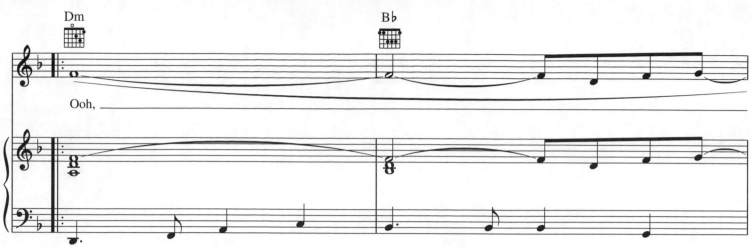

Ooh, _____

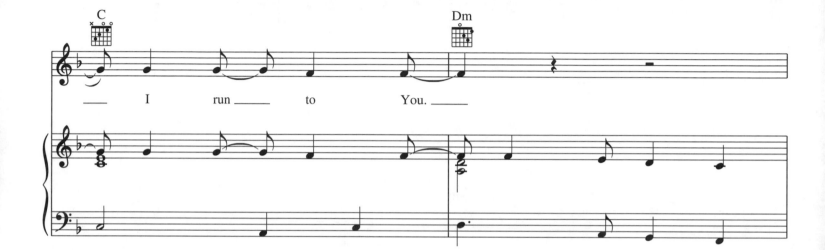

_____ I run _____ to You. _____

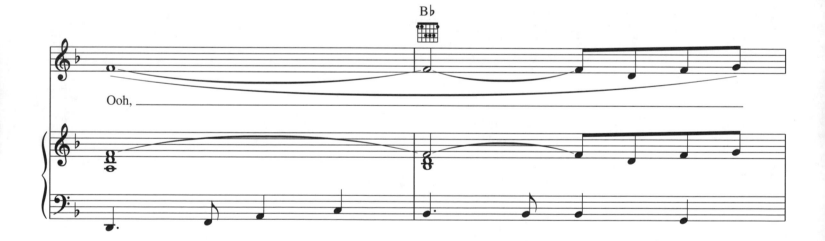

Ooh, _____

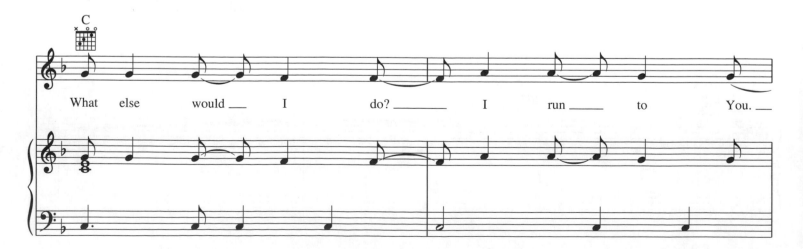

What else would ___ I do? _____ I run _____ to You. ___

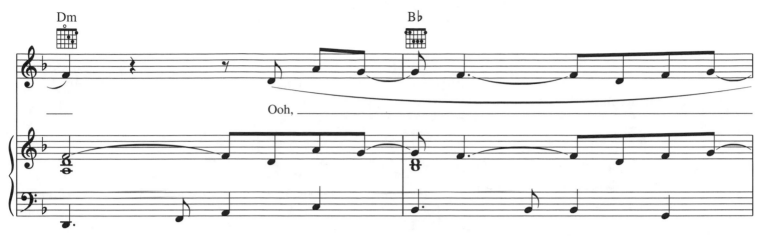

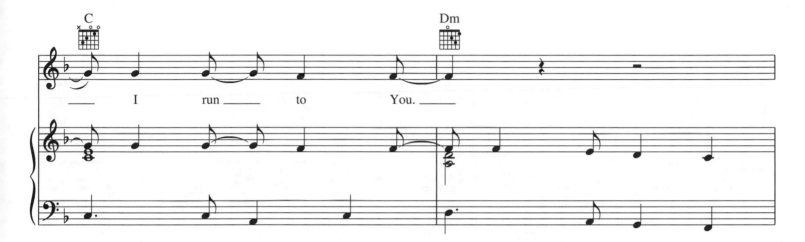

I run to You.

Ooh,

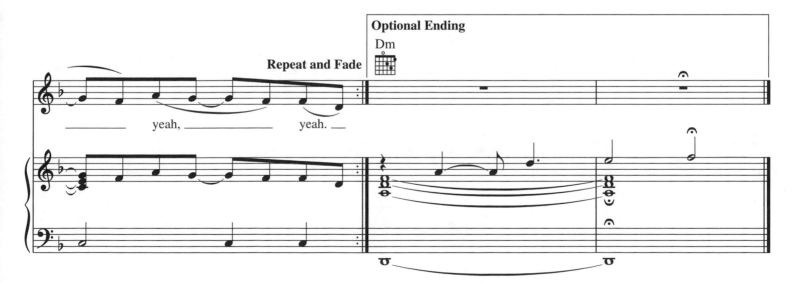

yeah, yeah.

Repeat and Fade

Optional Ending

SAVED THE DAY

Words and Music by
MICHAEL NEALE

The dark-est day in his-to-ry___ was o - ver; all was lost___ on the cross.___ Beat - en, bat - tered, bruised be - yond___ de - scrip - tion, You gave it all.___ What went wrong? This

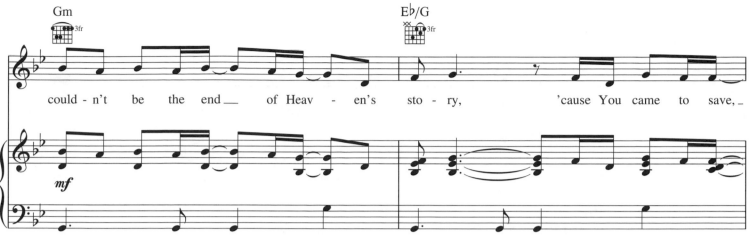

could-n't be the end __ of Heav - en's sto - ry, 'cause You came to save, __

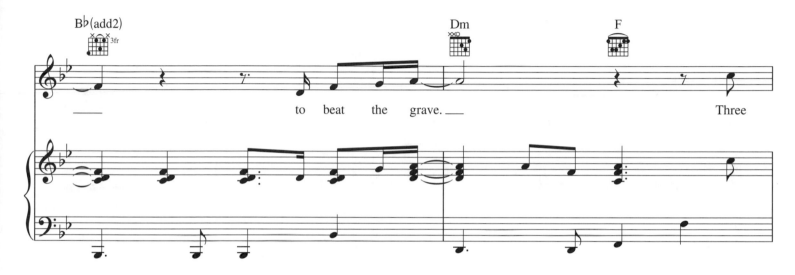

to beat the grave. __ Three

days, and now they're look-ing for __ Your bod - y. But You were gone, __

__ and now I know __ You saved the day __

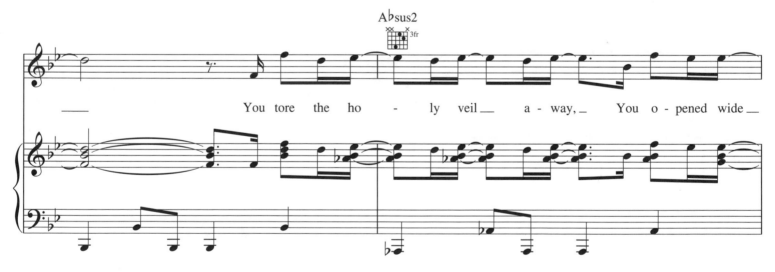

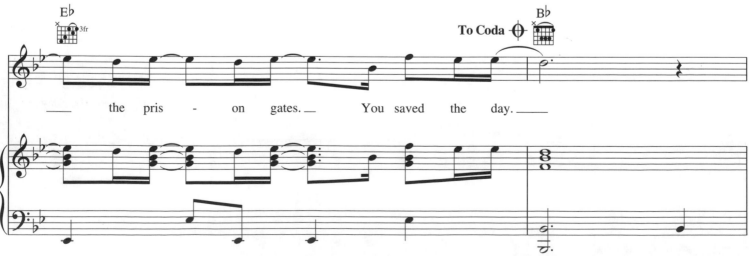

Res - cued from _ the shack - les of _ my fail - ure, in the dead of night _

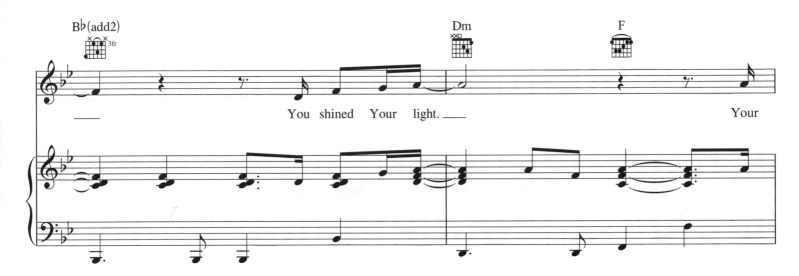

_ You shined Your light. _ Your

gift of love _ is hope _ that springs _ e - ter - nal. Be - cause of You _

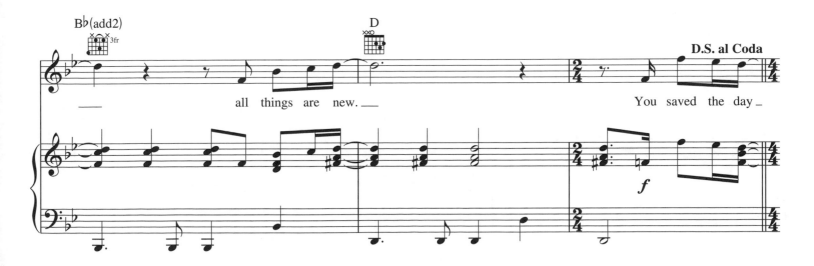

D.S. al Coda

_ all things are new. _ You saved the day _

CODA

Oh God, __ You res - cued me __

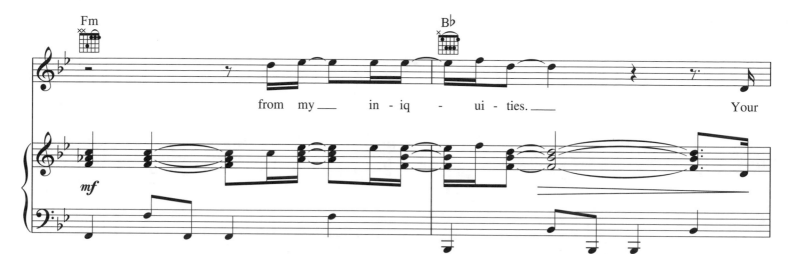

from my __ in - iq - ui - ties. __ Your

gift of love __ is hope __ that springs __ e - ter - nal. And be - cause of You __

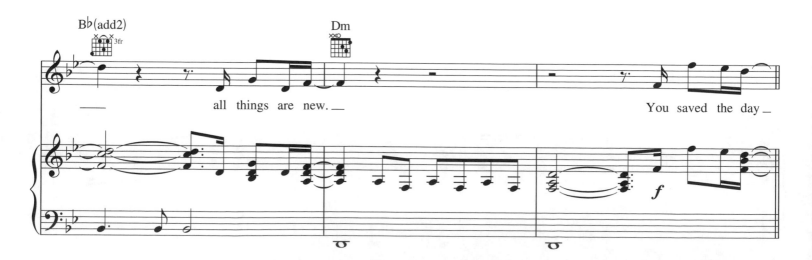

__ all things are new. __ You saved the day __

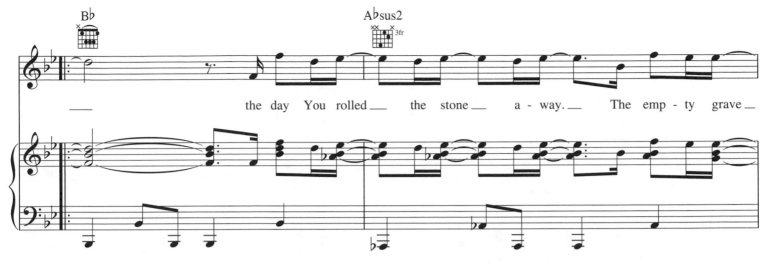

the day You rolled ___ the stone ___ a-way. ___ The emp-ty grave ___

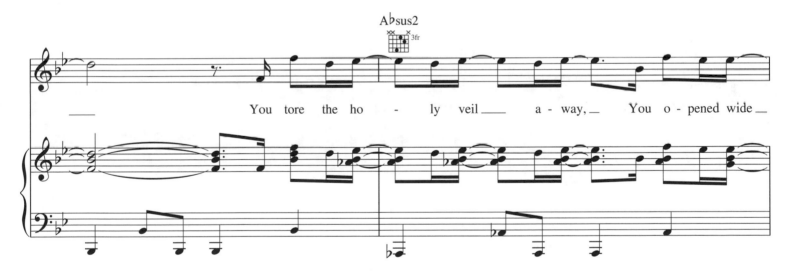

___ is there ___ to say, ___ "You reign!" ___ You saved the day. ___

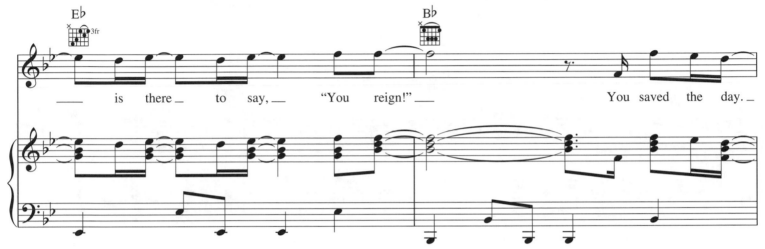

___ You tore the ho-ly veil ___ a-way, ___ You o-pened wide ___

___ the pris-on gates. ___ You saved the day. ___ You saved the day ___ ___

SIMPLE THINGS

Words and Music by KEITH THOMAS,
AMY GRANT, WILL OWSLEY
and DILLON O'BRIAN

In a steady four

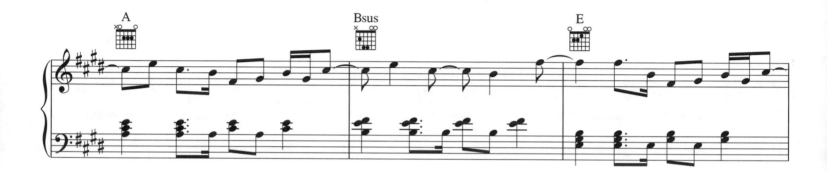

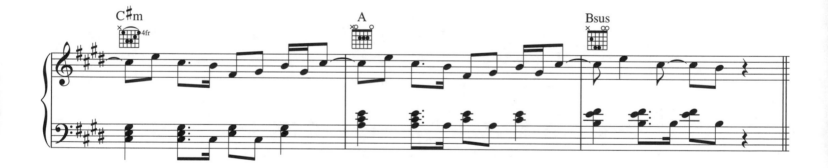

Wake up, ba-by, look a-round. ___ Birds sing, ooh, that sound ___ re-minds ___

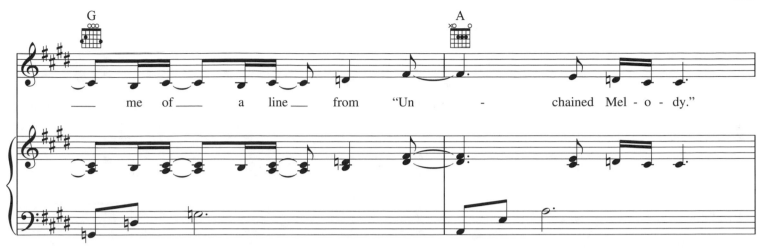

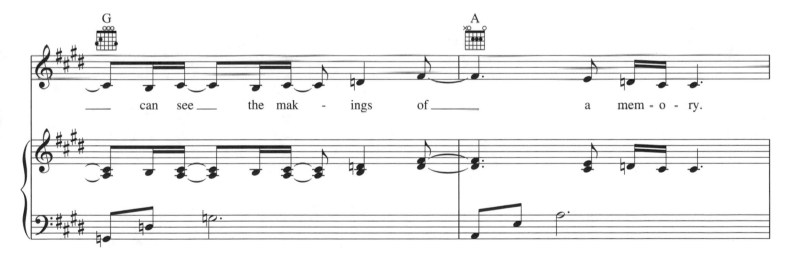

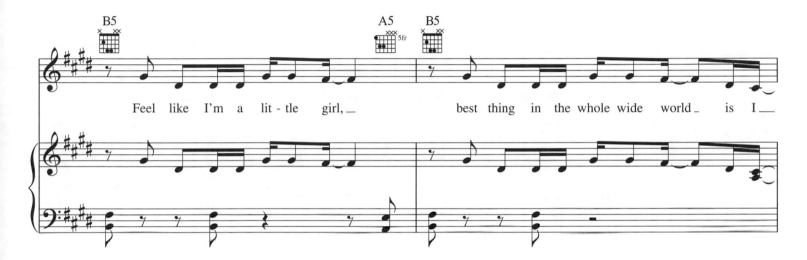

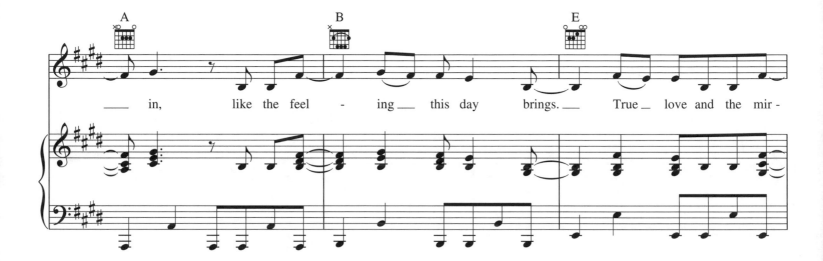

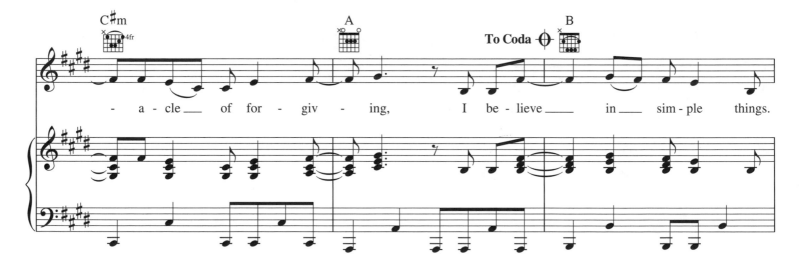

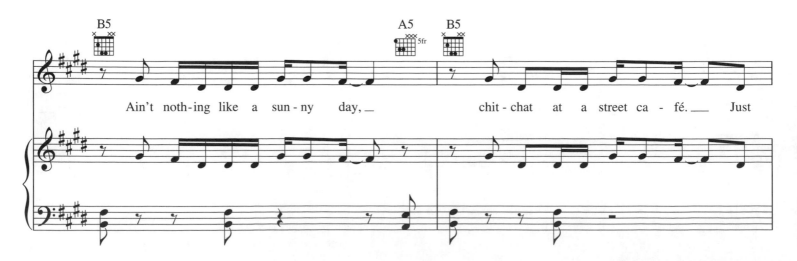

paint the pic - ture, ba - by, where ___ you wan - na be.

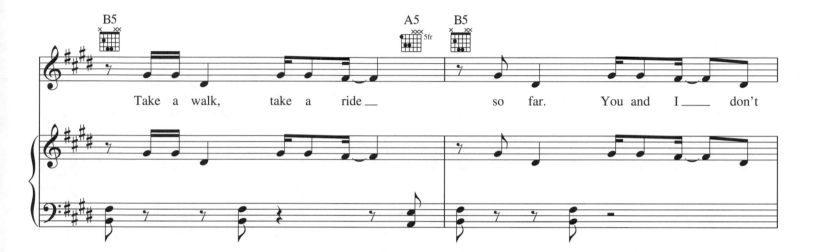

Take a walk, take a ride ___ so far. You and I ___ don't

need a plan ___ when we ___ can share ___ this rev - el - ry.

I re - mem - ber how I used ___ to want ___ it all. ___

D.S. al Coda

Fun - ny, now the big_____ things seem ___ so ___ small.

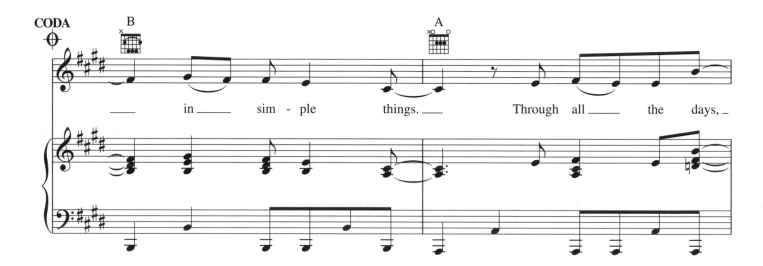

___ in ___ sim - ple things. ___ Through all ___ the days, _

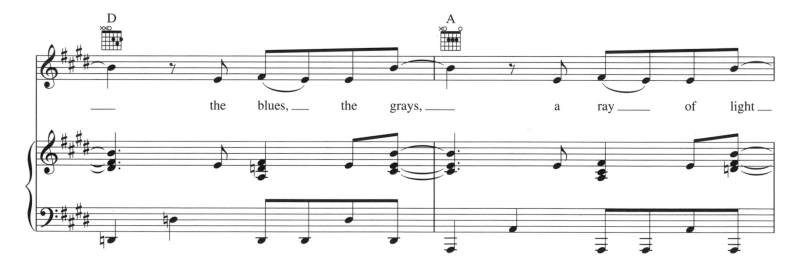

___ the blues, ___ the grays, ___ a ray ___ of light _

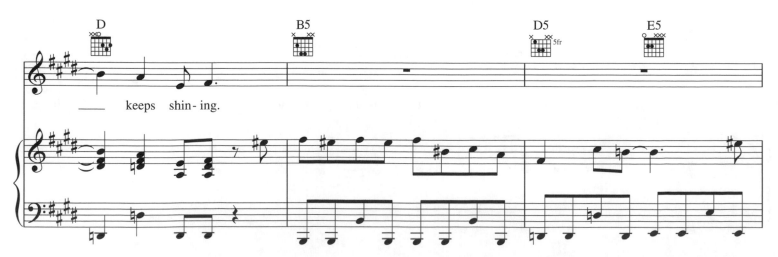

___ keeps shin- ing.

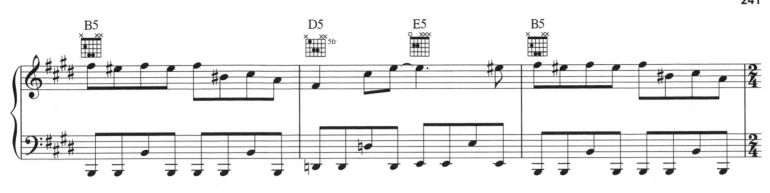

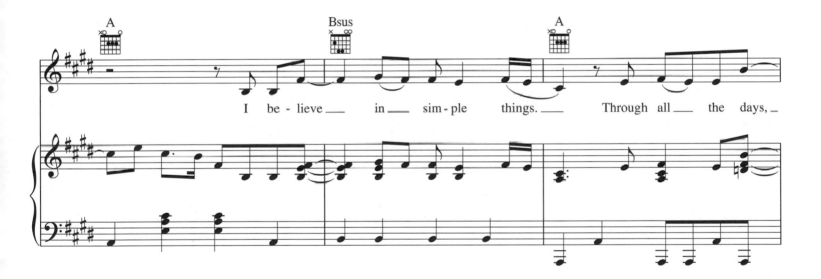

I be - lieve ___ in ___ sim - ple things. ___ Through all ___ the days, ___

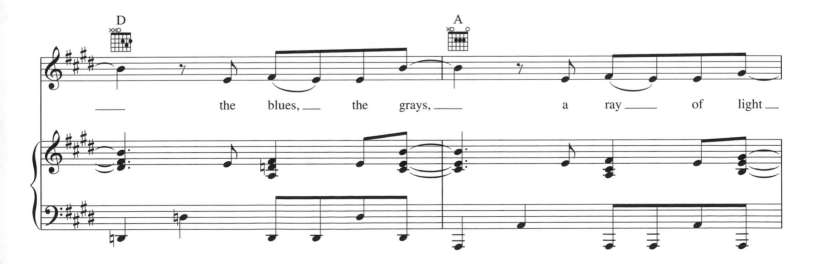

___ the blues, ___ the grays, ___ a ray ___ of light ___

was shin - ing. I dream of sim - ple things I can be - lieve

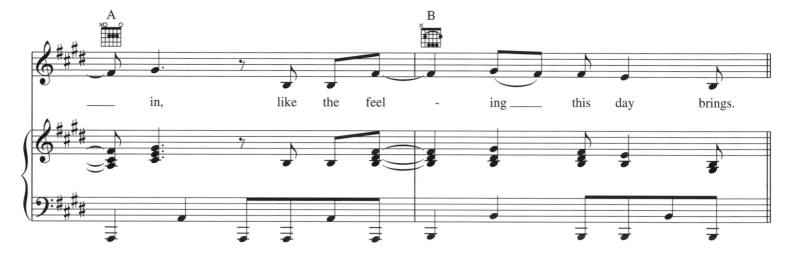

in, like the feel - ing this day brings.

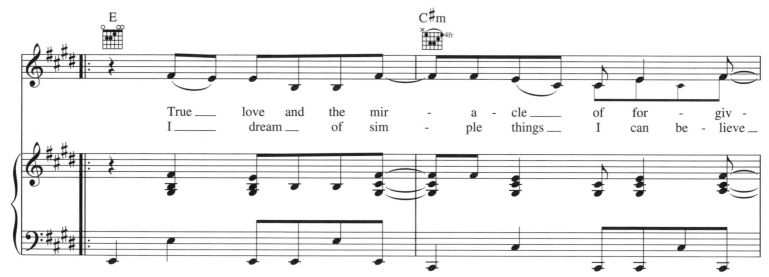

True love and the mir - a - cle of for - giv -
I dream of sim - ple things I can be - lieve

- ing, I be - lieve in sim - ple things.
in, I be - lieve in sim - ple things.

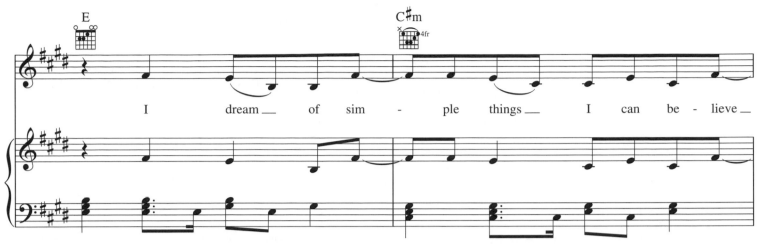

I dream __ of sim - ple things __ I can be - lieve __

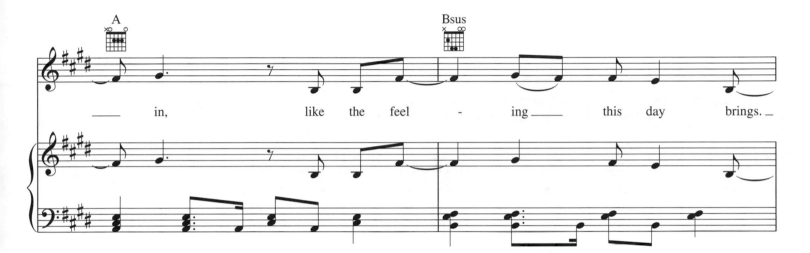

__ in, like the feel - ing __ this day brings. __

__ True __ love and the mir - a - cle __ of for - giv -

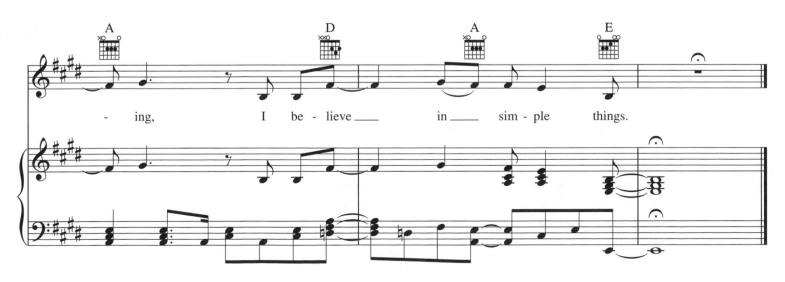

- ing, I be - lieve __ in __ sim - ple things.

STEADY ME

Words and Music by SCOTT DENTE,
CHRISTINE DENTE and CHARLIE PEACOCK

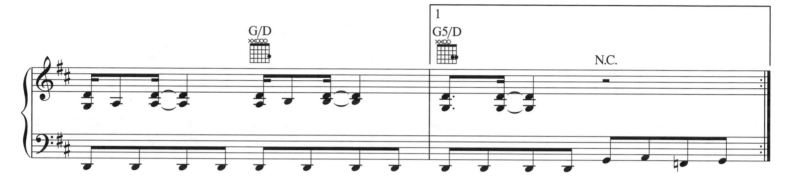

Some-times this life of mine

feels like a tight-rope, I'm go-ing slow, watch-ing where I walk.

245

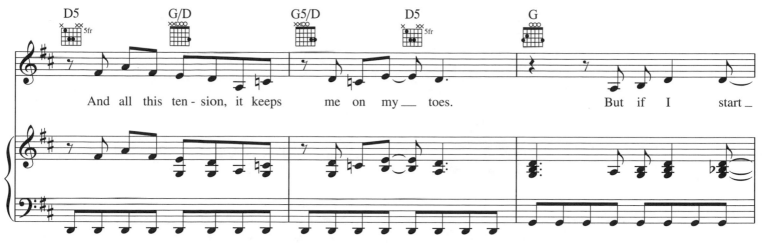

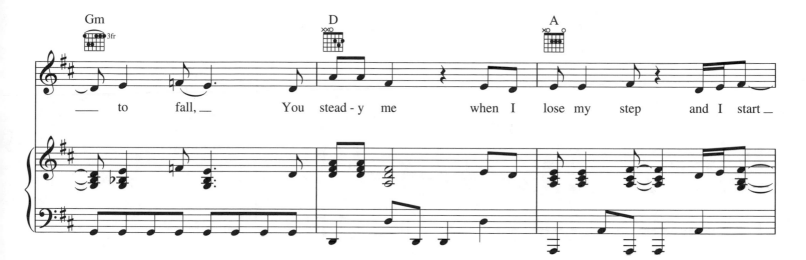

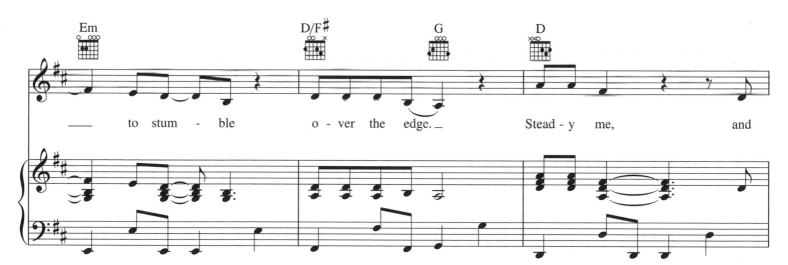

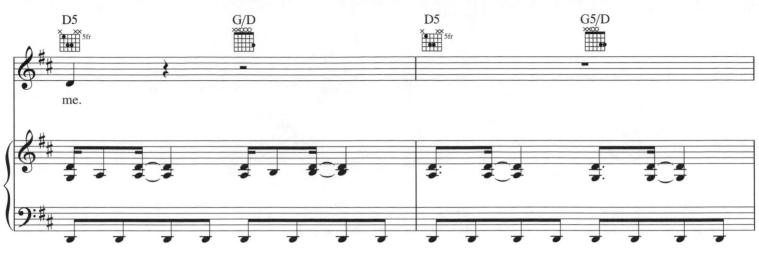

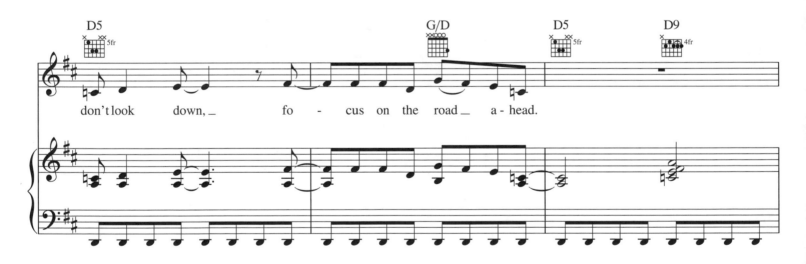

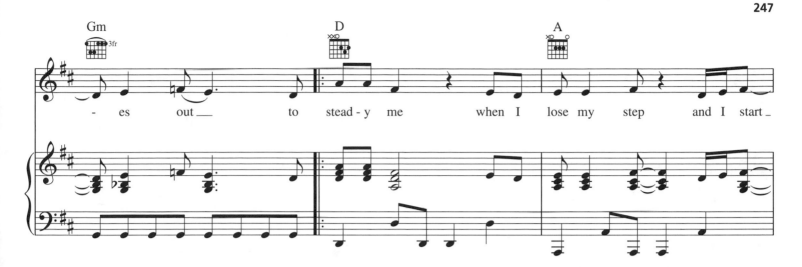

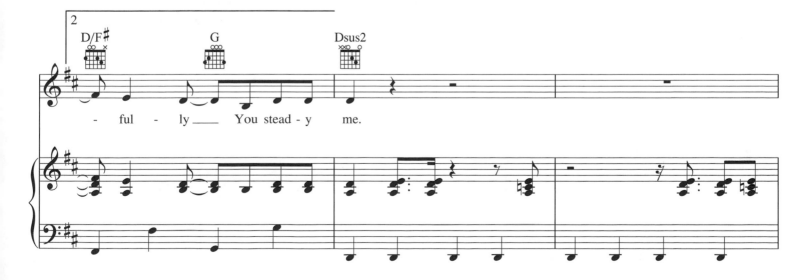

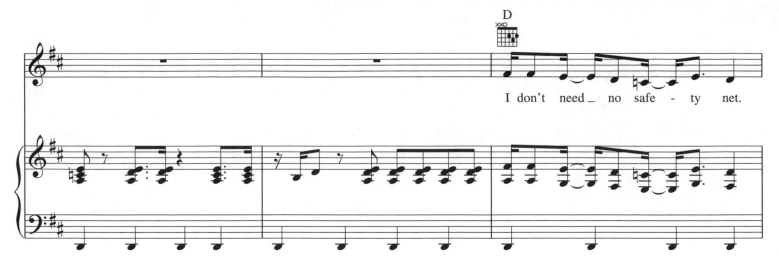

I don't need _ no safe - ty net.

I know You _ will nev - er let __ me ____ down.

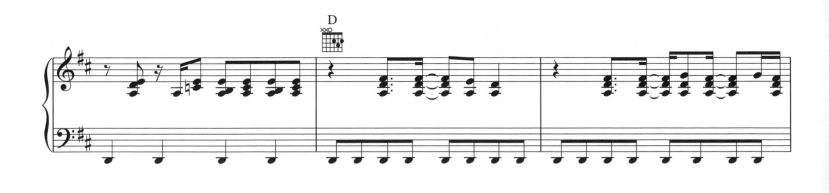

I don't need_ no safe - ty net. I know You_ will nev - er let_ me_

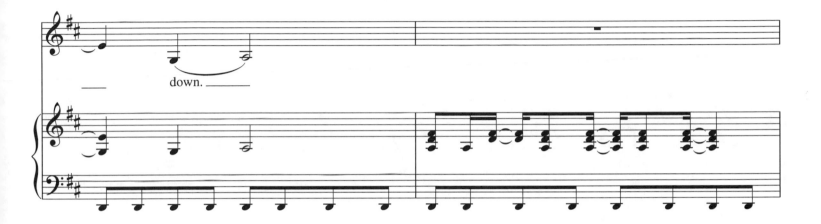

_ down._

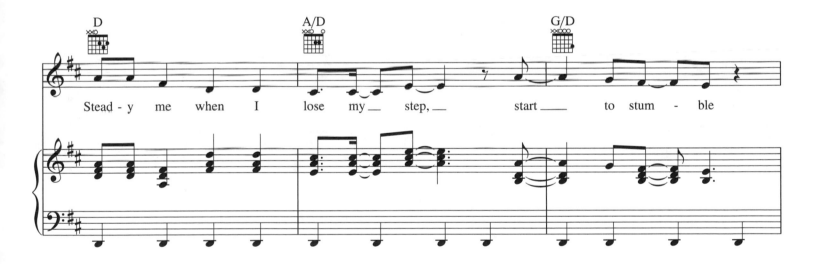

D   A/D   G/D

Stead - y me when I lose my_ step,_ start_ to stum - ble

D   Dsus   D   A/D

o - ver the edge._ Stead - y me, stead - y me once a - gain._ It a - maz -

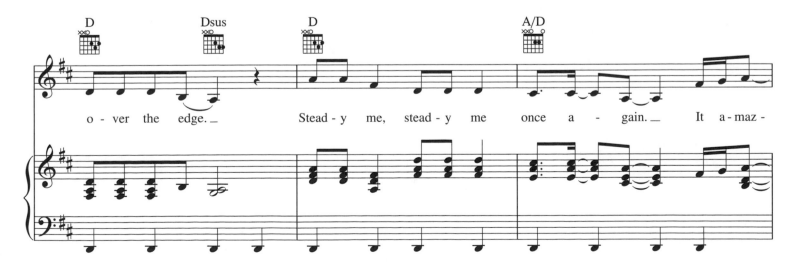

- es me__ how grace - ful - ly You stead - y me. Stead - y me when I lose__

__ my step and I start__ to stum - ble o - ver the edge.__

Stead - y me, and once a - gain, it a - maz - es me__ how {faith - {grace -

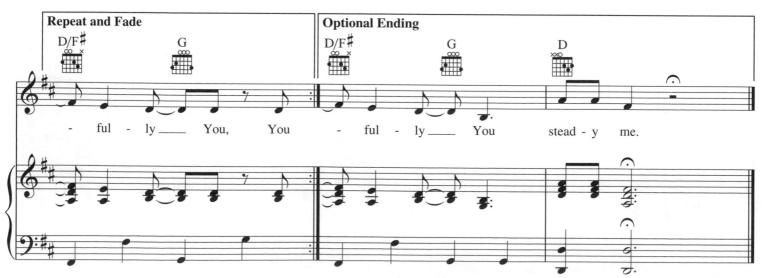

Repeat and Fade

- ful - ly__ You, You

Optional Ending

- ful - ly__ You stead - y me.

STORY OF LIFE

Words and Music by GORDON KENNEDY,
WAYNE KIRKPATRICK and JERRY McPHERSON

Moderately, in a funky grove

Some-times life ___ is frag-ile, seems like it's com - ing un - done. ___

Some-times you're o - ver a bar-rel, some-times you're un - der the gun.

Some-times life ___ is eas - y, just a walk ___ in the park. ___
Some-where there's some-one walk-ing. He is the watch-er of me. ___

Recorded a half step higher.

Some-time life's _ a gam - ble,   just a shot _ in the dark.
He gives the sto-ry mean-ing,   gives me a rea-son to be.

An - oth - er   day _____ in oth-er words. _____
For it is   writ - ten in _ words. _____

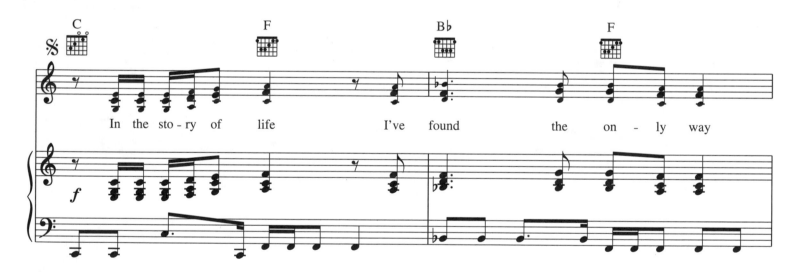

In the sto-ry of life   I've found   the on - ly way

I can ev-er sur-vive _   is read-ing by the light of my faith.

And hope is a-live ___ and love turns an-oth-er page. ___

And heav-en is mine ___ when the au-thor signs his name on my heart ___

To Coda ⊕

___ in the sto-ry of ___ life.

___ life. ___

TAKE YOU AT YOUR WORD

Words and Music by GRANT CUNNINGHAM
and PAUL FIELD

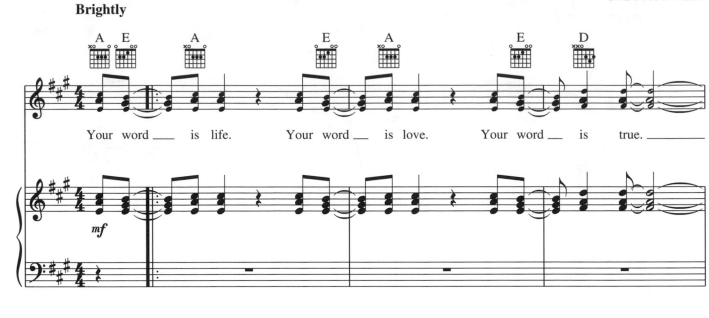

Your word ___ is life. Your word ___ is love. Your word ___ is true. ___

___ Your word ___ is life. Your word ___ is love. Your word _

___ is true. ___ Your word ___ is life. Your word _

Oh. _____ Oh. _____

Lord, I love_ You, oh, ___ and I trust_ You. As ___ I live I've learned_

___ I ___ can take You at Your word._

Your ___ Your word _ is love. Your word_

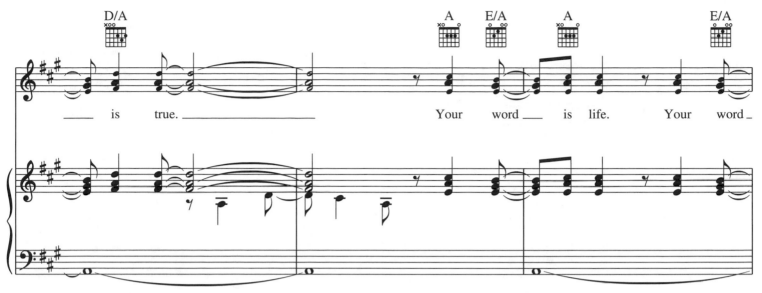

is true. _____ Your word __ is life. Your word _

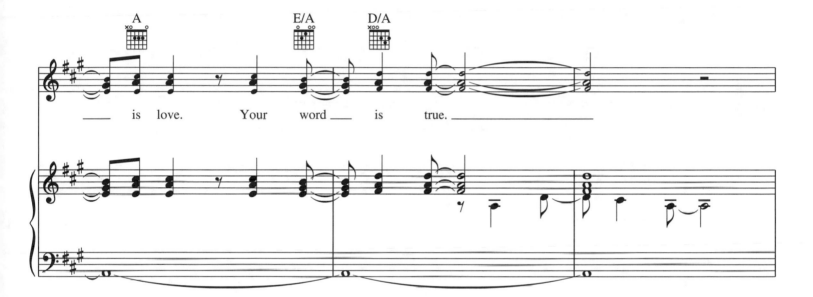

__ is love. Your word __ is true. _____

Yeah   yeah   yeah   yeah

Say   You   say ___ Your word.   Yeah, You say ___ Your word.

Oh. _____ Oh. _____

Lord, I love ___ You, oh, ___ and I trust ___ You. As ___ I live I've learned ___

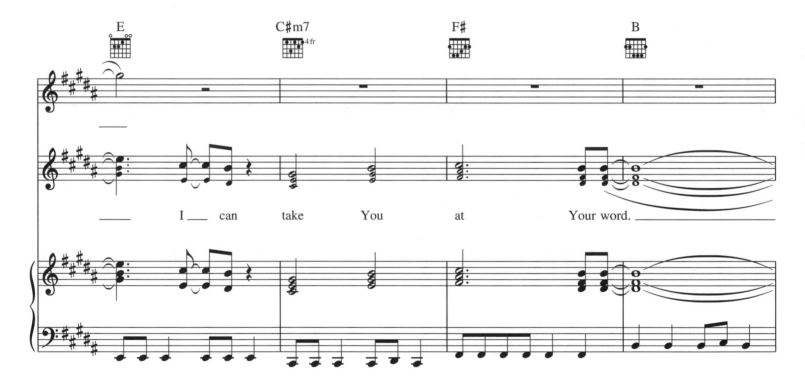

___ I ___ can take You at Your word. _____

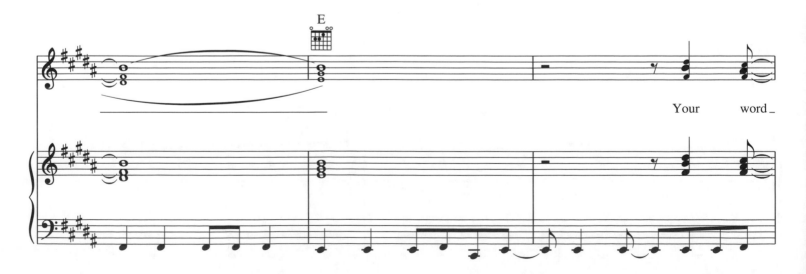

_____ Your word ___

Oh _____ Lord, I trust ____
____ is life. Your word ____ is love. Your word ____ is true. _____

____ in You. _____ Ev-'ry-bod-y's look-ing for some - thing to ____ be - lieve ____
____ Your word ____ is life. Your word ____ is love. Your word ____

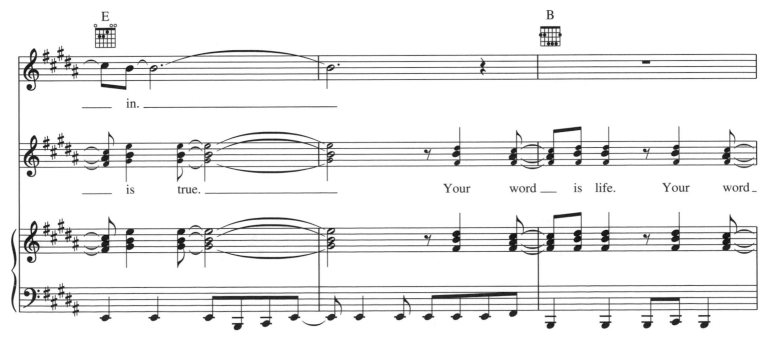

____ in. _____
____ is true. _____ Your word ____ is life. Your word ____

I will trust ___ in You, ___ to be-lieve ___ in.   Your word ___
___ is true. _____   Your word ___ is life. _____

___ is love.   I will trust ___ in You. ___
___ is true. _____   Your word ___

Your word ___ is love.   I will trust ___ in You. ___
___ is life. _____   Your word ___ is true. _____

THIS MYSTERY

Words and Music by
NICHOLE NORDEMAN

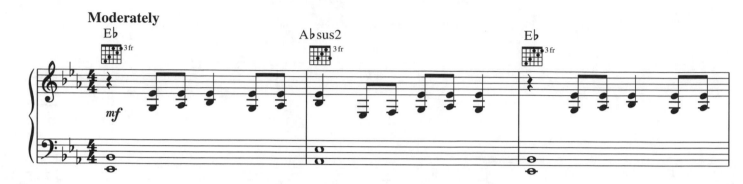

Say good-night to the light of the set-ting sun. ___

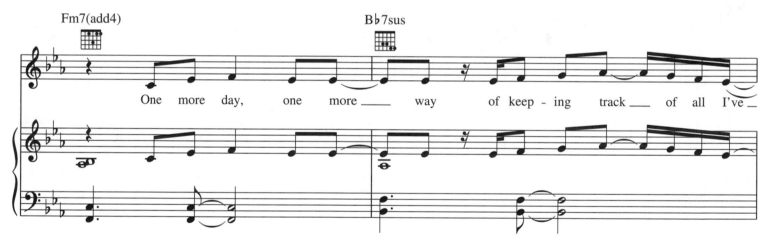

One more day, one more ___ way of keep-ing track ___ of all I've ___

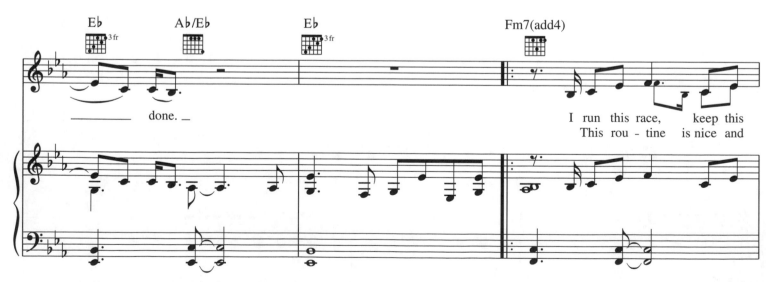

___ done. ___

I run this race, ___ keep this
This rou - tine is nice and

want us to breathe a-gain? _ Say good-bye to the lines that we've col-ored in ____

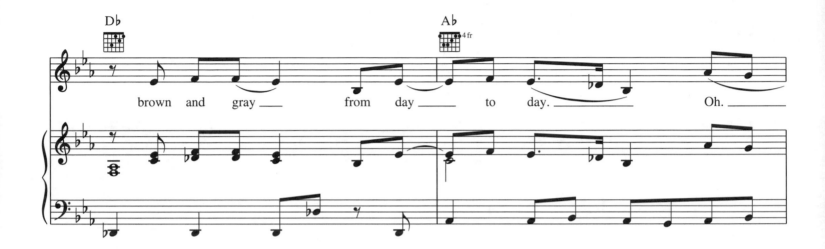

brown and gray ___ from day ___ to day. _____ Oh. _____

____ Do You cry, do You hope for all things made ___ new? _ Try and try to in-

voke us to live in You _ that we might be _____ the hands _

_____ and feet _____ of this mys - ter - y. _____ Yeah. _____

mys - ter - y. _____ Oh. _____

We _____ take stock _____ and we punch

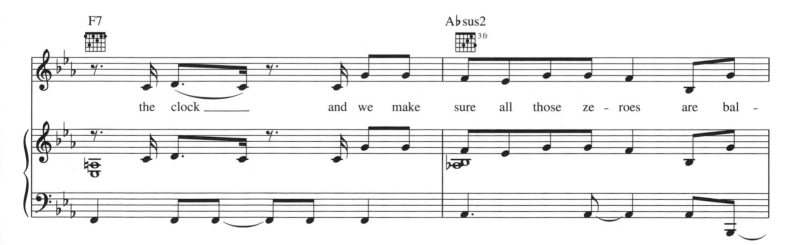

the clock _____ and we make sure all those ze - roes are bal -

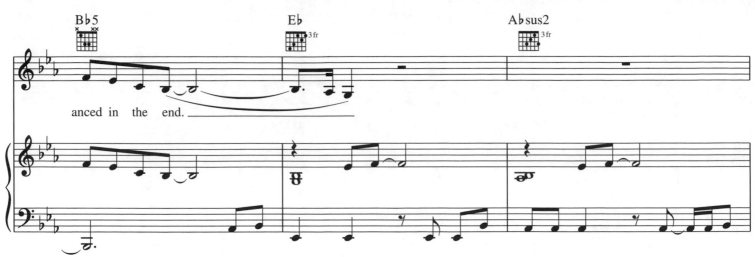

anced in the end. _____

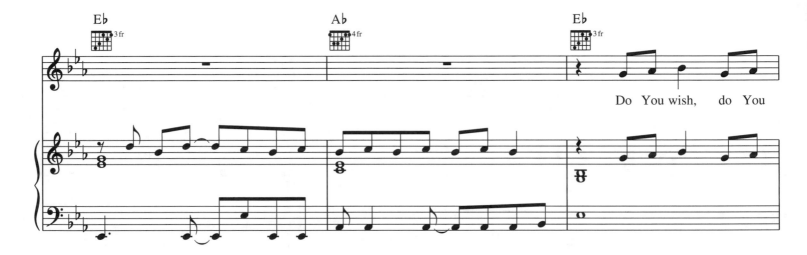

Do You wish,   do You

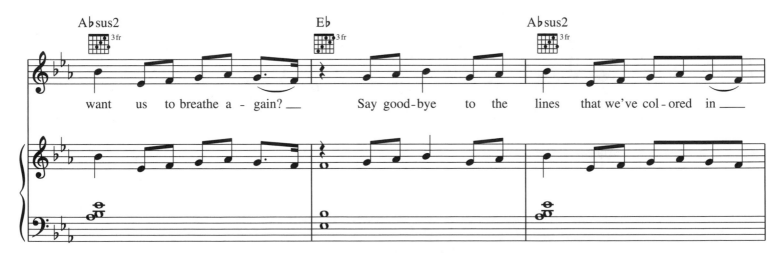

want   us   to breathe a - gain? ___   Say good-bye   to   the   lines   that we've col - ored   in ___

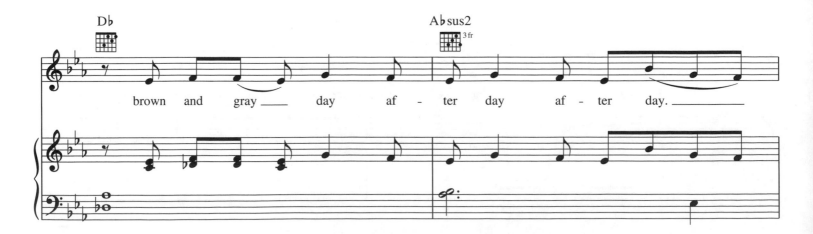

brown   and   gray ___   day   af - ter   day   af - ter   day. _____

Do You cry, do You hope for all things made ___ new? ___ Try and try to in-

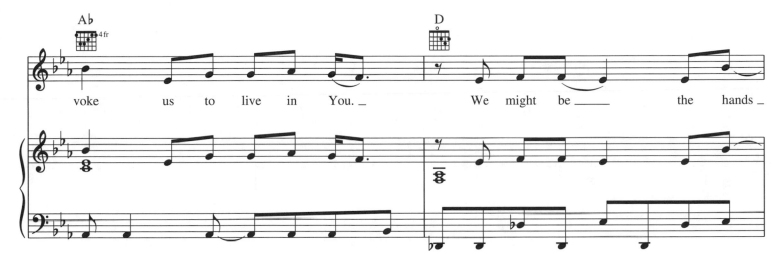

voke us to live in You. ___ We might be ___ the hands ___

___ and ___ feet ___ of the next mys - ter - y. ___ Ah. ___

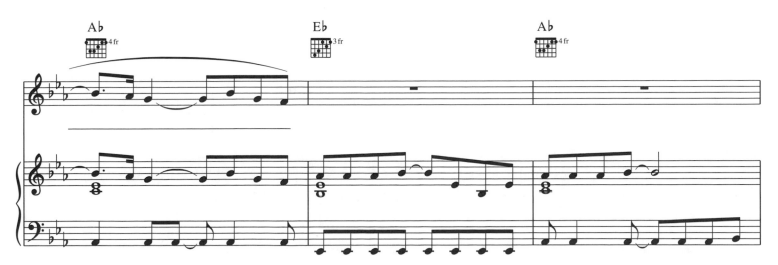

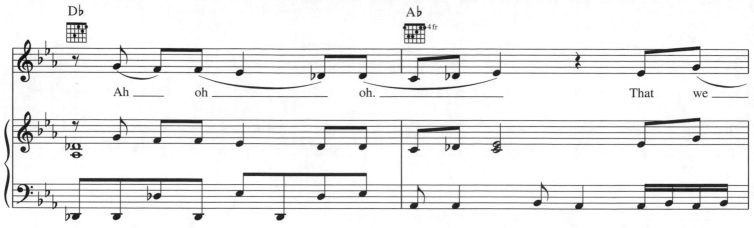

Ah _____ oh _____ oh. _____ That we _____

_____ might be _____ the hands and feet, that we might be _____ the hands _____

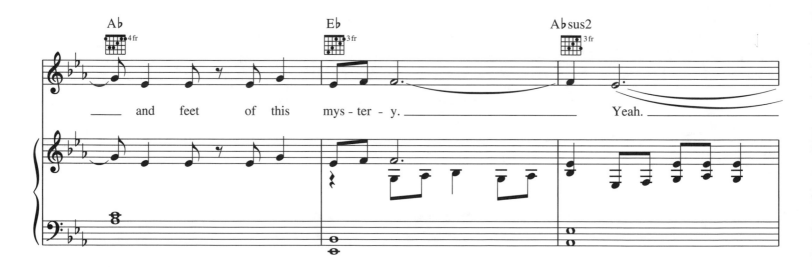

_____ and feet of this mys - ter - y. _____ Yeah. _____

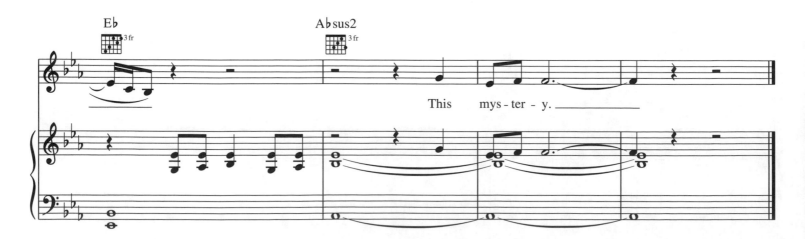

This mys - ter - y. _____

TO EVER LIVE WITHOUT ME

Words and Music by BLAKE SMITH,
BRIAN WHITE, JOE BECK
and CHAD CHAPIN

Choic - es, _____ e - ven though You knew _ the lines You'd have _ to cross _
Help - less, _____ that's hu - man - i - ty _____ with - out _ Your sav -

_____ for me, _____ You made them an - y - way. _____
- ing grace. _____ So mis - led. _____

Voic - es, ___ as You knelt there in ___ the gar - den 'neath ___ the ol -
Self - less, ___ You could have called ten thou - sand an - gels down ___ to take ___

- ive tree, ___ You heard me call Your name. ___
___ Your place, ___ but You took mine in - stead. ___

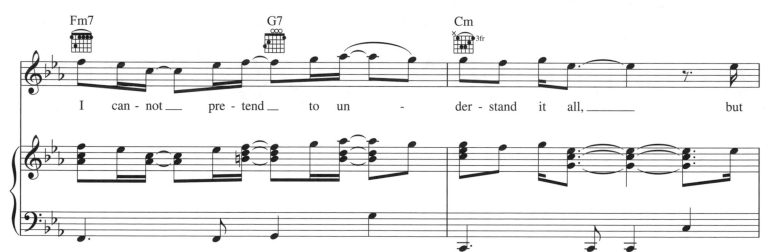

I can - not ___ pre - tend ___ to un - der - stand it all, ___ but

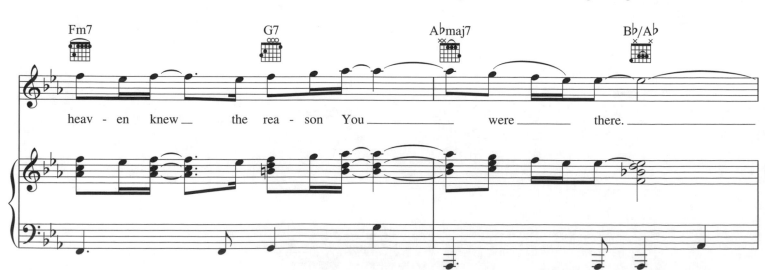

heav - en knew ___ the rea - son You ___ were ___ there. ___

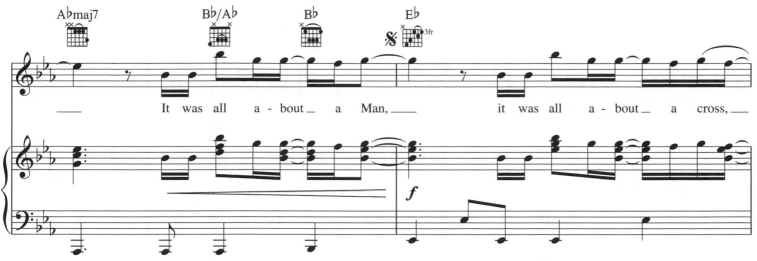

It was all a-bout___ a Man,___ it was all a-bout___ a cross,___

___ it was all a-bout___ the blood___ that___ was shed___ so I___ would not___

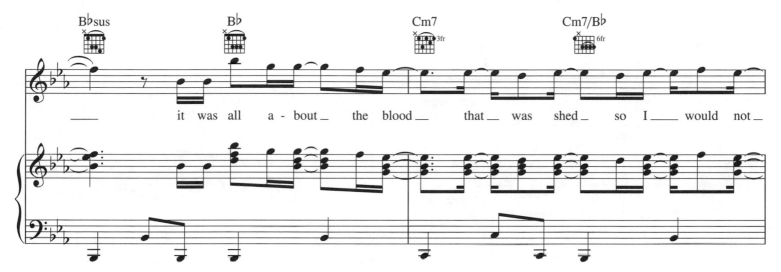

___ be lost.___ It was all a-bout___ a love,___ that was big-ger than___ a life.___

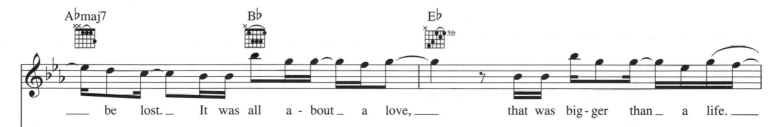

___ It was all a-bout___ the free - dom that___ was giv-en through___ Your sac-

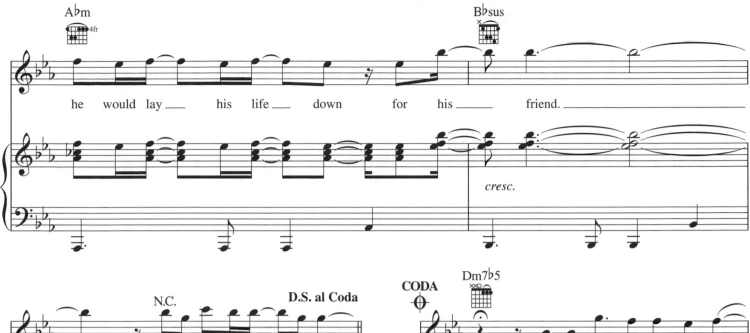

he would lay ___ his life ___ down for his ___ friend. ___

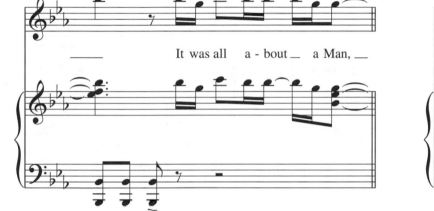

D.S. al Coda

N.C.

It was all a-bout ___ a Man, ___

CODA

than to ev - er live with - out ___

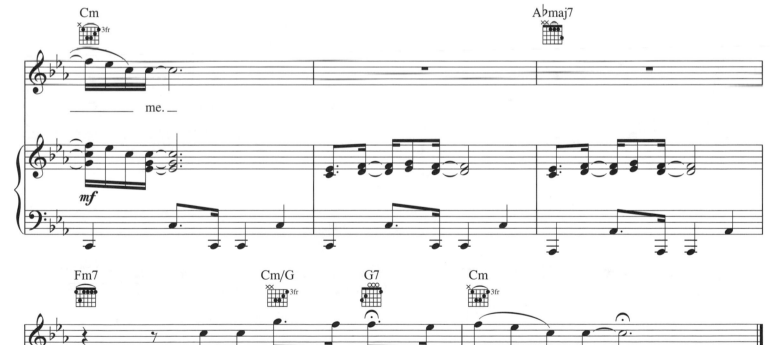

_____ me. ___

Than to ev - er live with - out ___ me. ___

WAIT FOR ME

Words and Music by
REBECCA ST. JAMES

Moderately slow Pop

Dar - ling, did you know that I, ___ I dream a - bout ___ you? Wait - ing for the look in your

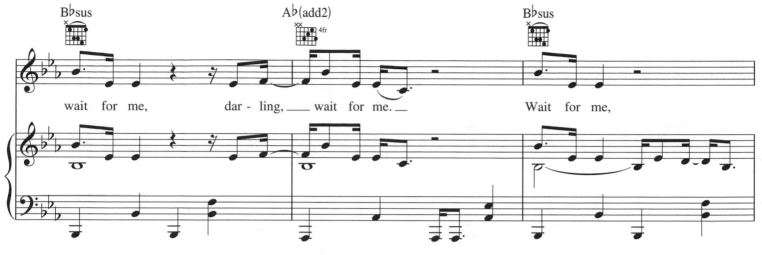

wait for me, dar-ling,___ wait for me.___ Wait for me,

wait for me._____ 'Cause I am

wait-ing for, pray-ing for___ you, dar-ling.___ Wait for me,_____

___ too.___ Wait for me as___ I wait___ for you. 'Cause I am

WHAT IF

Words and Music by JADON LAVIK,
ADAM WATTS and ANDY DODD

What if I were ev-'ry-one's first choice, ___

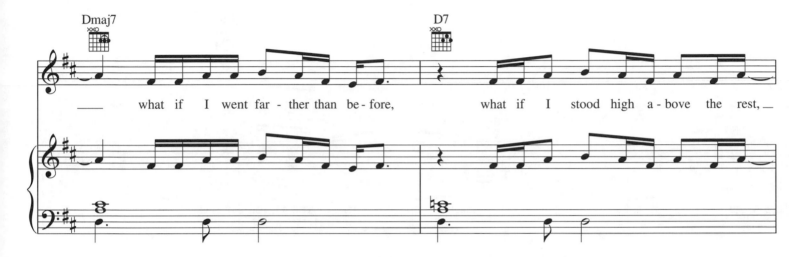

Dmaj7 ___ what if I went far - ther than be - fore,   D7 what if I stood high a - bove the rest, ___

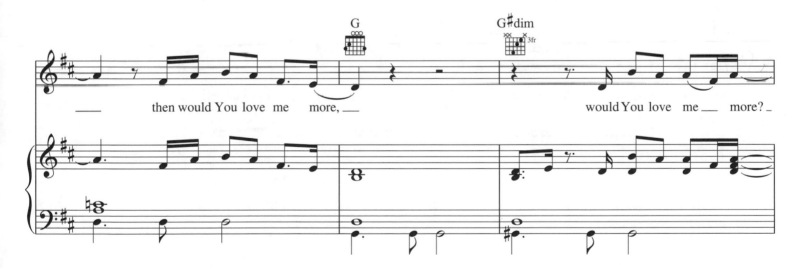

G ___ then would You love me more, ___   G#dim would You love me ___ more? ___

D

D   **Dmaj7**

What if I ig-nored the hand __ that fed __ me, what if I for - got to con - fess, __

D7

__ what if I stum - bled down __ that moun - tain, then would You love me less? __

G   **G♯dim**   **D**

Lord, would You love me __ less? __

What if I were ev - 'ry - one's last choice, __

what if I mixed in with the rest, ___ what if I failed what I passed be - fore, ___

___ then would You love me less? _____ Lord, would You, ___

___ would You love me ___ less? ___ Oh no, ___

___ oh no, ___ oh no. ___ You say I be - long ___ to You ___

a - part from the things __ I ____ do.

You say I be - long __ to You. ___ I'm in awe of why __ You do, __

___ You do, ___ You do, ___ You do. ___ What have I

done to de - serve Your Son, ___ sent to die ___ for me? __

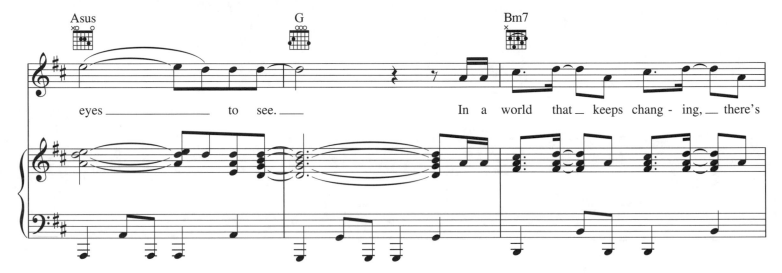

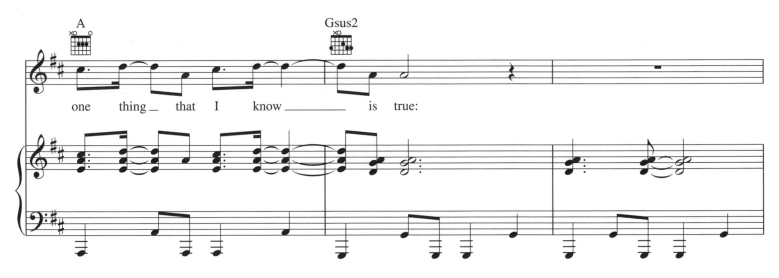

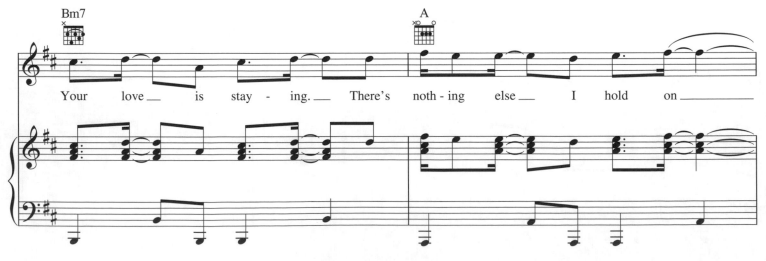

to.

You say I be-long __ to You __

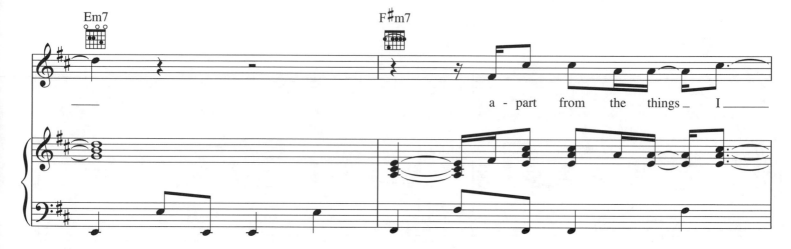

a - part from the things __ I __

do.

You say I be-long to You.

I'm in awe __

of why You __ do, _____ why __ You do. ____

I'm ___ in awe _____ of ___ You, ___

I'm ___ in awe _____ of _____ You. ___

The way You love ___ me, _____

the way ___ You do. ___

Optional Ending

Repeat ad lib. and Fade

WE LIFT YOU UP

Words and Music by
BRIAN LITTRELL

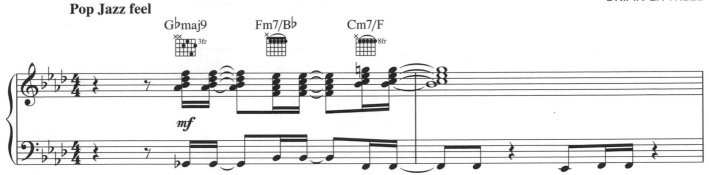

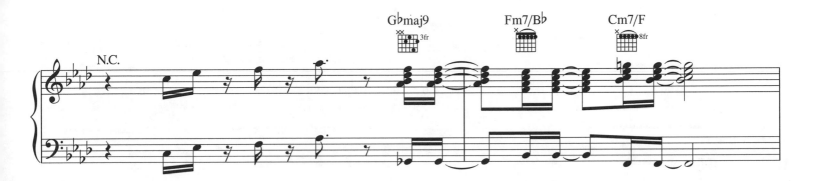

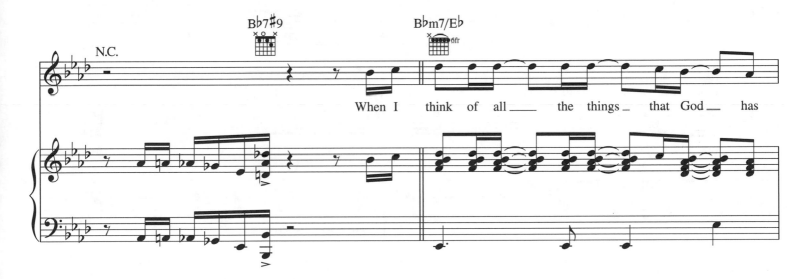

When I think of all ___ the things ___ that God ___ has done for ___ me, ___ and how my faith ___ has al - ways con - quered ad -

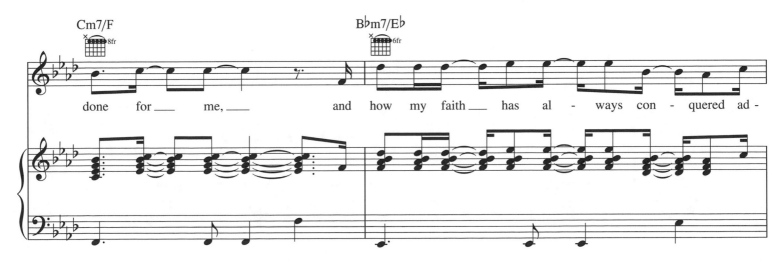

gave to save___ my soul.___ And that's why we lift You up

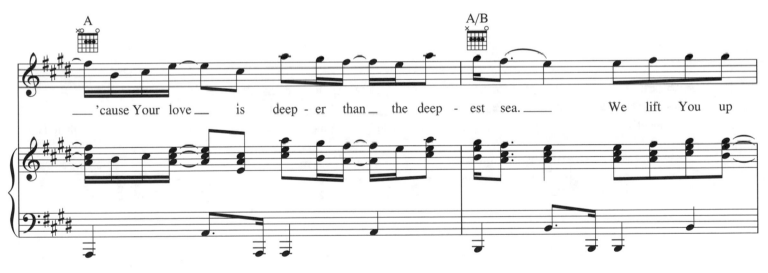

high - er than___ the heav - ens.___ We lift You up___

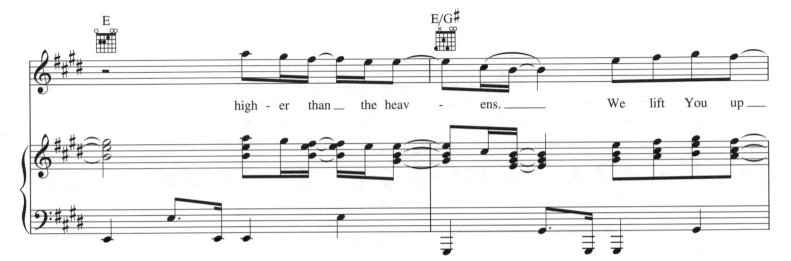

___ 'cause Your love___ is deep - er than___ the deep - est sea.___ We lift You up

high-er than___ the moun - tains. We lift You up.___ He died for you___ and me,___

yeah. Let me

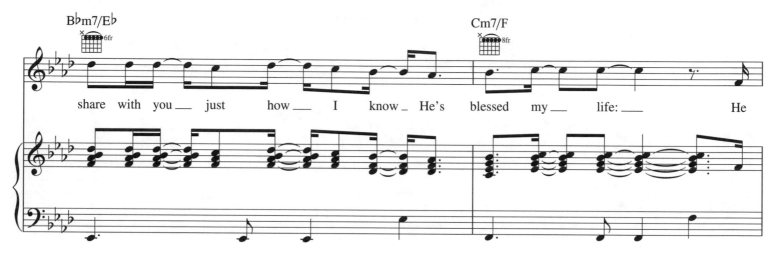

share with you ___ just how ___ I know ___ He's blessed my ___ life: ___ He

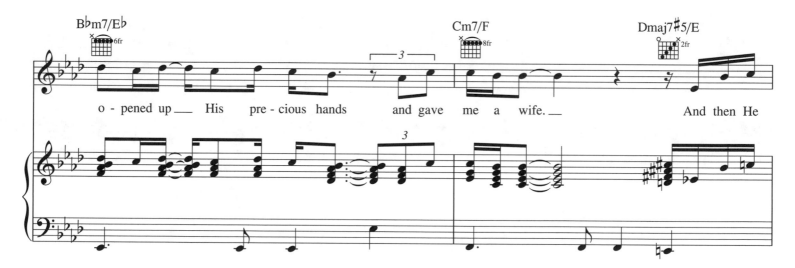

o-pened up ___ His pre-cious hands and gave me a wife. ___ And then He

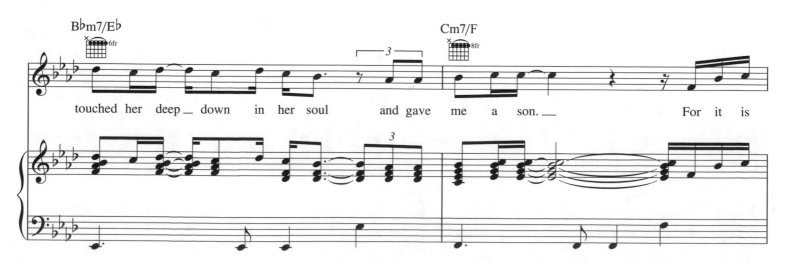

touched her deep ___ down in her soul and gave me a son. ___ For it is

He that knows — no great-er love, for He is the One. And at

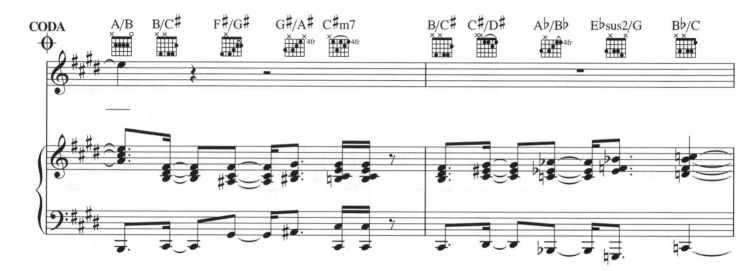

We lift You up high - er than — the heav -

- ens. _____ We lift You up _____ be-cause Your love is deep - er than _ the deep -

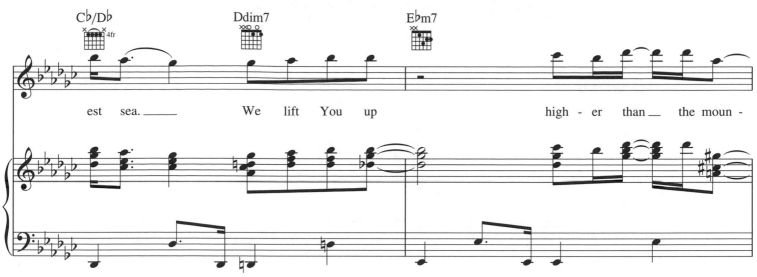

est sea. _____ We lift You up high - er than _____ the moun -

- tains, oh _____ yeah. _____ We lift You up. _____

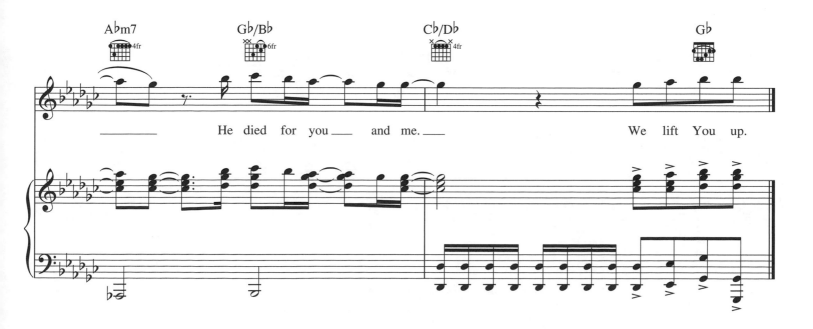

_____ He died for you _____ and me. _____ We lift You up.

YOU ARE LOVED

Words and Music by
REBECCA ST. JAMES

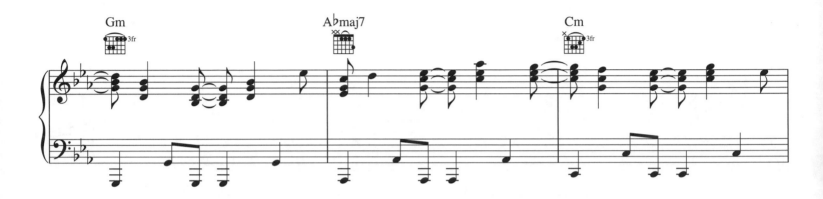

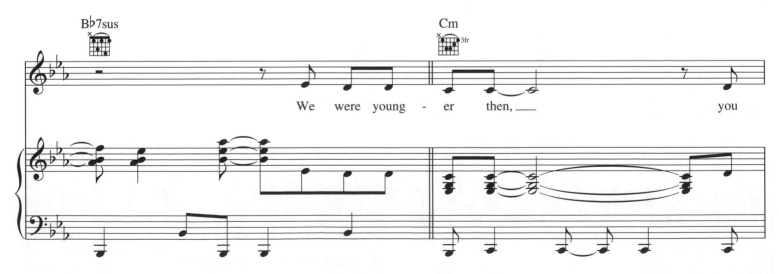

We were young - er then, ___ you

ing out,   'cause I _____ re - mem - ber. ___

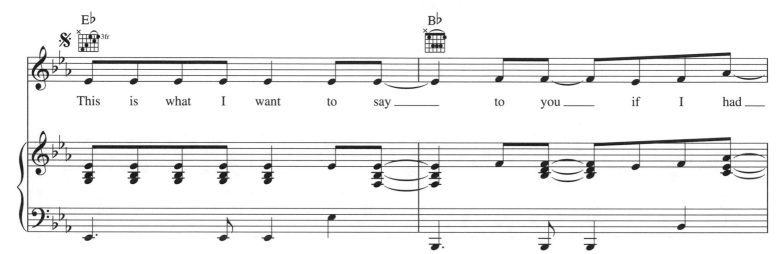

This is what I want to say _____ to you _____ if I had ___

___ one chance __ to speak __ to your heart: You are loved __

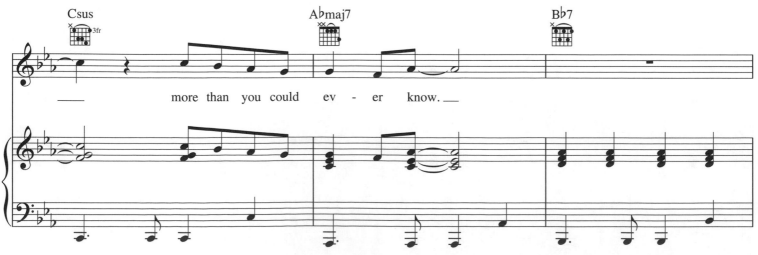

___ more than you could ev - er know. __

This is what I want to say _____ to you _____ if I had _____

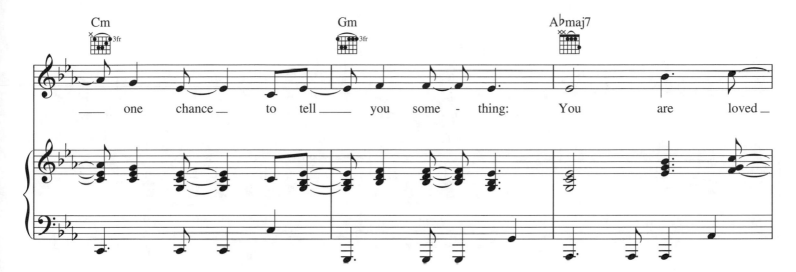

_____ one chance _____ to tell _____ you some - thing: You are loved _____

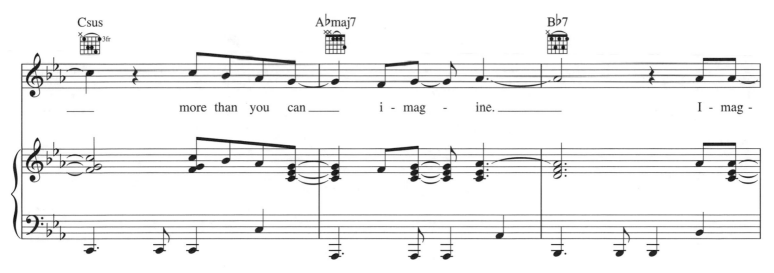

_____ more than you can _____ i - mag - ine. _____ I - mag -

To Coda ⊕

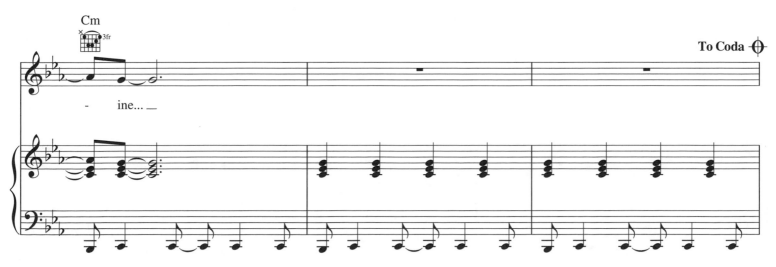

- ine... _____

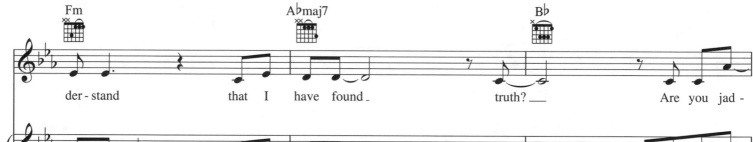

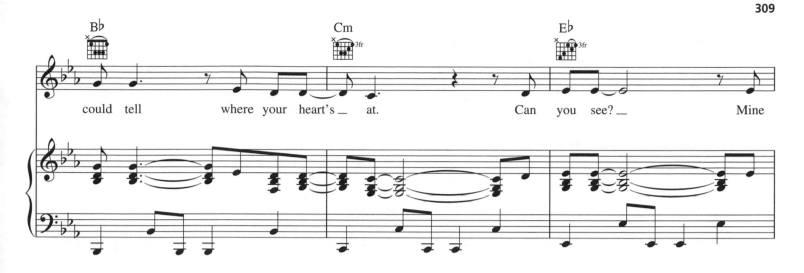

could tell where your heart's _ at. Can you see? _ Mine

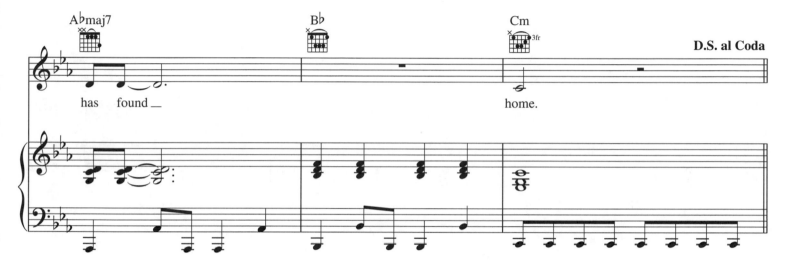

D.S. al Coda

has found _ home.

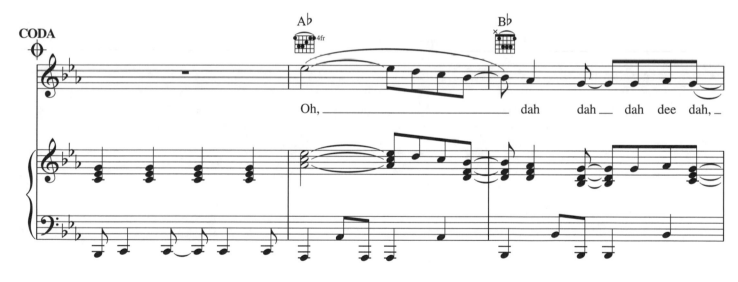

CODA

Oh, _____ dah dah _ dah dee dah, _

_____ dah dah dah _____ dah dah _ dah. Hey, _____ oh, _____

dah dah dah dee dah, dah dah dah dah.

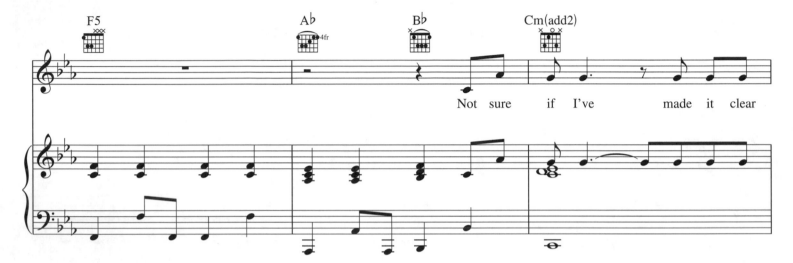

Not sure if I've made it clear

e - nough. It's not ___ my love I sing a - bout. Ev - 'ry - bod -

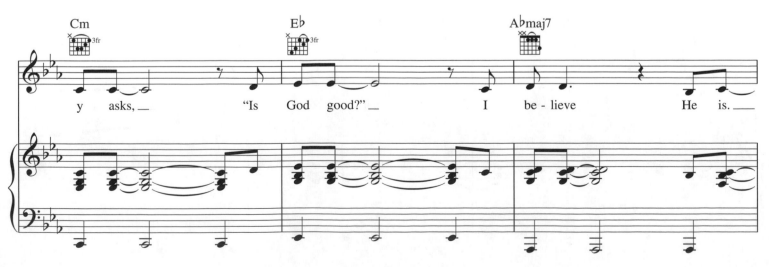

y asks, ___ "Is God good?" ___ I be - lieve He is. ___

more than you could ev - er know.

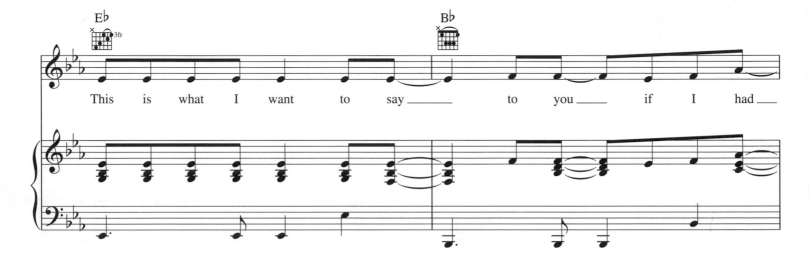

This is what I want to say to you if I had

one chance to tell you some - thing: You are loved

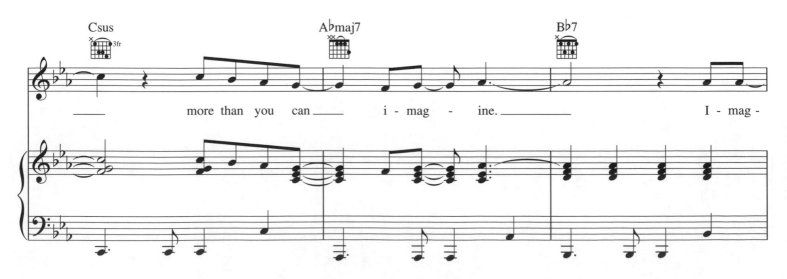

more than you can i - mag - ine. I - mag -

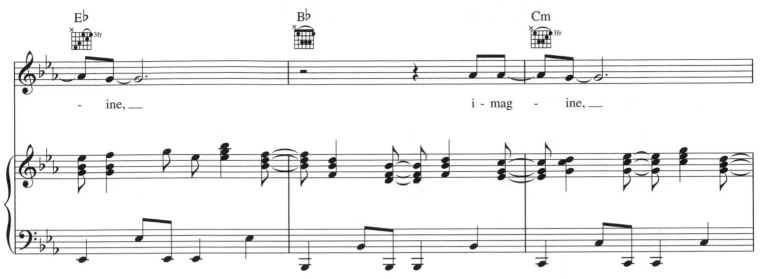

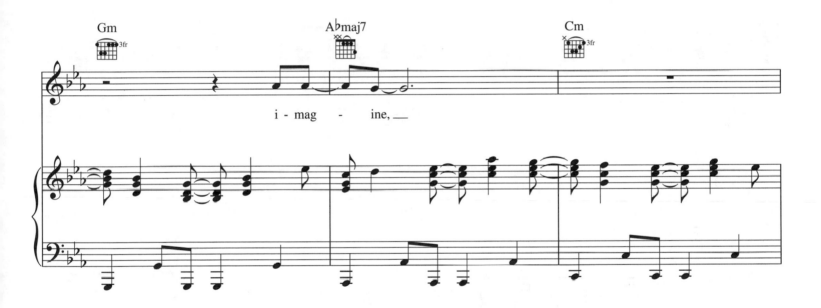

WHAT IT MEANS

Words and Music by
JEREMY CAMP

*Recorded a half step lower.

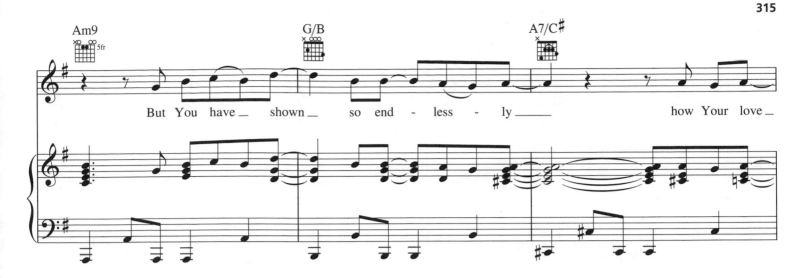

But You have __ shown __ so end - less - ly _____ how Your love __

__ pours o - ver __ me. ___ No pic - ture can __ re - cre - ate __ the __ beau-

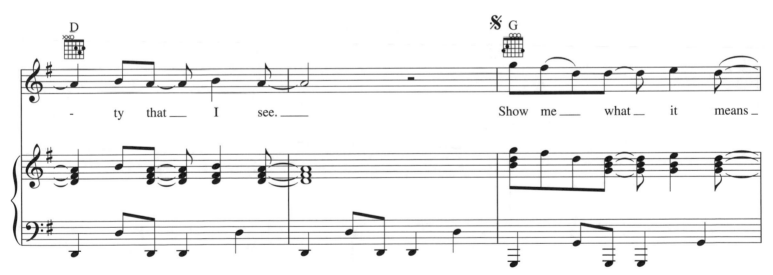

- ty that __ I see. ____ Show me ___ what __ it means __

to live my life __ a sac - ri - fice. ___ If

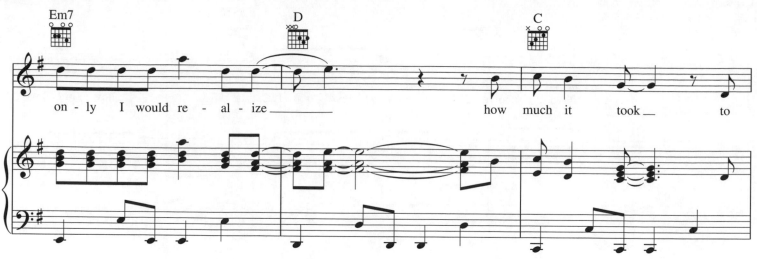

on - ly I would re - al - ize _____ how much it took __ to

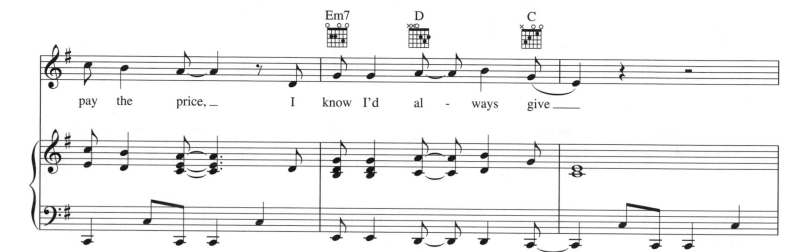

pay the price, __ I know I'd al - ways give ____

ev - 'ry - thing __ to You.

I want this __ world __

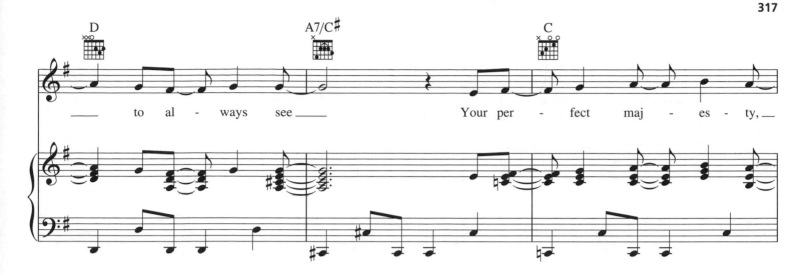

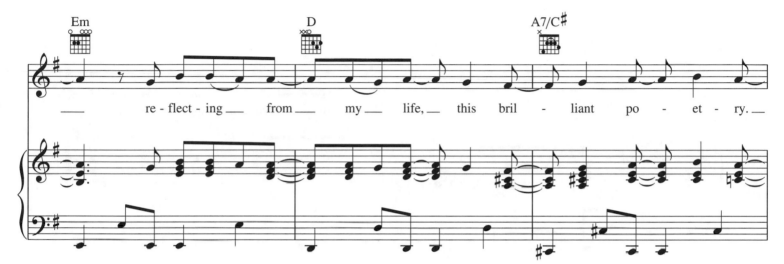

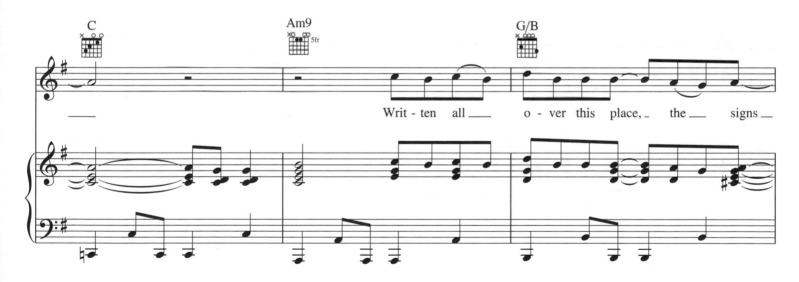

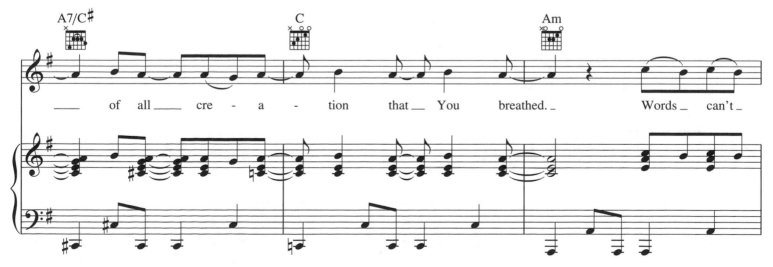

D.S. al Coda

e - ven state __ how __ much __ You mean __ to me. __

CODA

I want to __ face __ my ver - y __ crime __

__ of not giv - ing __ all __ of mine. __ But I can __ feel __

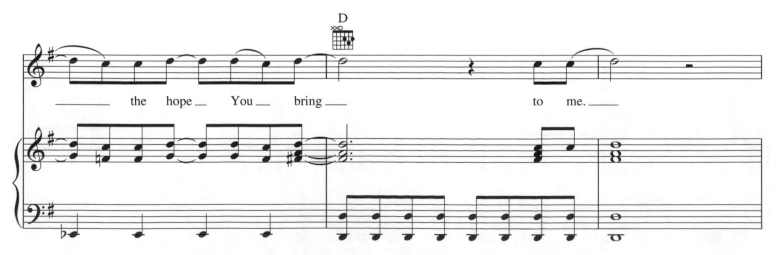

_____ the hope __ You __ bring __ to me. __

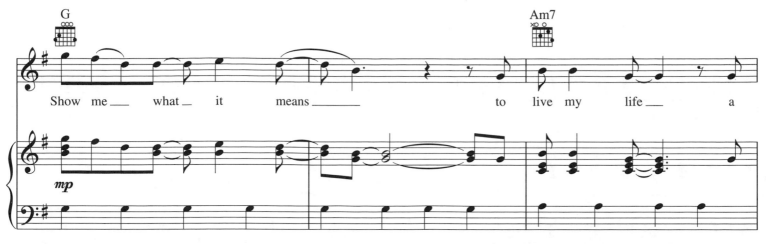

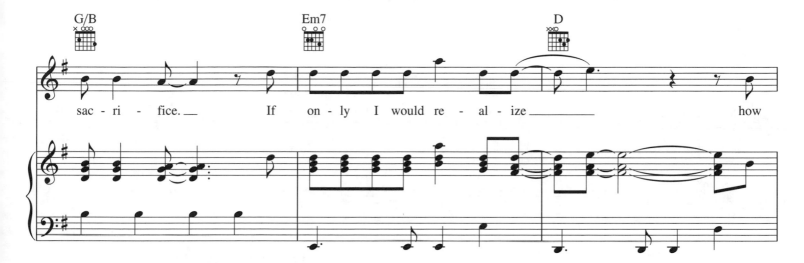

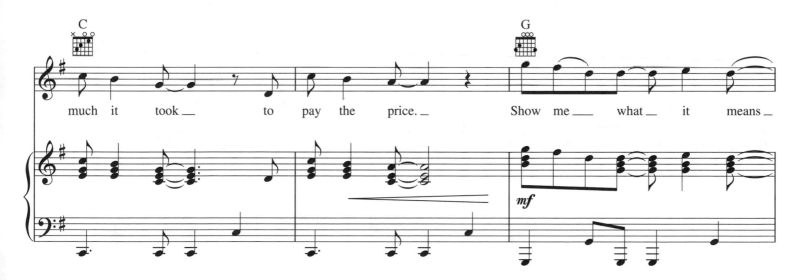

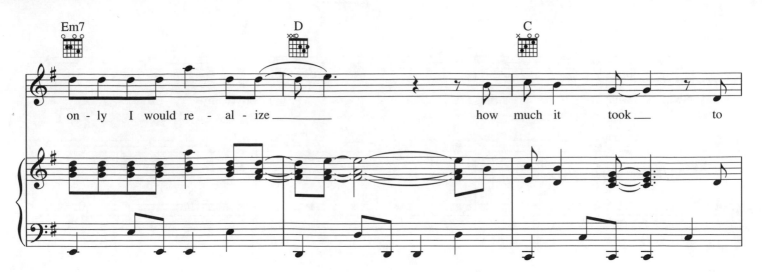

on - ly I would re - al - ize _____ how much it took ___ to

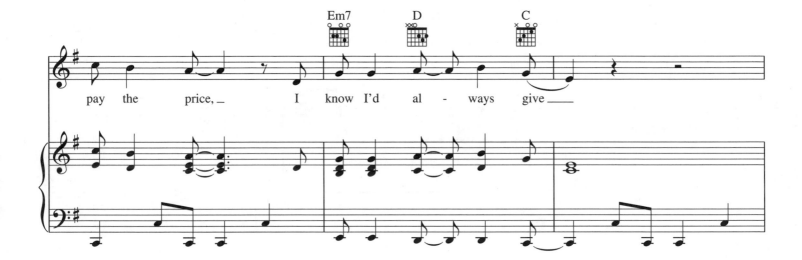

pay the price, _ I know I'd al - ways give ___

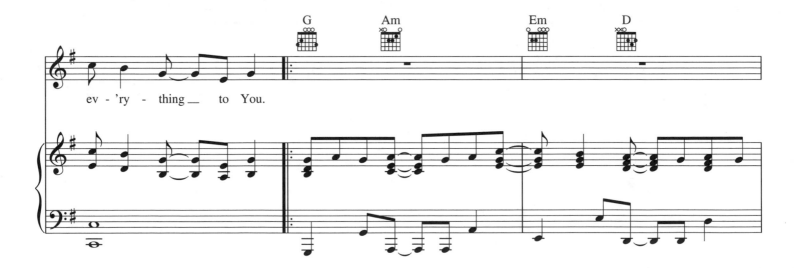

ev - 'ry - thing _ to You.

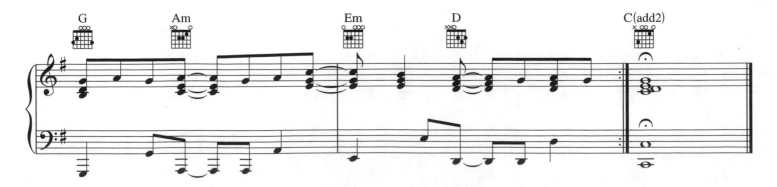